SPORTS FOR SALE

David A. Klatell & Norman Marcus

SPORTS
FOR SALE

TELEVISION, MONEY, AND THE FANS

New York · Oxford
Oxford University Press · 1988

Oxford University Press

Oxford   New York   Toronto
Delhi   Bombay   Calcutta   Madras   Karachi
Petaling Jaya   Singapore   Hong Kong   Tokyo
Nairobi   Dar es Salaam   Cape Town
Melbourne   Auckland

and associated companies in
Berlin   Ibadan

Published by Oxford University Press, Inc.,
200 Madison Avenue, New York, New York 10016

Oxford is a registered trademark of Oxford University Press

Library of Congress Cataloging-in-Publication Data
Klatell, David A.
Sports for sale : television, money, and the fans / David A.
Klatell and Norman Marcus.
p.   cm.   Bibliography: p.
ISBN 0–19–503836–3
1. Television broadcasting of sports—United States. 2. Sports-
Economic aspects—United States. I. Marcus, Norman, 1934–
II. Title.
GV742.3.K53 1988   88–18789
070.4'49796'0973—dc 19   CIP

Printing (last digit): 9 8 7 6 5 4 3 2 1

Printed in the United States of America
on acid-free paper

To my parents, Jack and Arla Klatell, for setting high standards; to my wife, Nancy Lauter-Klatell, and my daughters Jenna and Devon, who have continued to inspire me.

D.K.

To my wife, Dawn-Marie Driscoll, for her extraordinary patience during yet another lost summer; and to my son, Chris, for being so special.

N.M.

PREFACE

PUBLICATION of this book follows more than a decade of research and teaching of the subject. Because we are both great fans of the medium, the years spent watching and discussing television sports have passed pleasurably. To be sure, on numerous occasions the obligation to conduct "serious applied research" (by watching several events on TV—often simultaneously) has dramatized the burdens of scholarship and tested the endurance of our respective marriages. We hope that our appreciation and enjoyment of the subject matter has helped make the information in the chapters that follow accessible to the average fan.

This book started with a desire to examine sports programming with the same seriousness of purpose as other aspects of the television and cable businesses, many of which have been the subject of numerous studies and publications. Sports is among the most popular forms of programming, has set all-time ratings records, and generates billions of dollars' worth of business annually. By some measures it is the most innovative kind of television, taking fullest advantage of the technology while relentlessly testing new production techniques and program formats. Television sports has repeatedly pioneered new equipment and program concepts later adopted by news and entertainment programs. Many of the industry's best and brightest original thinkers have come from sports. And yet, what little has been written has focused on individual personalities, sociology, and psychology. Comparatively little attention has been paid to its growth and maturation as an industry.

Our intent is to explain, rather than judge the business of television sports, accepting as we do the innately commercial orientation of both television and sports in the United States. One can debate endlessly the philosophy of sports and television in our society, with reference to what might be a more perfect union. Our purpose, however, is to describe and discuss what *is*, and to make the realities of the television/sports interaction understandable to its consumers. Armed with this knowledge, hopefully they may arrive at their own conclusions about the role and impact of sports television. Most important, perhaps, is our desire to treat the topic seriously, thereby extending a measure of respect to the business and its consumers alike.

In 1975, when David Klatell proposed that Boston University establish an informal study center, later to become the Institute in Broadcast Sports, the idea was greeted with considerable skepticism by many in the academic community, and with a hint of suspicion from working professionals. However, thanks in good measure to the efforts of Craig Aramian at Boston University, and the invaluable assistance of Jack Craig of the *Boston Globe* and Professor Robert Berry of Boston College Law School, the Institute soon took root and grew. When Norman Marcus joined the faculty in 1978, the research and teaching were given new energy and impetus, leading to year-round tracking of major industry trends and new developments.

As prominent executives frequently offered guest lectures at the Institute's annual summer conference, the early suspicions turned to gracious cooperation and generous contributions. We have benefited immensely from the insights, analysis, and raw data provided by dozens of guest lecturers, whose comments and correspondence have frequently sparked productive inquiries on our part, or offered new perspectives on the analysis of relevant information. In many cases, we have found that our willingness to treat them and their profession with seriousness and respect (in a field commonly demeaned because "it's only sports") has been reciprocated with long-term productive exchanges of information.

In 1978, John Wright of Oxford University Press first proposed a book which would accomplish the goals we have adopted for ourselves. John's vigorous support, optimism, and flexible deadlines nursed this project through its early years. Our appreciation too, to Sheldon Meyer, who inherited the authors' tendency to continually extend the publication deadline, in hopes of incorporating information from one more year of contract negotiations, ratings, and programming changes. We valued his steady imperturbability in the face of our constant experimentation with organization and structure.

Preface

Special note should be made of the Contributors whose essays appear in Chapter 11. Their gracious assent to our request for predictions of the future is appreciated, as is the vigor with which they undertook the task. The results offer some provocative prescriptions, and their variety demonstrates the breadth of opinion which invigorates the industry.

As much as possible, we have avoided the temptation to concentrate on personalities; this reflects our belief that although some of them are quite interesting, they are less important than the underlying business policies and procedures that govern decision-making. In addition, we believe that perceptive viewers already understand the on-air side of the business well enough to reach independent judgments about individual personalities. The book contains selected illustrative examples of salient business practices and strategies, and attempts to explain the on-air products which therefore result. It would be impossible to cover every sport, every programming format, or all the amusing anecdotes in a comprehensive manner; all of us—readers, the authors, critics, and people within the industry—have our own favorites, but to include them all would render the book both unwieldy and daunting to the average reader. And it is the general public to whom we address this work, because it is they who support the entire industry as paying customers of television sports. Ultimately, the powers of ownership are theirs.

Boston   D.A.K.
February 1988   N.M.

ACKNOWLEDGMENTS

WE WISH TO EXPRESS our appreciation to the great number of people who have contributed to the development of this book. Some have, by their encouragement and enthusiasm, spurred us to make the information contained in this work accessible to the general public. Others have graciously made available personal remembrances, and have confirmed or amplified much anecdotal information. A few have made specific editorial contributions, shaping the manuscript and offering suggestions for organizing the material. Still others have generously offered guest lectures at the Boston University Institute in Broadcast Sports, and their discussion of relevant issues has provided the starting point for many of the ideas upon which we have expanded. Finally, we wish to thank those contributors who have granted us access to corporate documents and data, but who wish to remain anonymous.

Seth Abraham, Dick Alford, John Andariese, Robert Apter, Robert Berry, Dick Bresciani, Carroll Bowen, Dick Button, Robert Caporale, John Carroll, T. Barton Carter, Bob Cochran, Jeff Cohen, Sharon Cohen, Scotty Connal, Beano Cook, Jack Craig; also Len DeLuca, Donald Dell, Ricky Diamond, Joyce DiBona, Eddie Einhorn, Bob Fishman, Barry Frank, Ed Garvey, Curt Gowdy, Nate Greenberg, Bud Greenspan, J. William Grimes, David Halberstam, Julie Hall, Greg Harney, Phil Hochberg,

ACKNOWLEDGMENTS

David Hoffman, Rob Ingraham, Stan Isaacs, Fern Kaplan, Paul Kelley, Bowie Kuhn; also Rex Lardner, John Lazarus, Carl Lindemann, Jr., Jack Mahoney, Carl Meyers, Gil Miller, Chuck Milton, Don Ohlmeyer, Kevin O'Malley, Glenn Ordway, Jack O'Rourke, Andrea Poch, Bill Rapaport, Scott Rasmussen, Betsy Richardson, Andy Rosenberg, Ron Ryan; also Tina Santi, Sam Schroeder, Bob Schron, Ginny Seipt, Jay Severin, Helaine Siegle, Harry "Chip" Shooshan, Chet Simmons, Charles Smiley, Charles Tarbox, Stu Tauber, Mike Trager, Jan Volk, George Wallach, Bob Warner, and Carolyn Weidman.

CONTENTS

SPORTS FOR SALE

1

WHAT WE ARE WATCHING: THE VIEW FROM THE COUCH

RODNEY DANGERFIELD ought to be the patron saint of television sports—viewers and sports program producers alike get very little respect. Despite the fact that sports programming is among the most popular, original, and spontaneous forms of television worldwide, viewers are frequently characterized as low-brow, passive spectators, whose preference for sports programming is vaguely antisocial. The dedicated men and women who produce the programs are most often prophets without honor in their own companies. It is not uncommon to hear the Sports division of a network disparaged as "lightweight" because it is not so imposing as News, so creative as Entertainment, so profitable as afternoon Soaps, so important as Sales. Besides, it looks like such fun to work in Sports—lots of travel, weekdays off, attendance at exciting events, the chance to rub elbows with famous athletes—why, it's hardly like work at all.

This attitude galls the highly skilled professionals whose job it is to bring a unique version of sports to television viewers. It ought similarly to gall thoughtful viewers, because it denigrates their ability to perceive the differences among program formats and select attractive, interesting sports events. In how many households have sports viewers been told to shut off the "boob tube"? Why do television sports fans put up with being called "Joe six-pack" or "the couch potato"—often by members of

3

their own family? Who decided that it is socially acceptable for intelligent adults to become hopelessly addicted to *Dallas,* or *Hill Street Blues,* or *As the World Turns,* but that equally compulsive baseball viewing is somehow childish?

Why, then, don't we give up and turn off the set? It is because of the personal experience of having seen for ourselves a tiny memorable moment which can be shared around office water-coolers for days—and replayed in our memories forever. The lawn will have to wait, because the next game, the next play, the next moment might be the magic one, and the suspense is killing us.

At its best, television sports is the finest programming television can offer. In many respects, sports may be the quintessential television program format, taking fullest advantage of the role television plays in our daily lives. Sports on television have visually attractive elements—splashy colors, attractive locations, motion and movement galore. They have expansive vistas, exquisite details, and larger-than-life images. Compared with the austere hush and "studio" sound of most programs, sports are alternately loud and brassy, and painfully hushed: you can tell the moment you hear the sound of the crowd what's going on. There is drama, tension, suspense, raw emotion, real anger, unvarnished joy, and a host of other responses. Most of all, you are watching real people compete for real, as unsure of the outcome as the viewer. The script, being written in front of you, is subject to few constraints common to the formulas of standard entertainment fare. In sports television the "bad guy" of the script often wins, unexpected things happen, virtue doesn't necessarily triumph, and goodness is not always rewarded.

Although many television program formats rely on the viewers to project their own fantasy of stepping through the screen to join the action, few do so as instinctively as sports. Many viewers of *Dallas* must have thought to themselves how wonderful it would be to be as rich as J. R. Ewing and to live his lifestyle. Few, however, ever believe even the most remote combination of circumstances could ever make such a dream reality. Sports viewers, on the other hand, share an almost universal sense of mutual interest and personal expertise in sports, and many, if not most, have played some. They commonly believe that were it not for unhappy circumstance, or childhood injury, or too-strict parents, or time constraints, they could have been the athletes now gracing the screen. Walter Mitty lives in all of us: "Boy, if I only got in shape, I could do that!," we think. On television we watch long stretches of unimaginable athletic excellence, hoping to catch an occasional reflection of some ability of our own.

The programs can also be viewed in a much more detached, almost casual manner. Sports are perfect for those drowsy weekend afternoons when one feels somewhere between taking a nap and cleaning out the attic. You can watch a bit, leave, come back, and watch some more. There's no dialogue to follow, no crucial scene to miss (in sports, you'll never miss all the replays), no complex serial plots from last week's show. Sports can be a sort of visual Muzak, playing quietly in the background, while other activities dominate your attention. When something of particular note happens, you will be alerted by the announcers, or the crowd noise. By and large, the competitors and events are familiar and need neither explanation nor rapt attention. They go on for hours, so what's the harm in a ten-minute lapse of attention? In short, you can watch sports just about any way you feel on a particular day. You can control the relationship between program producer and audience, simply by the way you choose to watch.

The drama inherent in athletic competition is sometimes taken for granted, usually by non-sports fans. To them, all baseball games look the same, all announcers sound the same, all crowds act the same. They have no sense of the pride, passion, and pain embodied in the competitors; no sense of the theatrical performance witnessed by the stadium crowd; no sense of the reporters and announcers describing simultaneous snippets from a dozen or so biographies unfolding in public. And no sense of having witnessed one of those rare, transcendental moments when sports really do become an allegory for life. As in many other areas, some sports clichés are actually true. There really is a thrill of victory, an agony of defeat, as ABC's Wide World of Sports mentions every week. The gritty realities of competition convey an underlying passion that no scripted television drama—no matter how carefully crafted—can regularly bring to the small screen.

Sports transforms itself into dance, into song, into drama, into comedy, into news—often when one least expects it. It embodies aspects of ethnic, community, regional, and national pride. It produces heroes and villains, rule-makers and law-breakers. It magnifies the striving accomplishments and tribulations of athletes raised high and fallen low. It is often candid, sometimes voyeuristic; often reassuring, sometimes disturbing. On some occasions, you can't turn away, on others you do so readily. Such moments are most special when they happen unexpectedly, when you want to call out to others, "Hey, come in here and watch this!" How often does this happen in any other television program format.

The television audience has been studied by a variety of research methods, ranging from purely anecdotal comments to highly sophisticated demography and in-depth psychological profiles of "typical viewers." Despite the sheer tonnage of such research, producing popular and profitable

5

programming remains an elusive goal in the vast majority of cases. The failure rate for Hollywood entertainment programming is staggering, especially when one considers the dozens of scripts and story ideas killed even before they pass the stage of a "pilot" program. Even the best guesses of the most experienced producers fail with numbing regularity. Anticipating correctly the changing mood of the American population is nearly impossible, particularly when society itself is changing in the short term, and commitments to programs must be made on a long-term basis.

Sports television must deal with these uncertainties all the time, and the problems of providing the audience with sports programs they will enjoy several years in the future are staggering. Although most reputable major sports events are sold to television in multi-year packages, it is nearly impossible to predict which teams or which sports will be attractive and entertaining by the time the package ends; it resembles blind bidding when the networks head to the bargaining table. Further, there is no way of knowing, for example, whether Magic Johnson and Larry Bird will still be in the National Basketball Association, or will still be playing for their present teams, or still ratings winners, over the life of the next contract, and yet network executives must bid anyway. Sports programmers have no way of knowing, for example, when they prepare to commit millions of dollars in rights fees to an event like the Belmont Stakes, whether they will end up with a Triple Crown race, or just the tired third race in an uneventful series.

The audience, like society itself, is also constantly changing, although in subtle ways that seem to baffle most programmers. We can observe certain trends, such as the growth of leisure time, and the visible increase in the awareness of health, fitness, and participatory activities, and still not know whether it means people will watch more television sports or less in the next few years. We can note the emergence of females in industry and commerce, and their greatly increased purchasing power and decision-making regarding disposable income. What we cannot know is whether this means television should produce more women's sports, or sports believed to be more appealing to women. For many years certain sports, principally soccer and tennis, have been enjoying a participatory boom across the country. Children and adolescents—the television viewers and consumers of tomorrow—are playing these sports (and others) more and football less. Why, then, have repeated attempts to produce successful television soccer packages all gone down in flames: why will they play but not watch?

The difficulties of programming sports television are daunting enough. Essentially, we ask network decision-makers to anticipate, years in advance, the participants in major public events, the tenor and tone of the actual contests, and the composition and purchasing power of the audience which will watch them. We then expect these network executives to mortgage a healthy chunk of their company's future on these assumptions, without even knowing the state of the economy, the advertising business, or the public mood during those crucial years. In addition, they have no way of predicting how the television business may have changed by the time the events take place.

Naturally, their competitors will certainly not stand pat but will engage in "counterprogramming" designed to defeat the best-laid plans. New communications technologies, such as cable television, satellite dishes, and videocassette recorders, are diminishing the audience available to network sports. Whole new networks, both national and regional, are being cobbled together by consortia of competitors looking to acquire the rights to major events, or at least drive up everyone else's operating costs and reduce the rate of return on programs. Advertisers are shifting their marketing plans to segments of society reached more efficiently through other program formats.

Most troubling, something truly drastic may go wrong with the event itself, such as the cancellation or boycott of the Olympics on which your company has bet the balance sheet, or a players' strike in professional sports that leaves your weekend programming devoid of both quality and quantity for weeks or months. Things may be no more predictable within your own company, at a time when corporate mergers and acquisitions are sweeping the broadcasting business, leaving the sports divisions at the mercy of tight-fisted accountants who could not care less who wins the NASCAR race, or which basketball player is retiring on-air, or whether Fenway Park's obscure nooks and crannies really deserve two extra cameras and crews to cover the games there. The rug may be yanked out from under you by your own employers, concerned more with their fiduciary obligations to stockholders than with any particular program format, especially one so expensive and visible as sports.

The production of a major live sports event can be television at its most exhilarating. It can also be an enormous, and frequently unrecognized, challenge to the resources, expertise, and daring of the production crew. They must extract, from an unscripted and unrehearsed event, sufficient entertainment, news and information to satisfy a knowledgeable and demanding audience. Frequently working under daunting physical conditions, they must incorporate complex technological innovations without the benefit of real field-testing. They must attract and hold the interest of an audience large enough to be profitable, sometimes when the event itself is boring, one-sided, or arcane. All this must be accomplished while living and working in a series of hotel rooms, cramped production trucks, and the inevitable airport waiting rooms. It is a challenge to make the productions seamless, and a far greater one to make them look easy. Yet, that is what viewers demand.

Many television sports fans are (or regard themselves as) experts regarding the program content—that is, the actual playing of the game, the players, rules, strengths, weaknesses, and strategies of the teams. Armchair coaches all, they can pick apart any zone, always call the right play, and reliably send the pitcher to the showers at the right moment. This is not surprising, given the attention lavished on watching such contests through the years, and it is one of the essential ingredients in the loyal relationship between fans and their chosen favorites.

These fans will not be satisfied by a cursory description of the events they are watching, nor with camera shots that miss the key moment, isolate on the wrong player, or omit the most telling replay angle. Their patience with announcers who restate the obvious, misidentify players, talk too much, or commit the unpardonable sin of appearing to be biased against the team they are rooting for is minimal at best. They are sports experts and critics simultaneously. This critical viewing skill is also applied by viewers of entertainment television. Loyal viewers of soap opera serials or situation comedies can be depended on to understand the story line and characters well enough to notice any deviation or mistake in the content.

What is more surprising, however, is the emerging understanding that many sports viewers have become, often without conscious effort, or even awareness, critical experts on the process of making sports television. They understand the underlying mechanics of getting an event on the air, as well as the unstated intentions of the production team in illustrating and describing the event to fit the demands of art and commerce. They have, essentially, learned the idiom of television sports—its techniques, pacing, formating and rhythms—from watching so much of it.

There are very few viewers who can explain their understanding in technical terms, but they certainly know when to expect certain program elements, including replays, slow-motion, promotional announcements, commercials, and even sequences of shots. They seem cognizant of and comfortable with the cadence and pace of each production, and they are sufficiently perceptive not only to differentiate between superior production values and the relatively mundane, but actually to critique those they find lacking. In no other television format must the producers and directors anticipate, and essentially compete with, the audience's own practiced directorial instincts.

For example, consider the relatively slow, short, and simple sequence that begins when a batter approaches the batter's box: he digs in (while the announcers discuss him), faces the pitcher, gets his statistics flashed on the screen (from a third base camera with a lefty, first base for righties), looks over the players in the field and their relationship to any baserunners, receives a stare from the pitcher, whose back is then turned to the audience by a centerfield camera which sets the catcher, umpire, and batter in perspective; the pitching begins, followed by commentary, shots of coaches, fielders, and dugouts, replays, crowd shots, and a repeat of the whole sequence for each pitch and for each batter. The longer the turn at bat, the closer the camera moves in, increasing the tension and the sense of human drama. When a ball is finally put into play, a whole other sequence is released, gushing forth fast edits, fleeting glances at speeding targets, and the blossoming of wide, encompassing shots.

It all has a wonderful, soothing, and familiar rhythm, one which conveys a sense of time and place, so that the viewer can say, "Ah, yes, this is baseball, not football or basketball, and it feels right." Each sport has its own analogous "feel" and timing. Each contains whole series of sequences which act not only as descriptive illustrations of the game at hand but also offer the experienced viewer subtle clues into the mindset of the show's producer and director, as they weave together the story line. Consider the quarterback breaking the huddle to survey the defense, or the basketball player at the foul line, or the golfer over a putt. We may think of each as a single image, but in reality they are composites of numerous sights, sounds, and actions. Audiences have learned how to watch, and what to watch for, and woe unto the director or producer who misses a step in this intricate dance.

Sports viewers expect still more from a production. They want to experience a different view of the game than is garnered by ticket-buying customers at the ball park, and that view had better be more detailed, more comprehensive, more illuminating, and more dramatic. It also has to live up to, or exceed, the home viewers' sense of their own expertise, so that it shows them things they couldn't have seen, or wouldn't have noticed, by themselves: exquisite details, microscopic closeups, unusual angles, realistic sounds; in-depth information and unique commentary, interviews with participants; technical analysis, non-stop action, perfect sightlines under any playing conditions; endless replays, isolations, and slow-mo shots without missing a play, and of course, suitable opportunities to head for the refrigerator or bathroom thrown in for good measure.

Oddly, the viewing public often seems to rely on these production techniques to validate what they have just seen with their own eyes.

They want to watch the replays again and again, as if suspending disbelief through the use of videotape. This trend has spawned an interesting phenomenon at the ball parks, to which many of these same fans now bring their own television sets to watch on TV what they have just seen, live, right in front of them. Many stadia and athletic facilities have now installed giant replay screens, so the paying customers won't be at a disadvantage relative to those who stayed home to watch from the living room couch. They are further reassured that waching at the stadium will be comparable to watching at home—a progressive reversal of logic no one would have believed a few short years ago. It is now almost instinctual to look for a replay in sports stadia of any quality, and many spectators feel a real sense of loss, should none be available. And throughout the land, the prevalence of portable videotape cameras assures that even Little League is recorded for replay, analysis, and critique.

It is the realities of sports television that we remember. Certainly, we have many other options for sports news and information, especially newspapers, radio, and magazines. We rarely remember those accounts, however impressive they were. On the other hand, we not only remember certain television images, we also recall where we were when we saw them, who was with us at the time, and how they made us feel. We remember Olga Korbut's charm, O. J. Simpson's grace, Muhammad Ali's bag of tricks; Celtics' pride, Mets' arrogance, and Dodger Blue; Jabbar's goggles, "Refrigerator" Perry's girth, and Theisman's broken leg; Olympian heroes and the tumbling, crashing ski-jumper who became "the agony of defeat" on Wide World of Sports; and victorious Olympic hockey goaltender Jim Craig, wrapped in the American flag, emotionally scanning the celebrating Lake Placid crowd for his father. We remember announcers like Howard Cosell and Harry Caray and John Madden and Brent Musburger. We even remember some of the TV sports commercials. Of the most-watched programs in American television history, the overwhelming majority have been sports events, particularly Super Bowl games.

The large audiences assembled by sports' programming may find themselves exposed to a range of issues and themes far beyond the narrow confines of sports and competition. For many years, one of the main attractions of many sports programs (especially Wide World of Sports and other magazine-format or "anthology" shows) was their audience's exposure to international travel and cultural variety. Quite a few events were placed on American television because the rights could be bought at bargain-basement prices from promoters around the world—many of whom were amazed that American television would pay them anything at all for the rights to televise an edited version of their event—and because the event or locale were so strange and wonderful to behold back in the States.

When ABC began promoting itself as "Recognized around the world as the leader in television sports," it was an accurate, if not boastful assessment. For many years in the fifties and early sixties, ABC was the weak sister of U.S. networks, and its stable of obscure overseas events wasn't necessarily something to crow about (except in that clever promotional phrase). Being recognized by foreign promoters of ski races, Irish hurling, auto tracks, and cliff diving as "the leader" was a distinction ABC would have happily traded for recognition where it counted— among the rights-holders to the National Football league, Major League Baseball, college Bowl games, and in the board rooms of the big U.S. ad agencies.

Nevertheless, the inter-cultural aspects of television sports have grown to include elements of news, diplomacy, and public policy, as well as other, more subtle aspects of our own society. From "ping pong diplomacy" in China and a variety of international tournaments, athletes and sports organizations have been bellwether indicators of international relations and the relative level of mutilateral tensions. Traveling almost exclusively in the company of television production personnel, these athletic ambassadors understand that their performance will be judged not simply on the winning and losing; the pictures, descriptions and accounts of their travels will have impact far beyond the world of sports.

One unfortunate aspect of international (or inter-cultural) sports television is the constant problem of the intrusion of politics, nationalism, and the associated "isms" including racism and sexism. Our encounters with athletes and sports organizations from around the world are frequently portrayed in simplistic, stereotypical terms. The more visible the event, the more likely someone is to claim that the other nation's teams are really professionals (as compared with our pristine "amateurs"); they are automatons, working at sports every waking moment, with no other interests (as compared with our students); they are on drugs (yes, we still make this accusation against others without irony); their women are really men, their Little-Leaguers really men, and their men really monsters.

Part of it is hype, simply to attract higher ratings, as in the endless series of U.S. vs. U.S.S.R. matches in boxing, gymnastics, hockey, etc., and ritualistic periodic confrontations with other nations which can easily fit the bill as the foreign menace. Another part of the equation seems to be the transference of legitimacy and importance onto the event simply because it entails foreign competition. In fact, some of the events exist almost entirely in a televised vacuum. They are contrived for the benefit of American television audiences, and often sold to advertisers seeking to establish a reputation as sponsors of international goodwill and multi-national business opportunities. Their actual importance to the athletes, or to international sporting organizations, may be minimal.

When indisputably important events such as various amateur World Championships, Pan American Games, the Olympic Games, Grand Slam Tennis, the America's Cup, and Canada Cup Hockey do come along, much of the hype is toned down, because the excellence of the events sells itself, and because the relatively sophisticated audience they attract won't fall for it anyway. Every sporting contest seems to require a bogey-man (hopefully foreign, but at least *different*) or two to root against, and promoters, team leaders, and politicians are only too willing to cast the event in terms of "us vs. them." Thankfully, in the major events, the networks seem to be a restraining influence, tempering their coverage with in-depth profiles, background information, and the "up close and personal" style which reveals more similarities between athletes from around the world than the differences others would exploit for commercial advantage.

One indisputable benefit of multi-cultural television sports in particular, and many other forms of television sports as well, is the instructional nature of the telecasts. While some "formal" education is provided by programs and videocassette actually designed to teach the techniques of particular sports, a much more pervasive, almost universal education is provided the casual fan on a regular basis. At its simplest, how can anyone watch hundreds of hours of skilled professionals plying their trade without picking up some of the skills, attributes, and behaviors of the experts? In some cases, this means copying Michael Jordan's dribble; in others, aping John McEnroe's tantrums. Want to know what makes Bulgarian weightlifters, Turkish wrestlers, Soviet hockey players, or Rumanian gymnasts so good? Just watch—as casual fans, young athletes, and coaches do with great regularity.

Among children especially, the influence of their athletic heroes (many of whom they have never seen except on television) can be profound, and it permeates certain segments of our society. The powerful images of success, accomplishment, high status and income are beacons to the young. What lessons can young people learn from watching television sports? All the lessons one can learn from watching most other activities in a concentrated and prolonged manner. One problem may arise from the simple fact that many young people, already predisposed to watch enormous amounts of television, are further encouraged by what they see to concentrate ever more intensely on sports. Television sports may appear to them as an open door beckoning them toward the success it portrays.

Like Oz, it shimmers in the distance, and like Oz, it is only a dream for 99.9 percent of all the dreamers.

It is probably pointless to observe that, if they were to spend so much time and energy watching, say, a carpenter at work, they and society would be better off. Young people cannot be blamed for participating in an activity which has been carefully structured and refined precisely to attract them, and which causes no evident harm at the time. In fact, given the realities of modern societies, it may be one of the lesser evils for young people thus to spend their time.

As many prominent sociologists have pointed out, however, the lasting damage may be done to a segment of that audience which grows to maturity believing that excellence on the athletic field or gym floor is the easiest and most successful route to achieving the glamour, status, and respect seemingly enjoyed by those televised athletes. The image of success is often highlighted on television sports. Few people wish to watch failure, despair, frustration, and pain, and even fewer television producers wish to broadcast it, or advertisers sponsor it. Failure is often treated by the athlete or team simply disappearing from future broadcast schedules. And yet, disappointment is statistically many times more common than success.

Competition, luck, injury, opportunity, and a host of other factors will conspire to rob the overwhelming percentage of athletes of their vitality, their self-image, and their livelihood. Television should not be blamed for its failure to insert this message in its programming, but it must be acknowledged that the images of success we see on television sports are, for the vast majority of viewers, simply that—images.

One subject almost universally ignored by television sports reporters and commentators is a most uncomfortable one for them: their own contribution to the problems, principally through the flow of television money into sports. When literally billions of television dollars are available just as war chests to bid for broadcast rights, and hundreds of millions more are available in equipment, facilities, salaries, and promotion, the impact on athletes, sports organizations, and the general public cannot be ignored. Television now effectively subsidizes several professional leagues, and many a salary structure is based on the flow of television money. If the problem of modern sports in this nation is indeed money (a situation which long predates the major impact of television), then television must accept a good deal of the blame, for providing what amounts to an addictive substance in great quantity to people not often prepared to handle it.

Television reporters very rarely do stories about how television has taken over the economics of sports, and what that has meant to the competitor or the fan. Never given to introspection or public hand-wringing, the television sports industry often decries the symptoms of trouble in paradise; only rarely the root causes.

Other ironies abound in the lasting imagery of television sports. Problems of racism persist in both sports and broadcasting. While it is true that in 1987 former Dodgers executive Al Campanis caused a national furor with his ill-chosen remarks about why there were no blacks in baseball management, his attitudes were no surprise to anyone familiar with the game and its hierarchy. Other organizations (notably the NFL, which has never had a black head coach) fared slightly better in the public eye only by avoiding so public an embarrassment. The executive suites of the television industry, and TV sports in particular, are also the preserves of white middle-aged males. What few black employees there may be are usually in highly visible positions, such as on-air talent or commentators. Rarely they are in decision-making positions or in control of budgets, administration, or even remote production crews. The record is slowly getting better, as attempts are being made to hire and promote minorities and women (partly as a consequence of the Federal Communications Commission's oversight function), but television sports could thank Campanis for inadvertently diverting the criticism, at least for a short while.

In January 1988 the problem again burst onto the front pages, this time directly threatening the public perception of the NFL and network sports. On the eve of the NFL conference Championship games, "NFL Today" analyst Jimmy "The Greek" Snyder was summarily fired for making remarks as outrageous as had Campanis. Ironically, Snyder was responding to questions about the legacy of Dr. Martin Luther King, Jr., when he offered the opinion that blacks were better athletes than whites as a result of selective breeding by slave-owners. He also noted that if blacks became NFL head coaches, "there'd be nothing left for white guys"—which he later claimed was said in jest. Snyder, at age seventy, had heretofore been spared CBS's rigid retirement policy, and was earning nearly half a million dollars annually as a thinly disguised oddsmaker for "NFL Today." Despite statements of support from black colleagues and a few prominent figures, including the Rev. Jesse Jackson and NFL Players Association head Gene Upshaw, Snyder was unceremoniously dumped by CBS, with none of the hand-wringing which accompanied Campanis's fall from grace. Perhaps both dismissals were fully justified; perhaps they represented the inevitable search for a scapegoat. The two cases focused public skepticism on the mixed and often conflicting values emanating from the network and sports establishments.

Similarly, viewers are accustomed to seeing public service announcements, in which well-known athletes speak out against drugs, drink, and other problems or endorse various worthwhile charities. These announcements, made at some considerable expense by the participants, represent a sincere attempt to help people in need, using the immense power of television to sway public opinion. Particularly when well-known athletes appear in these roles, the message can be effective in changing attitudes about the problems, as well as about athletes themselves. The message, however, often must appear hard on the heels of the ever-present beer or wine ad, often starring a galaxy of recently retired athletes. Without alcohol-related advertising, many a telecast booth and several stadia would go dark. The irony seems to escape most television sports announcers and executives.

A related problem is that of gambling, an activity which is frequently illegal, as well as corrosive to the fiber of society, and which can become an addictive disease in some individuals. In addition to its legal and medical ramifications, even a hint of gambling is sufficient to cast a dark cloud of suspicion across the sports landscape. Betting scandals, point-shaving, illegal payments, unsavory characters, and "fixed" results are all too commonly perceived by fans and viewers, particularly when they are dissatisfied by the outcome of a contest. Certainly nothing can so threaten the integrity of athletics, as well as the loyalty and support of the paying public, as allegations of gambling or related offenses. Players and coaches have been suspended and disciplined, others actually investigated by law enforcement at the behest of their employers, when even a casual association with gamblers was suspected.

However, television once again seems most blind to its own influence and behavior, as it sprouts on-camera experts such as NBC's Danny Sheridan to tout thinly disguised point spreads. On the more daring cable television services, you can watch actual bookmakers and bettors making choices and totaling wins and losses—there's no attempt to sugar-coat what's going on. It is estimated that a very considerable portion of the average audience for some sports, especially the NFL and NCAA football and basketball, is comprised of viewers having a financial stake in the outcome, from small office pools to Las Vegas wheeler-dealers.

Television may argue that the broadcasting of betting information is simply a harmless acknowledgment of reality, and to ignore the audience's interest in this information would be foolhardy. Perhaps, but it may also be seen as one more action that helps compromise a system based on implicit trust. The whole subject of on-air talent and expert commentators is a touchy one. The "star" announcers and commentators—the Maddens, Giffords, Musburgers, Michaels, and Cosells of the industry—are so removed in salary, visibility, and status from the humble local announcers or nightly sportscasters that they hardly seem employed in the same business.

In fact, a case can be made that they are not employed in the same business. The million-dollar salaries and incessant promotional campaigns mounted by their employers place them at a level equal to or higher than that of the athletes they are covering. In some cases, the television announcers, their associated personnel and vans full of high-tech equipment, have overwhelmed the event and its erstwhile participants.

In many instances, the broadcast booth, rather than the action on the field, has become the center of the telecast, with multiple on-air personnel orchestrating a combination of entertainment, network promotion, and commentary for the benefit of non-sports fans and their impact on ratings. This trend is supported, in part, by the technical complexity built into each major production, and the obligation for the star sportscaster to serve as ringmaster.

The role of announcers has been greatly changed by the growing battery of omnipresent cameras, videotape machines, computer graphics, and microphones; how much can they really add to a shot we can all see from four different angles at three different speeds? Instead, they often are relegated to anecdotes, memories, commentary, humor, or simply coordinating the mass of information, commands, queries, and signals flowing from the director in the truck. And as television production has grown more complex, they need to be more expert in television than their predecessors, more expert, even, than in sports. Knowing how to work with all the replays, commercials, statistics, promotional announcements, fellow announcers, and the entire production crew demands intense preparation and concentration. Preparation and experience are required when facing the unpredictabilities of covering live events: talking your way smoothly and informatively through rain delays, technical problems, disruption, and demonstrations requires skills best acquired long before the need arises.

Some announcers are better than others at knitting together the broadcast production; some are easier to work with, and more dedicated to their profession; some are insufferable egomaniacs, others delightful and generous. The only common attribute they must share is the ability to draw and hold viewers. Aside from providing grist for an endless number of insoluble arguments, one's personal preference for one announcer's style over another is bound to remain just that—a personal preference. There are few empirical methods of deciding who is best at what in the announcing field, since the whole matter is a subjective one.

In some cases, in fact, notoriety plays as well as popularity. It is important to remember that television executives and advertisers don't really care why we watch—only that we do. Howard Cosell regularly finished at the top of the list for "Best Announcer" and "Worst Announcer" at the same time. ABC skillfully capitalized on his powerful personality, building controversy and attention, and was delighted whether you watched him to love him or hate him—just so long as you watched. Other major network announcers have survived for years because their ratings value exceeded whatever limitations each brought to the calling of an event.

More troubling is the role of "color commentators"—usually ex-athletes promoted to the broadcast booth after retirement. Some admittedly distinguished talents have emerged from this system, including Frank Gifford, Pat Summerall, O. J. Simpson, John Madden, and others. However, for every commentator with sufficient knowledge, perception, communication skills, and originality to enhance the description of an event which the audience can see with its own eyes, we are treated to dozens of on-air try-outs resembling nothing so much as a public-speaking contest at the local grange. The selection—and surprisingly the training—of color commentators is both random and spotty. To sit through a newcomer's inaugural broadcast will make even the most dedicated viewer alternately squirm with impatience and doze off, waiting for the expert actually to illustrate a point before being cut off by the play-by-play man or a commercial.

These former athletes have taught us several valuable lessons: it isn't nearly as easy as it looks; being good at an activity like sports is not the same as being good at understanding or explaining it; mediocrity is so commonplace anyone with a little spark or originality will shine through. Apparently networks are eternal optimists. They seem to believe that next season, the next group of color commentators will arrive fully fledged from the playing field, ready to settle into the broadcast booth, and that new viewers will tune in to see them. They must believe that, because they keep hiring the same type, and these people are, almost without exception, white males. Some critics have noted over the years that quite a few veteran middle-aged white males seem to have incredible staying power, despite mediocre ratings and audience delivery, while the few minority males and women placed in the booth are more rarely given repeated opportunities to improve initial weak performances.

Most sports announcers (some notable exceptions are Jim McKay, Howard Cosell, and Dick Enberg) are ill-equipped to comment on the many issues now swirling about sports. The landscape these untrained observers must describe is as complicated, turbulent, and impassioned as the rest of society, and sports in the 1980s offers no refuge from all the many problems in society at large: drugs, money, gambling, dishonesty, selfishness, racism and sexism, hero-worship, peer pressure, and educational issues are all apparent in some segments of sports. Television frequently illuminates these problems almost by accident—not through dogged journalistic enterprise, but through the process of magnifying the athletes and their actions—so that we, if we are at all observant, cannot help but take notice.

Announcing "stars" are, of course, given the greatest support, because their employers have invested the most in them. They get plum assignments to big events, plenty of technical and personnel assistance, promotion, and perks. Famous athletes and others make themselves available for interviews and on-camera appearances with them. In short, the star announcers move from event to event like minor potentates. What about the little-known regional announcer hired on a temporary basis to telecast an obscure game, which will be shown on tape-delay only if there is a rainout of another event? Working with local crews, small budgets, and none of the technological bells and whistles afforded the heavyweights, can his performance fairly be compared?

And how about that other category of television sports announcer we are all so familiar with—the local station's sportscaster on the evening news? To put it mildly, it is more than a few blocks from ABC Sports in New York to the 11 p.m. news at WNEW-TV: it's a different world altogether. The role of local sports anchors is difficult to define, even by practitioners of the craft. Are they expected to be reporters in the same sense as the straight news journalists employed by the same program? Does the local audience, which watches them hundreds of times per year (as opposed to even the most omnipresent network stars, who work a fraction of that schedule), perceive them as independent journalists, home-team boosters, or just attractive on-camera readers of the scoreboard?

In many markets, the relationship between individual stations and local teams is either uncomfortably close or chilly and distant. Functioning in such an environment, can a local sportscaster really perform a job that is part hype and entertainment, part business partnership, and part enterprise reporting? What even the most sophisticated viewer may expect or depend upon will vary dramatically, with different markets and individual sportscasters.

Television executives generally are more forthcoming about the most pervasive and obvious influence their industry has had on sports: the scheduling and playing of the athletic contests and the rules of those games. They point out, and correctly so, that, without television's money (and the event promoter's willing agreement as part of the rights negotiations), many events would no longer exist or prosper. In return for its all-important investment in the sport, television expects reciprocity, cooperation, and accommodation—the sports' investment in television. This generally takes the form of adjusting the location, timing, duration, and pace of the event to accommodate it to the demands of the television program scheduling and production techniques.

To make the event a more entertaining television program, emphasis will be placed on different personalities and program elements than might appeal to the on-site fans. The stadium becomes, in effect, a giant television studio, and the event a controlled, inevitably stage-managed affair. This is not necessarily bad, simply the reality of our time. Surprisingly, as the years have gone by, fewer and fewer fans or athletes seem to be offended. The former realize that without television their ticket prices would assuredly skyrocket, and the latter know full well where next year's salary increase is coming from.

Nearly every sport has made the adjustments necessary to earn the attention of television. "TV Time-outs" are commonplace in the NFL, NBA, and break-neck hockey. Two-minute warnings have become strategic points in football games. Tennis has tie-breakers; golf switched from match play to 72-hole total tournament scoring; professional basketball banned the zone and installed the 24-second clock. Night baseball became the rule, not the exception. Teams and leagues have sprung up in cities chosen for their television potential, abandoning others after years of loyal fan support. Expansion has proliferated.

Some sports, including soccer and ice hockey, have been condemned as unsuitable for national television, and languish on the fringe of the big time. Others, especially tennis, have experienced a roller-coaster ride of limited telecasts followed by grievous over-exposure, which resulted in virtual banishment from network television. In other cases, and with increasing frequency, sports are invented or cobbled together almost solely for the purpose of appearing on television. So-called "television leagues," such as the United States Football League, are predicated on the belief that success on television will engender popularity at the gate— a reversal of the traditional method of operation.

Another category of programming has sprung from the availability of considerable air time for sports-related events. Called "junk sports" by most people and "made-for-tv events" by the programmers and entrepreneurs who dream them up, a bewildering variety of contests, competitions, exhibitions, and plain craziness has flooded broadcast and cable television. Some, like "The Superstars" (and its various progeny) and "Skins" golf matches, have outgrown their shaky beginnings, achieving the legitimacy and fan interest of real sports. Others, like the Bobby Riggs vs. Billie Jean King tennis "match," achieved the level of spectacular kitsch, capturing our attention for a short, gloriously ridiculous time. Still others, from cliff-diving to wrist-wrestling; from refrigerator pulls to "Challenge of the Sexes" (or was it "Battle of the Network Stars" . . . "Battle of the Network Sexes" . . . "Challenge of the Network Sexists" . . . ?); from the world's strongest men to women's sixteen-and-under billiards, continue to exist in their original orbits, regularly passing across the screen for no apparent reason, save that of commerce, and then disappearing once more from our view.

These quasi-events have helped force us to redefine our definition of sports itself. By blending the elements of competition (however amateurish), entertainment (however curious), excellence (however rare in these events), oddity (a common feature) and novelty, made-for-television-events have blurred the comfortable distinctions between what is legitimate sport and everything else. Perhaps we watch because the performances usually feature well-known athletes and other personalities doing something other than that which they are famous for. We can take a certain pleasure in watching the famous and near-famous brought to earth by their utter inability to scale a wall, paddle a Hawaiian canoe, swim two laps, or ride a bicycle. It humanizes them and brings them to a level of competition and excellence no higher (and in many cases, lower) than our own. Never underestimate the drawing power of the Mighty humbled.

Before totally condemning these programs, one must ask a difficult question: Do we define sports in this nation by the proficiency of the participants, by the riches rewarded, by accolades and fame? If the local neighborhod pickup game, featuring all manner of inefficient athletic pretenders (each of whom is trying to win, with nothing more on the line than pride), can be counted as "real" sports (in fact, the very model of sporting competition, to some observers), why turn our noses up at rich professionals doing the same thing for money? This question owes its existence to television, as we begin to contemplate what television has done to our understanding of sport.

Made-for-television events are often nothing more than gussied-up program-length commercials for the resort hotel or equipment manufacturers sponsoring the competition. They exist to sell products in as many ways as possible: through endorsements, favorable coverage, demonstrations of the equipment, association with athletes, and public exposure. The commercialization of television sports has grown inevitably as other costs have risen. Television advertising alone is rarely sufficient to offset the expenses of event promoters, marketing firms, rights-holders, participants, and television itself. New and more varied revenue sources must be identified and developed.

The influence of television is felt in the ever increasing number of on-site advertising banners and logos and sponsorship tie-ins. Some athletes have become walking billboards for their multiple sponsors and equipment suppliers; athletic arenas are plastered with billboards and print ads; the sponsor's blimp, Official Car, halftime award, fan-participation contest, and public-service campaign are all now accepted parts of the average major event. Athletes endorsing products can expect to have major television advertising campaigns built around their appearance in televised games.

The commercialization of sports, even at the amateur level, continues apace, justified by the constant need to bring in more and more money, and limited only by initial resistance from the public, which inevitably overcomes its outrage and learns to accept yet more blatant salesmanship in sports as a necessary evil which subsidizes the undertaking. If in junk sports, it's tough to separate the junk from the sports, then in all sports it's equally tough to separate the business from the sport.

More subtly, the almost limitless number and variety of events now available to the typical viewer via networks, cable, and local stations lend a sense of dislocation to relationship between the viewer/fan and the athletes or event. A typical week offers a veritable blizzard of sports programs, some local, others national or international; some live, others "live on tape," or edited videotapes, or even reruns. Bleary viewers or workers on the late shift may watch all through the wee hours, seven days a week. It is possible, in fact, to watch television every waking moment, and never see anything save sports. Some of it may be hard to identify, and can be watched totally out of any context of loyalty or location or time.

Superstations carry "national" teams into the home markets of their competitors, testing the loyalty of viewers and advertisers alike. Networks build their schedules around selected teams and performers perceived to be more glamorous or successful in national marketing terms. Leagues, sports, and franchises deemed unfit for major television are condemned to the nether-world out of the glare of publicity, and far from the sources of significant revenues. It may be a cliché—but just barely—to say that without television you simply can't be a major sport. And since the roster of major sports which will prove profitable to the television business is relatively small, and getting smaller all the time, television concentrates the full glare of its attention on them, often ignoring the struggling smaller outfits.

The once extensive system of successful baseball minor leagues is moribund, its survivors clinging to the financial lifeline of major league sponsorship. Their territories invaded by distant signals and by the expansion of professional leagues (itself fueled by television), former hotbeds of lower-level professional support have either withered as their fans turned to the telecasts of distant glamour teams or have been left stranded, like inland backwater eddies in the vast stream of national sports commerce emanating from the major cities.

Do the Dallas Cowboys, Boston Celtics, New York Yankees, L.A. Lakers, and teams from Chicago, Philadelphia, and a few other media centers get an unfair amount of air time? Of course, and without apologies to the other franchises in their leagues, who appear rarely, and then only in a supporting role. Television openly courts the viewers in certain major cities, and cultivates a viewing audience for those teams throughout the country. The thought of a Montreal Expo–Texas Ranger World Series, or a Kansas City–Green Bay Super Bowl strikes fear and trepidation in the hearts of network sports executives. "America's Teams" are a frank acknowledgment that in television sports, as in life, some are always more equal than others. To be small, weak, dull, or from a smaller market is to be off national television.

But should it be any other way? Can commercial television really provide programming which responds to all the various demands we have thus far discussed, as well as many others, and still make a profit sufficient to offset competition for air time from other types of programming? Is it fair to expect television sports to be, all at once, a mirror of society, an accurate reporter of complex personalities and events, a business partner in an enterprise central to our enjoyment of life, a producer of sheer entertainment on a grand scale, a predictor of demographic change and lifestyles, an everyday presence in our homes, and a source of both private and corporate profit?

We take sports seriously, perhaps too seriously, but that seems a part of the national character unlikely to undergo a radical re-evaluation any time soon. Those involved in the system of organized sports are in the business of perpetuating its place in the hearts of the public, whose appetite seems insatiable. Simply stated, sports matter so deeply to so many people that they really can't be left to amateurs, or entrusted to unsophisticated hands. We have evolved a system which virtually demands a highly structured, centrally controlled edifice of commerce to function properly. Television, once an observer of that edifice, has become an indispensable bulwark of the structure itself.

As television and sports have become more and more interdependent, separating their functions and role in society has become increasingly difficult. The marriage of the two businesses—which continues to have its rocky periods, like any marriage—has produced a hybrid offspring: the television/sports complex which is neither pure television nor pure sports, and resembles each parent only in profitable bloodlines.

2

TV CAMERAS DON'T BLINK, ONLY ADVERTISERS DO

GUGLIELMO MARCONI never hit a hanging slider or threw a Hail Mary pass. He never sank a three-point shot or scored a short-handed goal. But he indirectly contributed to sports broadcasting in America by revolutionizing the way we listen to and watch others play games. Marconi gave us radio, radio gave us television, and television gave us Howard Cosell.

Now what does the inventor of modern radio have to do with the man that TV critics called "the sportcaster fans love to hate?" The answer is simple. Howard Cosell was provocative in a medium that celebrates cool. His on-air style entertained millions of viewers while he enraged them, and his notoriety contributed to the marriage of two big businesses. He helped make ABC—and almost everyone else involved in sports broadcasting in the 1970s and '80s—more successful. Live TV sports became popular prime-time entertainment and worked wonders for a business that transformed sports arenas and stadiums into live TV studios.

But back to Marconi. His genius for invention at the end of the nineteenth century led to the development of wireless transmission and to radio as we know it today. Marconi should probably share credit for paving Howard Cosell's way with a technician in the employ of Westinghouse Broadcasting. Prior to World War I, the young engineer sent transcribed music over the air from the privacy of his garage while experimenting on a radio transmitter, his company's latest invention. Imagine the shock and delight of those few people within range of the signal who suddenly heard music on their rudimentary radio receivers.

"Maude, come on in here, quick! Listen to what's comin' in on the crystal set. Music, Maude, music!"

"Henry, you been touching that Allegheny hooch again, ain't ya?"

"No, Maude, I swear. It's music. Sweet music. Right outta the air."

And from this early experiment came more than sweet music. By the end of 1920, radio was no longer a figment of the nation's imagination. It was for real. In November 1920 an inaugural broadcast told the nation that Warren C. Harding had become 29th President of the United States, and started America's love affair with and dependency on electronic media.

The cheers of that election celebration had no sooner died down when other types of programs made their way onto the dial. More listeners than station operators could have imagined became enthralled with the new medium. The question of financing radio programs was answered when, by the mid-1920s, radio and advertising fell in love. The advertising industry had found a dynamic new way to move clients' products off the shelves, and it wasn't too long before commercial benefactors brought America the sweet sounds of the Ipana Troubadors and the A & P Gypsies. Radio's programming horizons seemed limitless at the height of the pre-Depression jazz era.

By the mid-1930s, radio was the center of American home entertainment. The networks were the source of most prime-time programming, and advertising made it all possible. Radio supplanted newspapers as America's number one source of information in the mid and late 1930s as Hitler was making his move across Europe. The immediacy of radio gave broadcast news a substantial advantage over the print media.

Sports and radio were another happy, pre-World War II duo. Sports provided countless hours of appealing, long-form programming, and an early breed of sports broadcasters like Ted Husing, Bill Stern, Graham McNamee, and Harry Wismer mastered the art of bringing live accounts of college and professional games into the theatre of their audiences' mind. Sports fans no longer had to wait until the morning newspapers arrived to read accounts of yesterday's games. Live radio brought listeners the thrills of victory and the agonies of defeat long before television found Jim McKay.

By the end of World War II, radio moved aside for television, which had been slow to develop because the war had diverted critical materials and reordered the nation's priorities. Inevitably, though, television took its first steps in the late 1940s and found its economic legs by the early

1950s. Radio became secondary to television for family entertainment, and local stations created new formats to replace lost network programming. The networks turned their resources to producing television programs. Television advertising, whose roots were in radio, blossomed like so many wild perennials because television gave advertisers the luxury of showing off their products live, and eventually in color. With even more at stake in television than in radio, a word from the sponsor could either make or break programs overnight.

In television's earliest years, the network sports divisions were barely active, a far cry from the ultimate influence they had on professional and amateur sports, and on network profits. By the 1980s, professional football teams would receive nearly 60 percent of their revenues from TV, and major league baseball and basketball teams approximately 30 percent each. As for television, ABC, CBS, and NBC collectively earned $1.3 billion in sports advertising revenues in 1986. About 20 percent of a network's total revenues comes from sports advertising, a percentage second only to prime-time programming. However, huge production costs limit the profitability of sports. Compared with network weekday programs, which earn nearly the same percentage of revenues, network sports programs are about five times less profitable.

Many advertising minutes have been sold since the day when about 1000 households tuned in to watch the first televised game on experimental station W2XBS in New York. When Bill Stern bravely attempted to broadcast the play-by-play of the Columbia-Princeton game on May 17, 1939—with one camera following the action taking place on upper Manhattan's Baker Field—little did he know that this event would presage the evolution of sports broadcasting into more than a billion-dollar industry within half a century.

During nearly three decades, the tenuous love/hate relationship of sports, television, and advertisers has become a way of life in which mutual back-scratching occasionally draws blood.

❦The success of sports on TV, like that of any other program, rests on the number of people who watch, and it is really the fans who hold the TV/sports/advertising triangle together. Events that attract a large audience stay on the air. Those that don't, generally go off, unless the sport—golf or tennis, for example—has a demographic appeal for advertisers which compensates for the sport's relatively small TV audience. Perhaps one can better appreciate the economic interdependency of advertising and television by knowing how commercial television works. To say that advertising makes the business go is perhaps an oversimplification because this multi-billion dollar industry is more complex than that.

Commercial television is comprised of hundreds of independently owned TV stations, relatively small businesses located in more than two hundred markets across the country. This is the most influential segment of the television industry because station managers and program directors decide what programs Americans will see and hear on television each day. Stations, not the networks, are the first line of contact with the audience. Each station is licensed by the Federal Communications Commission (FCC) to serve its community, with technical considerations and market size helping to determine a station's geographic coverage area.

As a licensee, station management generally bases its programming decisions on two grounds, one legal and the other economic. First, the station must fulfill its license requirement to "serve the public interest." Because broadcasting is a business, however, decisions about which programs are selected and where they go in the schedule are made on the basis of a station's need to attract a large audience for its advertisers. Sometimes, regulations and economics come into conflict because programs deemed to serve the public interest aren't necessarily the same ones that appeal to a large audience.

A corporation may own as many as twelve TV stations, but it may not own more than one in a single city. The reason for this one-to-a-market rule is to ensure a diversity of ownership and to limit any possible private monopoly of the public airwaves. Station owners, who are responsible to the FCC for every program they put on the air, decide whether or not to be affiliated with a network, a relationship based on mutual need and dependency. Network-affiliate agreements may be terminated by either party at the end of two years. Independent stations are those which choose not to have network affiliation, opting instead to fill all of their air time themselves.

The FCC defines a network as "an entity which offers an interconnected program service on a regular basis for 15 or more hours per week to at least 25 affiliated television licensees in 10 or more states." ABC, CBS, and NBC, which also own television stations, qualify as networks. Fox Broadcasting, another corporation which owns a group of TV stations, provides programs to other stations on a part-time basis and does not meet the FCC's standard definition of a network.

In considering the network-affiliate relationship, think of a modern-day marriage in which both mates sign a pre-nuptial agreement, have separate careers, keep separate bank accounts, and go to bed together only when it suits their respective moods and schedules. Networks provide their affiliates with eminently promotable entertainment, news, and sports programs, and in return the affiliates deliver an audience. Networks pay their affiliates to clear their air time to carry programs in which the network sales department has sold commercials. About 60 percent of a typical affiliate's total weekly schedule—including daytime and week-ends—comes from the network, and approximately 85 percent of its prime-time schedule originates with the network.

Television stations have three sources of programs besides the network. They produce their own—news, talk-shows, coverage of local sports teams—and they buy syndicated programs which are either reruns of old network series or new programs which have been produced specifically to bypass the network for sale directly to stations. Examples of "first-run" series that were sold directly to stations on a market-by-market basis are Greatest Sports Legends and Light Moments in Sports.

While the broadcast and several cable networks have tied up the rights to many college football and basketball conferences, independent pro-ducers own the rights to a considerable number of individual events which they sell directly to stations through barter arrangements. In barter syndication, the syndicator retains a percentage of the available commer-cial air time in the program that he sells to advertisers. The station sells the rest of the commercials. In some instances, syndicators interconnect an "ad hoc" network of stations across the country to offer live sports events of either regional or national appeal.

The Mizlou TV network is perhaps one of the most active barter syndicators in sports programming, focusing primarily on national events which the networks have refused. Mizlou often clears as much as 90 per-cent of the TV markets in the country for post-season college football bowl games and NIT college basketball.

Barter syndication became profitable in recent years for a number of other sports syndicators such as Jefferson–Pilot Teleproductions (Atlan-tic Coast Conference college football, Southeast Conference college basketball, independent college football) and Raycom Sports (Metro and ACC basketball, Southwest Conference football). In a mood of muscle-flexing in late 1987, executives at Raycom claimed that their basketball telecasts delivered to advertisers 56 percent more homes than NBC, 68 percent more than CBS, and 153 percent more than ABC. All of these companies attributed their success to paying rights fees that were in line with the amount of advertising revenues that the programs could yield. They benefited from the earlier experience of such companies as Metro TV Sports, TVS, the sports division of Katz Communications, and several others which suffered heavy financial losses in the early 1980s because of having overpaid rights fees.

Feature film packages of full-length theatrical motion pictures are the third source of station programming. These are a particular staple of independent stations. Films are economical because they usually run two hours or longer and can be cut conveniently (and often indiscriminately) to fill the station's commercial time needs. Like films, coverage of local sports teams is an equally valuable source of long-form programming, although rights to local sports events are increasingly being bought by regional cable and pay-TV outlets, which are often willing to pay higher fees.

The economics of TV advertising and the network-affiliate relationship revolve around the "ownership" of air time. When an affiliated station airs a locally produced program, or one which it has bought through syndication, its sales staff and representatives sell commercials directly to ad agencies. Station profits come from these sales after commissions are paid to the ad agency which bought the commercial time and to the salespeople who sold it.

The commercials within a network program are sold by the network's sales staff, and networks compensate stations that carry their programs. The compensation, however, is significantly less than the amount a station would have made had it carried its own programs at the time. Then why carry network programs at all if a station can make more money by filling the time with its own programs? Simply because network programs attract a large audience in prime time (8-11 p.m.) which affiliates hope will stay tuned for the entire evening, including the station breaks between the programs. The air-time between network programs is "owned" by affiliates, which keep all of the money from the commercials they sell—at premium prices—during these breaks. While independent stations keep all revenue from the sale of their air time, they seldom attract a prime-time audience comparable to that of network affiliates, and their profits are generally much lower.

On the average, about 7 percent to 12 percent of an affiliate's total revenue comes from network compensation. The percentage differs according to market size, with major market stations less dependent than stations located in smaller markets on this source of revenue. The rest of a station's revenue (40-45%) comes from locally sold commercials and from spots sold to national or regional advertisers (40-45%). These percentages also vary according to market size. National advertisers generally find it more efficient to buy time in large and medium-sized markets, and smaller-market stations must sell more local advertising.

Affiliated stations can pre-empt the network at any time to carry programs which they feel are in their communities' best interest. When this happens, the network is free to release the pre-empted programs to other stations in the market. In general, however, pre-empted network programs seldom achieve the same audience size on other stations that they do when carried by their affiliate.

Over the life of the network-affiliate agreement, the relationship is marred by any number of issues. Occasionally, a controversial program makes its way onto the network schedule—Maude's abortion, *The Day After* a nuclear holocaust, or when Russia takes over *Amerika*. But occurrences of controversial network programs are rare, however, because commercial broadcasters shy away from controversy. Controversy is not good for business. Bones of network-affiliate contention more often have to do with who keeps whom from making money.

There are other sources of tension between a network and its affiliates. For example, when the network's prime-time ratings are a disaster, the affiliates feel the pinch, particularly if the 10 o'clock program is a poor lead-in to the affiliate's money-making late newscast. When the vacation schedule of the Tonight Show's Johnny Carson caused some NBC affiliates to lose audience, more than the peacock's feathers were ruffled. Many threatened to drop the show entirely rather than suffer as a result of Carson's absence. But the greatest cause of tension in the marriage comes from program clearance, or better yet, lack of it.

In the early 1980s, college basketball on NBC made the NBA on CBS look stale and tired. The professional game was struggling with many image problems that threatened to bury the NBA in network purgatory, a fate which befell the NHL when professional hockey failed to capture a large enough audience. The NBA was criticized for many reasons:

"Professional games are too predictable; all you have to do is watch the last two minutes because that's when the outcome is always decided."

"Pro basketball is all offense and the players are too good; too much perfection is boring."

The fact that professional basketball was increasingly dominated by black players, many of whom had honed their skills on the macadam pavements of America's ghettos, stirred a not-so-subtle undercurrent among many long-time NBA fans. Disenchanted viewers turned away from the NBA and found college basketball a more than fitting substitute.

NBC's college basketball games gave viewers what the pros did not—excitement and unpredictability; energetic players who, at least on the surface, approached the games with refreshing innocence; the spirit of pretty cheerleaders and pep bands; the silliness of undergraduate rooting sections filled with faces painted in the old school colors. Big Ten, ACC, Big East, Pac 10, and other conference rivalries were made for television at a time when the NBA was waiting to be rescued by Larry Bird and Magic Johnson. Was college basketball on NBC a natural winner? Not for all NBC affiliates.

Boston's WBZ-TV, one of the best and most profitable local stations in the country, decided to pre-empt NBC's college basketball package and schedule local movies in its place, many of them repeats. The reason was evident. The monetary compensation that WBZ received in return for clearing its time for the NBC feed paled in comparison with what the station would get by airing its own programs. Even though the ratings for the old movies were not significantly higher than what the basketball games attracted, the station kept all of the advertising revenue from its movies. The decision to pre-empt the network games came at a critical time in the television industry. The advertising market is generally slow in the first three months of the year because many advertisers commit their budgets to pre-Christmas campaigns. Commerical time in the first quarter of the year often goes begging, even though bargains can be had. NBC felt the pain of the WBZ defection because, when a network sells time to its advertisers it promises to deliver a substantial national audience. NBC lost revenues because it couldn't deliver the country's fifth largest market for this time period.

One fly in WBZ's ointment, in this case, was Bob Ryan, a *Boston Globe* sportswriter who is an acknowledged college basketball "maven." Ryan waged a one-man campaign against WBZ, describing the station's action in the most unflattering terms. He urged college basketball aficionados to write directly to WBZ, and he printed the program director's name and address in boldface type in each of his daily diatribes. The campaign had limited success, though, because commercial television lives by the axiom that "hell hath no fury like a profit-and-loss-sheet scorned." The station relented only to the extent of carrying several important late season games when conference championships were being decided.

While sports are traditionally carried on weekend afternoons and generally get a high percentage of station clearance, the invasion of prime-time games has caused its share of tension in the network-affiliate partnership. An affiliate station's overall success is primarily dependent on two things—how well its early and late newscasts do in the ratings and how well its network performs between 8 and 11 p.m. Programs aired in prime time provide audience flow into the affiliates' all-important profit center—"the late news." When network sports move into prime time, stations pay attention. Poor network performance affects affiliate revenues, and they often react the same way that WBZ management did with college basketball. They pre-empt. Detroit's WXYZ-TV dropped eight ABC Monday Night Baseball games in 1987 because these programs achieved less than half the rating that the station normally gets. In place of live Monday Night Baseball, WXYZ viewers saw old movies.

Network-affiliate relations were sorely tested in 1970 when ABC moved sports into prime time in a major league way with Monday Night Football. When Howard Cosell, Frank Gifford, Don Meredith et al. premiered at 9 p.m. that fall, the NFL became high entertainment. Most ABC affiliates reveled in the novelty of Monday Night Football's early years, because Tuesday morning discussions around office coffee machines centered as much on Howard Cosell's latest on-camera pronouncements as they did on the on-field heroics. But affiliates also offered silent prayers that Monday Night Football would not adversely affect prime-time ratings in the long run.

By 1984, viewer interest in Monday Night Football began to decline, parallelling a general growing loss of interest in televised professional football. Howard Cosell retired, and neither Joe Namath nor O. J. Simpson could help Frank Gifford and Al Michaels recapture fan interest or the Cosell mystique.

The loss of prime-time football ratings was nothing new to ABC affiliates whose network had become a perennial last in the three-way network ratings battle. Like sharks circling a wounded swimmer, they attacked their network with a vengeance over Monday Night Football. The issue was not so much the overall ratings decline, but rather the 9 o'clock starting time, which sent the games running well past 11 o'clock when local news was king. Stations bitterly complained about losing audience for their profitable late newscast which on most Monday nights could more properly have been called "Tuesday's Eye Opener News." Somehow, the stations bore this infringement more kindly during the Cosell era, but they were less sanguine now that the viewers had turned, along with the network's football fortunes. An 8 o'clock (EST) kick-off failed to mollify the stations.

By 1985, ABC was under new ownership which instituted unprecedented across-the-board cost-cutting practices. The sports division, like everything else at the network, came under close scrutiny as Capital Cities Broadcasting, the new owner, brought spending under control and looked for new ways to stimulate revenues. CapCities/ABC management proclaimed that "there are no more sacred cows. If Monday Night Football can't carry its weight, then it has to go." But before dropping Monday Night Football, CapCities/ABC floated a few old-fashioned tricks that tested the loyalty of its affiliates and tried their patience. "We'll minimize their loss at 11 o'clock by giving them some prime time spots for commercials," said CapCities/ABC. The network experimented in 1986 by giving its affiliates a 3½-minute "news window" to sell locally at halftime, and one additional minute to sell during the telecast. The experiment appeased some of the affiliates who were still bothered by the length of the games.

In 1987, CapCities/ABC turned up the heat a notch when it threatened to eliminate the local news window in order to reinstitute an entertaining halftime package of action footage which Howard Cosell had popularized. But the coup de grace was ABC's threat to drop all monetary compensation entirely. This proposal outraged the affiliates, nearly pushing them over the brink. Many threatened to drop Monday Night Football entirely. CapCities/ABC management, fearful that wholesale affiliate defections would become reality, compromised and restored the halftime local news window, the additional local advertising time, and compensation.

In general, television sports advertising is governed by the rules of supply and demand. When ABC, CBS, and NBC were the only—and most efficient—delivery systems for providing sports events nationally, they dominated the marketplace by vying for rights and entering into long-term agreements with sports leagues.

ABC, CBS, and NBC paid handsomely for exclusive rights to events, knowing that they could pass the costs on to advertisers who, in turn, would pass their costs along to consumers. When exclusive rights from soared (or in the case of the NCAA, when the courts stepped in to redefine who actually held the rights to college games), exclusivity became a luxury. Leagues sold their games in separate packages to whichever networks cared to share them.

But even this did not satisfy the bottom-line pressures the networks were feeling. In the 1986–87 season, CBS and NBC reduced the number of regular-season college basketball games they produced. NBC only broke even on its Major League Baseball deal, even though the network televised more regular season games and paid less for rights (due to its shared arrangement for games with ABC).

As a footnote to NBC's baseball deal, the network helped itself dramatically in its five-year agreement by securing exclusive over-the-air rights to Saturday afternoon games. Up until 1984, local TV stations could show home-team games in competition with NBC's national telecast. This competition held NBC ratings down, not to revive until the playoffs and World Series came around.

When the number of national outlets for sports was primarily limited to the three networks, demand by advertisers needing to reach the national sports audience was great. Commercial time in network sports was at a premium, and automobile companies, breweries, shaving product, and toiletry manufacturers—advertisers who target a sports audience—had limited opportunities. Demand for choice commercial time clearly exceeded supply, and the networks drove the price of commercial air time skyward every year. Advertisers were at the mercy of the networks, which regularly increased their ad rates by 8 percent to 15 percent annually.

Conversely, the television sports advertising marketplace is influenced by fewer than 20 companies which spend about half the total advertising amount committed to televised national events. When any member of this "exclusive" club shifts its buying patterns, the networks feel the tremors. For example, in 1984, when General Motors reduced its sports advertising expenditures from 68 percent of its total ad budget to approximately 10 percent the following year, reverberations were felt at all three networks, especially in light of GM's prominence in NFL telecasts.

In August 1986, *Advertising Age*, the industry Bible, dramatized the problem in banner headlines which proclaimed, SPORTS TAKES A DIVE, EVEN SUPER BOWL WILL "DEAL." The article reflected on four consecutive years of a soft advertising market and spelled out the near panic climate within network sports divisions. Instead of paying premium prices for reaching a targeted audience, advertisers now enjoyed discounts. Instead of committing to purchases before the fall and winter seasons began, they were getting bargain rates by buying as the seasons progressed. This reversed the traditional industry practice of rewarding early commitments and placing a premium on in-season buys. By the mid-1980s, network sports was a shopper's delight—a fire sale where the goods aren't damaged and everything must go!

Cable's emergence in the 1980s dramatically affected rights negotiations and the advertising marketplace. The number of venues where rights-holders could peddle their games multiplied, which served to fragment the sports audience, reduce network ratings, and lower the price that networks could charge advertisers.

College basketball is an example of cable's impact. Traditionally the domain of CBS, NBC, and a few regional networks, college games can be found on all three broadcast networks, in syndication, and on ESPN, USA Network, superstations, and many regional cable channels. NBC and CBS, both of which had originally negotiated the "best" packages in the early 1980s, were the most adversely affected by basketball's over-exposure. But basketball was not the networks' only big loser. Between 1982 and 1987, all network weekend sports lost 11 percent of the sports-viewing audience to cable, with the World Series and the NBA the sole network sports that gained. It is interesting to note that the networks have a virtual monopoly on both the World Series and weekend NBA games.

Advertisers who had long sought to counter the network monopoly have gained the most through audience fragmentation. They still pay premium prices for premium events like the Super Bowl and World Series, but generally enjoy lower regular season rates. Commercial time on cable is very cheap by network TV standards, and is perhaps the best advertising bargain in town. Many agencies, however, complain that while commercial time on cable is eminently affordable, they cannot get reliable audience figures, which makes media campaign planning risky.

The ultimate beneficiaries of the sports glut on TV and cable are the viewers, who have long suffered through countless minutes of barely clad nymphets on TV selling shaving cream, and endurance tests of trucks being dropped from mountain-tops. These inveterate viewers have been quick to capitalize on the wonders of new technology, from cable's multiple channels to VCRs and remote controls. They can now zip and zap their way through commercials in a never-ending procession of games, on more channels than they ever imagined possible. On a good day, four baseball or basketball games can be watched. With the magic of remote control, neither a pitch nor a free throw need be missed in any one of them. Two events happening simultaneously? Wife schedule you for a dinner party away from home on the night of a playoff game? Not to worry. The VCR can suspend or shift time to make possible otherwise unavailable events. Advertisers aren't too thrilled with society's modern betterments, because viewers who zip and zap through commercials can't join the debate about whether the beer tastes great or is less filling. But who are advertisers to complain? Their commercials only make the games possible.

While network revenue growth has slowed dramatically, the cost of labor and other fixed items has accelerated at a higher rate than income. Rights fees, which account for about two-thirds of a network's total sports expense budget, are inextricably tied to advertising revenues. When considering multi-year deals, it doesn't hurt for sports division planners to be one-third "jock" and two-thirds clairvoyant because not only must they know and enjoy sports, they must also be able to gauge accurately the volatile and changing sports advertising marketplace.

Networks have fallen into the unfortunate Draconian cycle in which they either must lower their bidding price or bid on fewer games. The stakes are high in the rights/revenue game, and a network's prestige is often on the line. This fact was no more evident than in 1983, when NBC paid $7 million for three-year rights to telecast the Rose Bowl, compared with the previous contract, which was less than $1 million per year. This extravagant amount stunned the entire TV, sports, and advertising world, which could only surmise that NBC's sports division had other motives besides profit in mind when signing the agreement. Perhaps retaining these rights was a way for the network to save face after its embarrassment in 1980 when the U.S. boycott cost them the Moscow Olympics.

When planning for rights negotiations, network programmers, sales people, and audience researchers engage in as much teamwork as do the players on the field. First of all, the programming staff must be attuned to the importance of various sports events when it puts a price on them. They are fairly sure about what the competition is planning and can usually anticipate any surprise strategies that may confront them. Then, the network sales staff understands the dynamics of the advertising marketplace, including which advertisers are likely prospects to buy commercial time. (In case you're counting, the networks have about 25–30 commercial minutes per game to fill, depending on the length of the event. The rest of the commercials are sold by affiliates when the networks "cut away" for local breaks.)

Audience researchers provide what one CBS executive calls "the alleged objective empirical." They balance the high ratings projections that programmers make with the more conservative ones of the sales staff. Programmers always feel that the events they've chosen are sure ratings winners. "The final round of figure skating from beautiful Sardinia? A guaranteed 15 rating! If we can't whip the competition with this one, we may just as well fold up and go into radio."

Sales people, on the other hand, are more conservative, if not downright pessimistic. "Sports is dead, ratings are dead, and we'll all be out of work if we think we can project more than a 4 rating on that dog!" they cry. Erring on the side of caution is an asset, because the networks generally guarantee advertisers a certain ratings delivery. When programs underperform, they repay the advertisers, either in the form of cash rebates or "make-goods"—commercial time elsewhere in the network schedule. ABC found this out to its dismay in the aftermath of the 1984 Olympics when the ratings were considerably less than promised. ABC made good on its faulty projections.

Audience researchers fill the happy middle ground between programming and sales by focusing on past ratings performance of similar types of programs. They consider the event, its season, and whatever scheduling variables apply such as network lead-ins.

CBS's success in winning the rights in 1986 to the NCAA Final Four basketball championships offers a scenario common to network negotiations. ABC and NBC were only sparring partners.

When CBS signed its three-year contract with the NCAA in 1986, it retained exclusive rights to the jewel in college basketball's crown. In fact, exclusivity was at the heart of CBS's negotiation strategy, which underlines its philosophy that "When you look for championships, you look to CBS Sports." But the cost of exclusivity comes high. CBS paid $166 million, 73 percent more than it paid in its prior agreement. Both ABC and NBC would gladly have become willing partners in a split arrangement that the NCAA proposed. This would have divided the championship games between two of the three networks.

Of the three bidders, CBS felt it had the inside track. It was, after all, the incumbent, having successfully carried the games through six earlier years which were profitable both for them and for the NCAA. The network's sales staff could sell championship college basketball based on CBS's actual experience. ABC and NBC's proposal could only rely on audience estimates.

CBS was also negotiating from another kind of competitive strength. Both ABC and NBC had in-house problems that critically affected their ability to negotiate freely. ABC had committed more than $300 million for the 1988 Winter Olympics with the disappointing results of its 1984 experience fresh in mind. The network, which faced potential staggering losses from one more Olympic undertaking, now labored under the mandate that the new CapCities management had set down. Strict, across-the-board budget guidelines forced ABC personnel to shoot for the NCAA basket with one hand tied behind their backs.

NBC had problems of a different sort. The NCAA wanted more games telecast in prime time. To comply with this, would NBC forgo The Cosby Show, which regularly attracted nearly half the TV households in America every Thursday and sold advertising time at unprecedented rates? Would they pre-empt any of their other runaway hits? NBC looked prime-time NCAA finals squarely in the eye, saw lost revenues from Cosby cancellations, and blinked. The network's Sports department, to its regret, was a victim of the shattering success record that NBC's Entertainment division was building.

Networks do not schedule sports in prime time casually. No matter how special the replacement program is, network programmers always consider the impact that sporadic pre-emptions create on their regular schedule. ABC may uneasily dodge the bullets that its affiliates aim at Monday Night Football, but at least these games are part of a long-standing, regularly scheduled network series that has built a loyal audience base over time. One-time only events like the NCAA finals, however, present different problems.

Networks calculate pre-emptive impact on the basis of how much money would be lost by replacing a regularly scheduled program with a one-time, non-entertainment special. If the regularly scheduled program is an original episode, the network may save money by pre-empting it and showing it the following week. This maneuver would actually extend the series later into the spring and command top-dollar ad rates when reruns are usually scheduled and ad rates have fallen. Pre-empting a rerun wouldn't save the network as much money because reruns do not ordinarily attract as large an audience as original programs. The networks would consider it a positive if their owned and operated stations profit from the pre-emption, while the network itself loses money.

In preparing their bid for the NCAA finals, CBS's programmers, sales staff, and audience researchers considered a number of different pricing options before recommending a final package offer. They took into account the cost of telecasting games on different days and at different starting times. They considered the impact of different dayparts—that is, what would it cost to broadcast games in prime time, late night, or daytime only, and what would the monetary return be in each case.

CBS's sales and research staffs computed the total ad revenues that the championship round would earn. They based their projections on the number of commercial minutes available and the price that CBS could charge advertisers for each unit of time.

CBS's finance people entered the pre-planning sessions, estimating the production costs for the event and all other payments such as affiliate compensation. CBS Sports has traditionally benefited from loyal affiliates, and boasts an average clearance rate of 95 percent for most of its sports schedule. This improves to almost 100 percent clearance for "quality" events like the NCAA Championships, Masters Golf, and NFL playoffs. Armed with a reasonably accurate forecast of income and expenses, CBS could project a double digit profit margin for the NCAA package, a target percentage consistent with all other CBS Sports undertakings.

CBS's winning bid exceeded ABC's and NBC's by about $4 million each. In return, CBS doubled the number of hours that it would broadcast in prime time—a total of five games or ten hours, allowing for some regional semifinals and one national final game when TV set usage is the highest. In addition, CBS expanded coverage of its Saturday and Sunday triple-headers by a half-hour, which gave the network more advertising inventory to sell on each of those days. Finally, CBS added an extra two minutes of advertising spots per game in each of the ten championship round telecasts. These additional twenty minutes of advertising time per game made all the difference in the world to CBS and would hardly be noticed by viewers who became inured to commercials shortly after Harding beat Cox in the 1920 presidential election.

The winning bid carried certain trade-offs. In making its selection, the NCAA committed CBS to televising the men's NCAA college baseball World Series for the first time, and guaranteeing continued coverage of other NCAA sports such as the women's basketball final, and men's and women's finals in volleyball, gymnastics, and outdoor track and field.

The impression that sales staffs and accountants run network sports is not far off the mark. Sales people are more like helmsmen on the bridge navigating the vessel through advertising's uncharted waters, while the accountants stay below, keeping track of profits. High ratings mean smooth sailing for the network. The reverse usually means that one or two vice presidents or executive producers are sunk.

How does a network spell success? R-a-t-i-n-g-s, the percentage of households watching a program at any given time. A rating point is equivalent to 1 percent of America's estimated 88,000,000 households. Thus, an NFL game on Sunday afternoon that gets a 15 rating reaches approximately 13,200,000 homes. The networks set their prices and advertisers use them to compare program performance.

The main categories of sports advertisers are beers, automotives, computer companies, insurance and financial service companies, and office products, all of which spend heavily to reach a target audience of men who are 25 to 54 years old. Some advertisers who would not ordinarily buy time in network sports look more to reach a particular demographic share of the audience instead of quantity. For example, Merrill Lynch and IBM are two "specialized" advertisers in search of high-spending, upper-income males who can be found watching golf and tennis. Golf and tennis are the least popular sports, with average ratings of 4.5 and 3.8 respectively.

While men are the primary target, sports advertisers are also aware of the women's audience which some televised sports attract. "Challenge sports" (Challenge of the Network Stars, Challenge of the Sexes, et al.) and horse racing, tennis, and professional football are most preferred by women, many of whom influence household purchasing decisions.

Ratings trends show that the NFL was the most popular event in network sports between 1980 and 1985. Regular-season games averaged a 16 rating, with major league baseball second, its five-year average rating at 11.1. Needless to say, the average cost of commercials in regular season football and baseball was the highest of all regular season events at rates of $118,600 per 30-second spot in football, and $71,900 per 30 in baseball. With costs this high, agencies regularly compare the cost of buying television time with other media.

Time buyers measure advertising efficiency by estimating the cost they pay to reach each one thousand homes with their commercials. This is referred to as the cost-per-thousand (CPM), which advertisers use to compare against the CPM for other TV opportunities. Thus, an ad in the NFL game mentioned earlier which cost $100,000 and reached about 13 million households, has a cost-per-thousand of $7.69—$100,000 divided by 13,000. (There are 13,000 units of 1000 in 13,000,000.) Compared with NFL weekend games, the CPM for ABC's Monday Night Football is about $10, and approximately $4-per-thousand for CBS's and NBC's college football.

Money is not the advertiser's only consideration when it comes to advertising in the Super Bowl or World Series. While they pay more, and at a higher CPM than regular season games, they also get residual benefits by associating with these world class events. The 1987 Super Bowl is a good example.

Advertisers paid $600,000 for each 30-second commercial. This was just the cost of the air-time. The cost of producing the commercials, which also ran into hundreds of thousands of dollars, was additional. The CPM was approximately $14 for the game, which was seen in just under half the homes in the country. In order to attract advertisers, CBS sold Super Bowl time as part of a larger package which gave advertisers bonus commercial spots in other CBS sports programs at bargain rates.

Pride of association becomes an intangible benefit, so many advertisers consider sponsorship of the Super Bowl as much of an opportunity to motivate their employees as to reach consumers. Many run incentive programs in which they reward their dealers and distributors for outstanding sales efforts. Top sales performers and their families are invited to the game and attend a week-long schedule of pre-event parties. Some companies create promotions and sweepstakes tied in to their Super Bowl advertising. Others, like Apple Computer, Inc., have used the occasion to launch merchandising campaigns. In 1984, the then young company devoted its Super Bowl advertising to introduce the Macintosh, inserting a commercial that cost $500,000 to produce and ran once in the course of the game. That event generated widespread news coverage for Apple, the value of which would be difficult to assess by conventional standards.

Ad agencies and clients all share one unspoken concern—what if no one watches the commercial? Six hundred thousand dollars is a lot of money for a little bit of time, and a lot of worry for more than a few ad agency account executives. To keep viewers in front of their TV sets throughout the 1987 game (or at least until their commercial aired), PepsiCo Inc. ran a print campaign in behalf of Slice, one of its soft drink products. One week before the game, PepsiCo announced a contest in which viewers could qualify for a $10,000 prize by calling in the score of the game when they saw the Slice commercial. For $10,000, who would leave the room? At $600,000 for thirty seconds of air-time, no gimmick is too outrageous.

The performance of the 1988 Super Bowl was of great concern both to ABC, which televised the game, and to advertisers who paid as much as $675,000 for a 30-second commercial. While ABC did not guarantee ratings for the Super Bowl (a practice the networks usually do on all other programs), the network clearly had some explaining to do to advertisers who had hoped the Redskins-Broncos matchup would be more attractive than the 1987 Giants-Broncos game (which drew a 46 rating).

However, both the 1988 Super Bowl and the Broncos under-performed, and the game averaged four ratings points less than the previous year. The reasons cited were the first-half blowout by the Redskins; lingering fan resentment and disillusionment in the year of the players' strike; neither team represented one of the top five TV markets which almost automatically increases the size of audience; and the use of the controversial people meters to measure the size of audience. (People meters are measuring devices which have shown that the size of network audiences in general is smaller than when the diary system was used to collect data.)

Whatever the reason, the networks, advertisers, and the NFL could gain small solace from what they hoped was only a momentary aberration in Super Bowl interest.

Much has been written about how television has changed the rules of the games, and no discussion of sports broadcasting would be complete without a look at how advertising has changed the way games are scheduled and played. Two-minute warnings before the end of each half, a gleam in Pete Rozelle's eyes when the NFL signed its first contract with CBS, are called solely for the purpose of inserting commercials. They may affect game strategy but are commercial bonanzas for television.

Television's golden arm has also warmly embraced college football, and the impact cannot be overstated. The bottom line: teams that play on television generally reap financial rewards that more than compensate for the intrusions. In a 1985 game between Syracuse and Maryland, for example, the Terrapins opened by driving for nine consecutive minutes towards the Syracuse goal line. Neither Syracuse nor television could stop Maryland's momentum. Once they scored, however, TV took revenge. The last six minutes of play were interrupted to show four minutes of commercials, and Maryland ultimately lost, never having regained its momentum.

TV timeouts have also altered the way NBA coaches coach. When Dick Motta was in charge of the NBA's Washington Bullets, his team was sent to the sidelines for a TV timeout. Given his choice, Motta would have waited until later to call time, but he was playing basketball by CBS's rules. He stuck his head into the huddle and said, "I have nothing to tell you guys, you're doing fine." He walked away while the Bullet players waited for the one-minute commercial to end and the game to resume. But if enforced commercial breaks each quarter slow down the game's pace, they also give players extra rest—whether they need it or not. More than one aging NBA veteran has added game minutes to his career thanks to the TV timeout.

In college basketball, two twenty-minute halves take triple the amount of air-time to accommodate the commercial load that fills network time and coffers. College basketball's 45-second clock is another TV-inspired innovation, designed to speed up games and take the deadening freeze away from defense-minded coaches.

Yellow tennis balls make lobs look prettier against azure skies, and even hockey was not immune from tinkering. Colored hockey pucks were once suggested as a way of adding greater visibility to a sport played too fast for television. Even this inspired creation was not enough to keep the NHL from becoming a network ratings loser. The sport's fast pace, its strong Canadian flavor, and its lack of appeal to the American Sun Belt did hockey in until ESPN came to its rescue.

Overall, sports have adapted well to TV's intrusions, and, in fact, television had added a dimension to viewing that often surpasses the enjoyment of watching a game in person. Slow-motion replays, isolated cameras, miniaturized equipment, electronic graphic illustrators, and the miking of on-field personnel, all heighten the at-home enjoyment. Satisfied TV viewers go hand-in-hand with good ratings.

However, there is one intrusion that threatens to turn the golden handshake between sports and television into something more akin to Roman wrist-wrestling. This involves the rescheduling of games to satisfy ratings and advertisers, mostly affecting ticket-buyers who have begrudgingly learned to accept the fact that TV pays the piper and gets to call the tune. It is no secret that gate receipts have long been outstripped by TV rights fees and advertising dollars.

Starting times of many games are often set to accommodate TV's scheduling needs. Ask Los Angeles Laker fans about championship games that begin at 6:00 p.m. (West Coast time) to meet CBS's prime-time needs in the East. Football kickoffs scheduled for 1:00 p.m. are delayed until 4 o'clock to allow network programmers to find a larger audience. Ticket-buyers sometimes never learn of the change until a few days before the game.

Contrary to its outward support, CBS schedules most of its regular NBA season games in the early spring when interest in college basketball has subsided. To keep CBS affiliates happy, coverage of NBA championship games is relegated to late May and early June, after the important TV ratings "sweep weeks" are over. In 1981, affiliates in every city but Boston and Houston were overjoyed when the network delayed weeknight championship round games until 11:30 p.m. CBS relented, by feeding the games live to those two markets, only when viewers in the contending cities threatened to blacken the network's eye.

One of the most egregious examples of network rescheduling to accommodate ratings involves the World Series, which became a night-time staple in 1971. That year, NBC began a three-year agreement which provided $700,000 in payments to each team. Once NBC saw its 1971 ratings increase by double over the prior year, mid-week Series games never again saw the light of day. They were all played at night on Monday through Friday.

Teams still played on Saturday and Sunday afternoons until 1985, when these day-time events went the way of the twenty-five-cent hot-dog and fifty-cent beer. In 1985, NBC and ABC were in the second year of their six-year agreement which offered more than $1 billion for rights to Major League Baseball. Come hell, high water, or frosty nights in Toronto, Montreal, or Pittsburgh, the networks were going to recoup their investment by passing the cost onto advertisers. They could do this only with the higher ratings that night games ensured. In 1987 the league and ABC relented, to allow a fifth game to be played on a Saturday afternoon, beginning at 4:00 p.m. (EDT).

If one overlooks the tradition of baseball, invented to be played under the sun, then the ratings performance and added commercial revenues justify the network's decision about night-only Series games. For example, in 1983 and 1984 two weekend games averaged ratings of 19.3 and 18.9 respectively. The 1985 and 1986 series, played all in prime time, averaged 25.3 and 28.6. In terms of advertising rates, a 30-second commercial in 1986 cost advertisers approximately $250,000. Similar spots during a weekend afternoon game would have cost about $125,000.

Clearly, the networks benefit more from night games than teams and fans. Viewers who want to watch the games in their entirety have to stay up later each night. When West Coast teams play, their fans get to the ball park early to see the first pitch thrown at 5:30 p.m., prime time for coveted East Coast television markets. Players in West Coast games also suffer from the schedule imposed by television. In the 1986 American League playoffs, Angels and Red Sox batters and fielders complained of poor lighting conditions. Faced with the prospect of hitting a Roger Clemens fast ball at twilight, Angels batters were little comforted to know that higher TV ratings mean higher ad rates; higher ad rates translate into higher rights fees; higher rights fees mean more money for each team (in the current baseball agreement, each team gets an average of $7 million per team annually); and more money per team means higher salaries for players.

If ratings and advertising drive TV sports, where does the fan fit into the equation? Basically, he's where he has been since he first saw his local heroes leave home for richer TV pastures. From Walter O'Malley's leap from Brooklyn into Chavez Ravine with the Dodgers to Robert Irsay's midnight ride from Baltimore to Indianapolis with the foootball Colts, sports fans are slowly learning to deal with the fact that loyalty if it counts, is a one-way street. Teams are owned by businessmen whose interests lie in making money. The days of sportsmen owners are long gone; at best, only a few remain. Most of today's owners operate on a level distinctly different from that of their fans, and both define success in different terms.

While sports fans blindly embrace Vince Lombardi's commitment that "winning isn't everything; it's the ONLY thing," most owners feel that not only is winning not everything, it's usually a pain in their assets. For them, being competitive until late in the season is ideal; coming in second on the last day of the season is perfection. When a team wins the championship, the hysteria of the moment is soon lost under the great expectations of players who demand higher salaries next year for this year's accomplishments. Fans want nothing less than for owners to spend recklessly in the off-season to ensure a home-town dynasty forever.

Higher ticket and concession prices can only go so far towards paying the added costs that go with winning teams. The pockets of the average fan are only so deep. At some point, their applause and jeers will be heard echoing louder in living rooms than in stadiums and arenas. For television's sake, they're usually not loud enough to drown out the commercials.

3

CABLE:
THE GOOSE THAT
CAN LAY GOLDEN EGGS

IF SIR ISAAC NEWTON said whatever goes up must come down, he never had the marriage of sports and new communications technologies in mind. Two seemingly unrelated events occurred in 1975 which were to contradict his age-old law of gravity. Ironically, each event involved the launching of something skyward, and these "somethings" are likely never to come down.

The first was the birth of cable television as we know it today. On April 10, 1975, Home Box Office, Inc. (HBO), a subsidiary of Time, Inc., announced it had reached agreement in principle with UA-Columbia Cablevision, Inc. (UAC). Under the agreement, HBO would supply 70 hours per week of pay TV programming to six of UAC's cable systems in the southern and western United States. The programs would be distributed on an RCA Communications System satellite, which was to be sent into orbit in December of that year. This decision legitimized the cable television business which, up to this point, was merely a struggling mechanism for redistributing over-the-air network programs and a limited amount of original material to areas that could not receive clear television reception.

The second event took place six months after the HBO announcement, when an important contract arbitration decision forever ended a system of employee relations that more closely resembled feudal servitude than twentieth-century personnel practices. From that day forward, player-owner relations in baseball, as well as in all other major professional sports, would never be the same, and player salaries began to soar as sky-high as the RCA satellite.

First, the launching of player salaries. In 1959, in the waning stages of Ted Williams's career, the Red Sox star returned his contract unsigned to owner Tom Yawkey. The contract called for a salary of $125,000, higher than any player in baseball was earning at that time but an amount identical to what Williams had earned the year before. Coming off a year in which he had hit only .259, Williams's contract rejection was not based on his feeling short-changed. To the contrary, he wanted his salary cut because he was embarrassed by his poor on-field performance the prior season. Yawkey reluctantly obliged by cutting his star's salary by 25 percent, the highest percentage allowed by league rules. To the collective regret of team owners then and forever more, neither Ted Williams nor 1959 was typical, a fact made amply clear some sixteen years later after the momentous arbitration decision.

In October 1975, independent labor arbitrator Peter Seitz was faced with a challenge to the option clause in the standard major league players' contract. The clause bound a player to a team at the team owner's option. He ruled that players would no longer be tied to their respective teams in perpetuity and was later upheld in the courts. This challenge to the baseball reserve system had been brought by Los Angeles Dodgers pitcher Andy Messersmith and by Montreal Expos pitcher Dave McNally. The offending clause dated back to 1879, and effectively bound a player to one team for as long as that team chose to exercise the option in the contract. This restrictive language gave baseball players two choices—dance with the team which brought them to the ball, or not dance at all.

The precedent-shattering Messersmith/McNally decision allowed baseball players to become free agents upon completing the last—or option—year of their old contract. They would, in effect, be free to sell their services to the highest bidder in baseball. The impact of this change regarding how the off-the-field game was played was later to be felt not only in major league baseball but in other professional sports as well. Professional athletes had gained a level of independence whose effects resounded each time a players' association negotiated a new contract. Joining the list of participants in the new world of sports labor negotiations was an added starter—the player agents whose very presence in the offices of team owners cast athletes into a role more on a par with entertainment figures than indentured servants.

Predictably, player salaries escalated as stars, pretenders to stardom, and even fading heroes exercised their new-found leverage over team owners. By the early 1980s, individual annual wages of almost a million dollars or more were commonplace, and sports fans became as accustomed to following salary disputes as they were to monitoring their team's place in the league's standings. By the latter part of the 1980s, baseball owners closed ranks and, under the guise of running their businesses more prudently, refused to meet the accelerating demands of free agents—demands often accompanied by threats of player holdouts. While a disgruntled players' union hurled charges of collusion among owners—a charge which ultimately stuck—individual players slowly came to realize that the marketplace for their services had changed.

Players in other sports were equally affected by the realities of the new economics, although each of the other major sports plays by different rules, deals with different unions, and works under different economic standards. For example, NBA owners, in an effort to deal with escalating salaries invoked a team salary cap, a complex arrangement that limited the total amount any individual team can spend on player salaries.

In professional football, the NFL Players Union sought a system of free agency similar to that enjoyed by baseball players. The owners, however, were concerned with declining TV revenues and escalating salary demands, particularly those of prized rookies coming out of college. Almost from the time of the first TV agreement, NFL team owners spent their share of TV rights money on player salaries. By 1987, however, a combination of long-term contract obligations to veteran players and higher than average salaries paid to such prized rookies as Vinnie Testaverde, Bo Jackson, and Brian Bosworth stiffened the owners' stance against any agreement that would further impact on profits. The players' strike in 1987 further hardened the owners' collective resolve to test the strength of the union. Almost as if in an act of defiance, NFL owners fielded teams comprising replacement players when the union walked out. The networks televised these games—playing to lesser TV ratings—until three weeks into the strike, when the union capitulated. Both sides went back to the bargaining table, with the players' quest for free agency becoming the equivalent in obsolescence of the drop-kick in football.

Whether you root for the owners or the players, one fact of professional sports life had become abundantly clear by the mid-1980s. The appetites of even the most voracious sports viewers were becoming overfed by the rich menu of televised events. The proliferation of sports events shown on the networks, through syndication, and on cable systems had fractionalized the viewing audience. Lower ratings followed oversegmentation of the audience, and network advertising stagnated. The large rights fees that owners could once command from television were in jeopardy, and commissioners and team owners had to face the realities of the new media marketplace. (Examples of rights fees de-escalating are about as common as World Series victories for the Chicago Cubs.) New revenue streams were clearly needed to deal with increasing player demands, soaring operational costs, and changes in the tax laws allowing team owners fewer business deductions.

The likely savior of the sports industry is cable, an industry that allows team and cable company owners to charge customers as if at an electronic box-office. Willing sports fans who subscribe to cable have to pay extra for the "privilege" of watching televised sports, a commodity they once enjoyed for free on conventional, over-the-air television, courtesy of advertisers. In the relatively short span of ten years, cable had made a major impact on sports viewing. If, in the mid-1980s, any questions persisted about the long-term viability of cablesports, the 1987 NFL agreement, which included ESPN as one of the participants, ended any lingering doubts. Network television's strangehold on America's most popular televised sports ended with ESPN's joining the ranks of the sports media elite.

This is not to suggest that cable and other new technologies have fully arrived. But neither had they been asleep regarding sports telecasts before 1987. To the contrary, wide-awake sports entrepreneurs had tried alternatives to television as far back as 1950, although with relatively little success.

Basically, the structure of the cable industry is more like retailing than broadcasting. The business is made up of wholesalers and retailers, each of whom marks up the price of his goods before passing these goods down the line. The local cable system is an electronic supermarket where customers (the subscribers) shop on a regular basis for the products they wish to buy. One major difference to remember between cable and traditional retailing, however, is that local cable systems are virtually unregulated monopolies. If customers don't like the programs that their local cable company offers, they have a choice—buy or don't watch. There are no other "stores" in town.

To many, the cable industry had always been an entrepreneur's dream. Former New York Mayor John Lindsay once called cable "an urban oil-well," referring to the untapped riches that would gush forth from the coaxial cables running beneath the streets of cities. For the public, these riches would be a wide variety of programs; for city officials, wealth would come in the form of levies and fees assessed onto cable companies lucky enough to win the rights to wire the town. (How ironic that less than twenty years after Mayor Lindsay's prophesy, several of New York's

boroughs had not yet been wired, the franchising process tied up in allegations of corruption and political payoffs. Meanwhile, in 1987, Yankee
owner George Steinbrenner, never a team owner known for his public
relations savvy, moved the majority of Yankee games from WPIX-TV,
the local over-the-air station, onto SportsChannel, a major regional pay
TV service. Thousands of deprived Yankee fans, outraged that they could
no longer see their beloved team for "free," protested in vain. For them,
it was either a trip to Yankee Stadium in the Bronx, or radio.)

While for many in the cable business the "urban oil-well" would be
more like fool's gold, the cable boom began in earnest after the launch
of HBO in 1975. Cable operators competed to win franchises and the
right to wire cities and towns across the country. In the early days of
cable's development, the big cities appeared to be the most obvious
choice for wiring. Population density was favorable, and most big cities
had sports teams with large followings that might translate into paying
customers when cable's promising electronic box-office opened. What
cable operators did not anticipate in the late 1970s was the difficulty of
wiring big cities and the hassle of municipal red-tape.

Cities grant easements that allow cable companies to use public rights
of way to lay their cable—either by digging trenches under the streets
or stringing the cable along existing utility poles. For this right, cities
expect to receive a portion of the cable company's profits. What many
cable companies discovered, however, was that the costs were prohibitive to wire cities that were overladen with high-rise buildings, heavily
commercialized, and bogged down in above- and below-ground traffic.
By the early 1980s, small became beautiful for cable operators. They
turned their attention to less congested suburban communities, where the
construction problems were not as severe and the demographics even
more attractive.

Cable systems are capital intensive, particularly in their early years
of operation. First there is the enormous outlay of money for laying the
cable. Underground installation costs nearly five to ten times more than
cable strung overhead along utility poles. Then there is the cost of building the system's head-end—the location within the community where the
programs from ESPN, TBS, USA Network, HBO, PRISM, and other
distant networks are imported via satellite or microwave and re-transmitted throughout the town to subscriber homes.

There is also the cost of installing converters in the homes of the
subscribers. Generally, a cable operator hopes to have at least 60 percent
of the town's population subscribe initially to the service. His ideal targets are middle and higher income families with several children and a
burning desire to dispose of their income by paying to watch television.

Finally, a cable company pays to acquire programs from the "wholesalers"—the national program suppliers.

Unlike commercial television, which earns its revenues from the sale of air-time, the cable business is subscriber-driven. Ninety to 95 percent of a cable company's revenue comes directly from subscribers. Direct marketing is at the heart of the cable business, and good customer service is essential to the success of any cable company. Like the electronic supermarket described earlier, each cable system prices its products in a way that will not only attract a large volume of customers but induce each of them to buy many high-priced items.

Local cable systems package the programs they offer in such as way as to attract the largest number of subscribers. These packages—or tiers— are lumped into two categories: basic and premium. The basic services generally include the advertiser-supported national services like CNN, ESPN, Arts & Entertainment, and a number of others for which the cable company pays about 5 to 25 cents per month/per subscriber/per service. Market research then indicates what packages are likely to be most profitable. For example, a cable system trying to attract the sports audience might place imported networks and superstations such as ESPN, USA Network, TBS, WGN, WOR, and WPIX, and perhaps one or two other channels, into a single package, and charge the subscriber anywhere from $8 to $10 per month. They hope sports fans who subscribe to cable will not mind paying for these precise services.

Premium channels are more costly both to the cable company and to the subscriber. Sold as something special, a premium network such as HBO markets itself for exclusive programming, although in the case of first-run theatrical films, it is not unusual to see the same ones repeated on HBO, Cinemax, and Showtime in the same month. Unlike the modest per-subscriber costs for basic programming, a cable company pays approximately $5 per subscriber-per month to purchase one of the premium services, and because of the exclusive nature of the programs, will often mark up the service nearly 300 percent when selling it to subscribers. Sports events, however, have virtually no re-run value and assure more exclusivity. Thus, national premium services like HBO, and regional premium services like PRISM, New England Sports Network, Madison Square Garden Network, Prime Ticket Network, and Sports Vision have become more prominent with their proprietary sports programming.

The history of the cablesports business is almost as old as the cable business itself. Cable originated almost simultaneously both in Pennsylvania and Oregon in the early 1950s, bringing local and network programs to communities where over-the-air reception was blocked by mountainous terrain. Cable operators in those areas contructed a master antenna on one of the highest locations in the region. This community antenna (which gave the acronym CATV) plucked television signals out of the air and redistributed them by cable to anyone willing to pay for the service.

Shortly after these few CATV systems started, other systems sprung up elsewhere in communities experiencing similar reception problems. One of these, in Palm Springs, California, was Telemeter, a small company started by two motion picture distributors who later sold 50 percent of their holdings to Paramount Pictures. By 1951 the new company, International Telemeter, was already an omen of things to come, for this early wedding of the motion picture and pay television industries was but the first clue of a marriage that would be fully consummated in the 1970s to the mutual benefit of both parties.

Die-hard sports-trivia buffs know that Telemeter presented the first sports event ever on cable on November 28, 1953, when approximately 200 subscribers in Palm Springs paid to see Notre Dame trounce the University of Southern California by a score of 48–14. The Fighting Irish were not the only winners that day. While the size of the cablecast audience was disappointing, International Telemeter began, with Paramount's financial involvement, a second pay television experiment in suburban Toronto. The primary attractions were Maple Leafs hockey and Canadian football, both providing about one-third of the new system's revenues in the early years of operation. But the early 1950s were still 25 to 30 years too soon for a pioneering venture of this sort to succeed, and Telemeter was sent to an early shower for lack of viewer interest.

The first professional sports event on cable occurred almost seven years after Telemeter's Palm Springs experience. About 25,000 cable subscribers in Arizona, Kansas, New Mexico, Washington, and Wyoming paid $2 above their regular monthly cable fees to watch the second heavyweight title fight between Floyd Paterson and Ingemar Johansson. This legendary bout was brought to them by Teleprompter, which was owned by Irving Kahn, one of the visionary men in the history of cablesports. Credited with developing the now-famous system which allows on-air talent to read their presentations while looking directly at the camera lens by using a "teleprompter," Kahn began operating cable systems in 1959. In a few short years he became the largest cable operator in the country by developing and acquiring CATV systems located for the most part in rural areas where community antennas were essential.

Kahn recognized the potential gold mine in promoting and televising major sports events for showing on cable or in theatres equipped to receive closed circuit feeds. His aggressiveness in seeking suitable sports events led to a court case in which Madison Square Garden sued Kahn.

MSG tried to block Kahn from transmitting a boxing match between Sugar Ray Robinson and Carmen Basilio to theatres throughout the country which sold tickets at premium prices to spectators willing to watch the fight via closed circuit on a large screen. Kahn won the court challenge, arguing that he had purchased "ancillary rights" to the event, a legality which was denied Kahn several years later when he tried to buy ancillary rights to major league baseball and football championships.

Two other ventures emerged in the early days of sports-for-pay, each using a delivery system different from cable, but which required the viewer to pay a fee. Subscription television (STV) involves sending a scrambled picture over a regular TV channel, usually an unused UHF station. Customers subscribing to the service pay to have a converter attached to their TV set which then unscrambles the STV picture.

In 1962, Zenith Radio Corporation joined forces with RKO General in an STV experiment using RKO's Channel 18 in Hartford, Connecticut. Zenith had tested its pioneering pay TV invention, Phonevision, in 1951 when it showed theatrical movies to a small sample of Chicago residents. The Zenith-RKO experiment added major sports events to its menu of films. The top box-office attractions in Hartford were the Sonny Liston–Floyd Patterson fight in September 1962, for which subscribers paid $3 per home, and their rematch the next year. In addition to boxing, Phonevision offered about seventy-five other live sporting events including collegiate basketball and football, and professional basketball and hockey originating from both Madison Square Garden and the Boston Garden. But STV in 1962 was an idea whose time had not arrived, and history will show that even when the time for paying to watch televised sports did come, cable was quick to supplant STV. Cable's ability to provide multiple channels was more than a match for STV's one-channel-only capability.

Another early sports–pay venture could have endured longer than the others, except for politics and the law. Subscription Television, Inc., was the brainchild of Matthew M. Fox, a classic entrepreneur whom *Sports Illustrated* once called "an international wheeler dealer." Fox had announced plans to offer Los Angeles Dodgers and San Francisco Giants games for pay on a system developed by Skiatron Inc., his electronic manufacturing company. Fox and Skiatron ran afoul of the Securities & Exchange Commission in 1961, however, because of some questionable business activities, and this put a temporary end to Matt Fox's bold scheme. Even in the midst of these legal problems, he was still able to get Subscription Television, Inc., off the ground by successfully raising the necessary capital from a number of private sources.

When Fox died in 1964, leadership of the company passed to Sylvester

"Pat" Weaver, whose contributions to broadcasting as head of NBC are legendary, and include the creation of The Today Show and The Tonight Show. Weaver's efforts to further the development of Subscription Television, Inc., in California were dealt a fatal blow when a referendum designed to ban all forms of pay television was passed. Sponsored by the National Association of Theatre Owners, and supported by a multi-million-dollar public relations campaign, the referendum reflected the fears of a segment of the motion picture industry, which saw its own survival at risk at the hands of this new electronic theatre. Subscription Television, Inc.'s, death signaled the end of the first era of cablesports in America, a period in which the seeds for pay-for-viewing sports were sown, but were not to blossom for another five years.

The drought which followed the death of STV in California lasted until the late 1960s when several regional pay television ventures began operation. But it took the launch of HBO in 1975 truly to thrust cable into the national limelight. Before examining some of the regional sports networks, first a look at the national "wholesalers." Their success changed the face of televised sports and promises to provide leagues, teams, and players the steady flow of money that over-the-air networks and television stations can never hope to match.

The major national players today are Home Box Office, ESPN, USA Network, several superstations, and a handful of other pretenders whose primary function, offered under the guise of diversifying their programming mix, seems only to glorify wrestling and roller derby, and dilute an already fragmented sports-viewing marketplace.

HBO is owned by Time, Inc., perhaps better known for its magazines than for electronic media. Time, Inc., first entered the CATV business in 1965 when it developed a number of cable systems in various parts of the country. One of Time, Inc.'s, partial holdings was Sterling Communications, whose subsidiaries included Manhattan Cable, a potentially lucrative franchise covering a significant part of the New York City borough. Time, Inc., purchased Sterling outright in 1973 and subsequently dissolved the company in order to form three wholly owned subsidiaries: Manhattan Cable, Inc., which continued to serve 60,000 CATV subscribers; Computer Television, Inc., which provided in-house pay-TV programming to major New York City hotels; and HBO, Inc., then only a regional pay TV service which provided feature films and sports via microwave to approximately fifty CATV systems in the middle-Atlantic states. (For trivia buffs, the first regional sportscast ever on HBO was a hockey game in 1972 between the New York Rangers and the Vancouver Canucks.)

Other early HBO sports offerings included boxing matches, New York

Knicks basketball, and some major league baseball games, a sport in which HBO had considerable interest and on which its management had hoped to capitalize during the network's formative years. However, HBO's presence was regarded as a threat to the league and to team owners, and the pay-to-watch network was unable to consummate a permanent relationship. "If the fans are watching television, they're not buying tickets at the ball park" was the prevailing sentiment of most owners.

While unable to win rights to "major" major league sports after the satellite launch in 1975, HBO sold itself to cable systems and subscribers as the exclusive network of special events such as first-run theatrical films, some HBO-produced entertainment specials, and sports. As a premium service for which subscribers pay an additional monthly fee beyond what they pay for basic cable, HBO was marketed as exclusive, commercial-free entertainment, suggesting that the customer is receiving "something extra" for his money. There are only certain events which lend themselves to this "special" quality, and most of these, like the Super Bowl, the World Series, and the NCAA Final Four, were still the province of the over-the-air networks.

Championship boxing, however, is a different story, and the marriage between HBO and fight promoters is seemingly made in heaven (although inevitable squabbles between HBO and the promoters have regularly caused this marriage to cohabit on a rocky bed of mutual suspicion). For the most part, HBO's exclusive rights to the main event, and the one-time-only nature of championship bouts play perfectly into HBO's marketing strategy. (Attesting to this is the 48 percent share of the 16 million pay-TV homes that watched the 1988 Mike Tyson-Larry Holmes fight on HBO.) The pay network meets the challenge by providing consistently high quality production (even for an event that by television sports standards is relatively easy to direct) and crisp, educated commentary.

While boxing, tennis, and some handsomely produced sports anthologies are the rich hors d'oeuvre that HBO feeds its subscribers, the pay network may one day play a bigger role on even richer playing (and paying) fields when the timing is right. While HBO was an unsuccessful suitor in the 1987 NFL rights race, nothing is forever in sports broadcasting, whether the sport be football, baseball, or the Olympics.

If by cable standards, HBO was a rich man's treat, ESPN started out as the blue-collar workers' delight. The 24-hour-all-sports network began operations in September 1979 with an eclectic program schedule filled with events for which rights were readily available—and cheap.

Its early programs included events the networks wouldn't look at even once. (At best, portions of some might be included on a rare Wide World of Sports or some other anthology show.) Slow pitch softball, secondary college sports, fila wrestling, hurling, sports-talk and news shows were staples on the early ESPN, many of which were repeated in the wee hours of the morning. This clever scheduling ploy not only filled time but also satisfied the appetites of the hungriest of America's insomnia-prone couch potatoes. More important from ESPN's point of view was that the rights to these events came for the right price—ESPN either paid no rights fee, or were paid by the event sponsors to air them.

While HBO's birth was carefully planned, ESPN was a love-child, born almost by accident. It was the brain-storm of William Rasmussen, then an employee of the Hartford Whalers, who conceived the idea while driving along the New England Thruway with his son Scott. (Soon after ESPN's debut, the younger Rasmussen left the cable network to try his hand at forming a national 24-hour all-sports radio network. Enterprise Radio met a fate different from its cable predecessor, going ingloriously out of business in less than six months for lack of listeners, advertisers, and station clearance.)

Seeking to extend the television coverage of University of Connecticut basketball games, the family Rasmussen hit upon the idea of renting transponder time on one of the several communication satellites that were being sent into orbit in the mid-1970s like so many Roman candles. From such an innocent concept came the next step. If satellite time were available—at no greater cost to deliver programs nationally than just to a local audience—why just UConn games? Why not more? It costs no more to transmit a program nationally via satellite than to do so locally or regionally. Father and son could only marvel at what lay before them—an untapped wealth of minor sports events, an increasing number of cable systems hungry for programming, and a sports audience that they counted on to be as enthused by the thrill of PKA full contact karate matches as it was with traditional network fare. From such humble beginnings grew ESPN.

While a few "major" minor sports made their way onto the 24-hour cable network—the NCAA College World Series from Omaha, Davis Cup and WCT tennis, and the early rounds of several major golf tournaments—the fly in the Rasmussen ointment was lack of operating capital.

Unlike the premium HBO, ESPN was primarily supported by advertising, and in its formative years very few ad agencies or sponsors were interested in the tiny audiences ESPN could deliver. Those that did participate were treated to very low ad rates, commensurate with the size of audience. In addition, ESPN actually paid cable systems to induce them to clear a channel and carry it. (Today, ESPN is still dependent on advertising income, and its rates, while low by television network standards, are nowhere near as embarrassing as in the early days. Cable systems now pay about 30 cents per month per subscriber to get the service. As testimony to its current popularity, ESPN's audience grew in 1987 by 103 percent as the all-sports program service became the most-watched cable channel in prime time.) Facing the prospect of running a revenue-starved network (which eventually lost more than $100 million in its first six years), the pioneering Rasmussens sought financial relief. They found it seven months before ESPN went on the air. In February 1979, Getty Oil, one of the few advertisers in the auto-motive and petroleum categories which did not have a major sports con-nection, gained 85 percent control of ESPN for $10 million.

Although cable penetration was slowly increasing, Getty continued to pad the ESPN coffers while sustaining enormous losses. With new owners came new management. ESPN and Rasmussen parted company, paving the way for two of sports broadcasting's pioneers to take over the still-struggling network under the Getty banner. Chet Simmons, former pres-ident of NBC Sports, and his executive producer, Scotty Connal, brought their wealth of network sports experience to ESPN.

Simmons's stay was almost as short as Rasmussen's, however—the for-mer network sports executive left in 1981 to become commissioner of the USFL. In a parlay typifying a classic case of vertical integration—or incest, depending on how one looks at the sports/broadcasting industry—Getty sold ESPN outright in 1984 to ABC Television. In that same year, ABC sold 20 percent of the company to RJR Nabisco, Inc., a major ad-vertiser. Don Ohlmeyer, a dynamic sports broadcasting executive who figured prominently both at ABC and NBC in the 1970s and early '80s, was now in charge of sports for Nabisco, and Ohlmeyer clearly under-stood ESPN's potential. The nose of network television was under the tent of cablesports.

Another veteran of the network sports wars, J. William Grimes, a former CBS, Inc., executive, replaced Chet Simmons in 1982, and ESPN's growth under Grimes would parallel the growth of the cable industry itself. By the mid-1980s nearly half of the American households could receive cable, with nearly 14,000 cable systems in operation across the country. This penetration level was not lost on advertisers growing dis-enchanted with the over-the-air networks' escalating costs and lower audience delivery. The agencies sought cheaper rates to reach a more easily targeted sports audience.

While ESPN's program staples are still considered minor, the 24-hour network under Grimes's stewardship blossomed with two major coups, the first of which only a specialized cable network could love. In 1983, ESPN had followed the America's Cup yacht race using a few water-level cameras and an overhead shot from a helicopter-mounted camera. The effect of this coverage was significant, but not so much for the small audience the race finals attracted, but for the fact that the exclusiveness of yachting and the unlimited airtime that ESPN devoted to such an esoteric event was clearly the kind of programming one expected from the cable network. Grimes put more than $2 million into the 1987 challenge race, held in Australia, sensing that the America's Cup could be turned into a viewer's delight and an advertising bonanza. Grimes was correct. Ten advertisers in search of an upscale yachting crowd totally spent more than $4 million to sponsor nearly eighty hours of racing. While the Anheuser-Busch company can be found in at least 85 percent of all professional sports on television, sponsors such as Cadillac, Crum & Forster personal insurance, Atlantic Financial's money market fund, and Schieffelin's Domaine Chandon champagne, products which seldom if ever see the expensive light of commercial television, paid handsomely to be associated with the America's Cup telecast.

ESPN's good fortune was not just the availability of a large audience—by cable's standards—and upscale advertisers. Advances in electronic technology gave ESPN new production credibility. Miniaturized cameras mounted on the masts of the competing yachts, and microphones placed strategically above and below deck captured the drama and hard work that are the America's Cup finals. These camera locations complemented a wide selection of blimp, helicopter, and boat-mounted stabilized cameras that covered the course from start to finish. The networks, always leaders in using dramatic on-the-spot technology—a camera mounted in a Daytona 500 race car; hand-held cameras in downhill ski races; and wireless microphones on out-riders at major horse races and on-field football officials—had met their match in ESPN's telecast of the America's Cup finals.

If the 1987 America's Cup was a maritime triumph for Dennis Conner and the American yachting community, it was a marathon tour-de-force for ESPN. An unprecedented audience either stayed up through half the night to watch the races (because of the time difference between Australia and the United States) or put their VCRs to use by tape delaying the races, a spectacle to be savored the next day while sipping white wine coolers and munching on Brie and crackers.

ESPN's next coup was the cable network's sharing in the 1987 NFL contract. But this rights victory was not without its detractors in the cable community. While ESPN emerged as a near co-equal with the over-the-air networks, it had to win out over other cable interests for the rights, including HBO and a consortium of cable system owners. In addition, ESPN sought to tax local cable systems with an additional surcharge beyond the usual monthly per-subscriber fee. This move put complaining local cable systems in the awkward position of either paying the fee, passing the costs onto their subscribers, or blacking out the games. With big-time success come big-time headaches. By 1987, ESPN was beginning to enjoy a major league migraine, the pain of which was lessened considerably by the audience and kudos the network earned for its superb coverage of the NHL Stanley Cup championship playoffs.

USA Cable Network is another national cable service whose roots lie in the world of sports. This basic cable service is supported primarily by national advertising, with local cable systems paying a few cents per month per subscriber to receive the network. Operating since September 1980, USA Network is the offspring of the Madison Square Garden Cable Network, which began in 1969 as a local cable programming service offering New York Knicks and Rangers games to cable subscribers in Manhattan. The 1975 launch of HBO thrust the Madison Square Garden Network into national orbit, however, with a five-year agreement which allowed HBO to carry New York's professional basketball and hockey teams across the country. A 1977 merger of Madison Square Garden and UA–Columbia Cablevision led to the formation of USA Network, whose programming consisted of a potpourri of soft feature material designed specifically for families and younger cable audiences, and sports. In 1982, USA Network signed an agreement with CBS Sports, one more sign of the commercial networks' interest in cable.

USA Network was unable to negotiate rights to most major sports events, which continued to be the domain of over-the-air commercial broadcasting networks, or ESPN and HBO. While Major League Baseball found its way onto the cable network for a series of Thursday night games in 1982, for the most part sports on USA Network has been of the minor league variety. One-time-only events like secondary college bowl games (the Liberty Bowl), the ubiquitous National Hockey League, Major Indoor Soccer League, boxing, college basketball, and a number of lesser tennis tournaments are its sports staples. However, the continued existence of a national cablesports entity such as USA Network attests to several facts: for every sports event, there's a cable programmer willing to fill up time and cable capacity; for every cable service showing sports, there are thousands of people willing to watch; and for thousands of viewers, there are always advertisers willing to pay some of the freight. As the size of cable audiences increases, ad agencies are beginning to include cable as a regular part of their clients' total advertising strategy. Nearly half of USA Network's roster of sponsors and spot advertisers buys into sports, paying low rates for audience delivery that is minuscule by commercial network standards.

Superstations are the last of the important national cable programming services. Spawned in the mid-1970s, a superstation is a two-headed monster which typifies the cable industry's image and identity crisis. On the one hand, a superstation is a local TV station licensed to serve a particular market. On the other hand, superstations use a satellite to transmit their signal across the country for pickup by local cable systems. Thus, programs that were once the sole province of a single community are now available nationally, and the issues of advertising fees, rights payments, and audience measurement now become national in scope.

Media baron Ted Turner first saw the potential of the superstation concept in 1976. In hot pursuit of product for WTCG-TV (the former call letters of what is now TBS), his Atlanta-based independent television station, Turner was quick to take head-on the forces of major league baseball, football, basketball, the FCC, and anyone else in the sports broadcasting firmament who cared to stand in his way. In addition to owning the TV station, Turner bought the NBA's Atlanta Hawks and baseball's Atlanta Braves, and by virtue of these properties had laid claim to two-thirds of a national sports triangle—rights to the teams' games and production capability. What he needed now was the means to distribute his product. Satellites gave him the third leg. Since December 1976, Turner has operated what looks and sounds like a fourth network—an independent station that offers first-run sports and the usual mix of syndicated sitcoms to a national cable audience. (Ted Turner didn't earn the title Captain Outrageous solely on the basis of his aggressive sailing prowess. Having created CNN and CNN2, two 24-hour cable news networks, he played hardball with cable system owners by coercing them into carrying all of his cable networks. If not, they would have to pay a premium price for those they simply selected individually. To many in the broadcast and cable business, Turner has been a refreshing visionary. To others, he is nothing more than a brash opportunist.)

Since the 1976 launch of TBS, Turner has artfully negotiated rights to major sports events, often outbidding the commercial networks and ESPN. Undaunted, with an "it's only money" attitude, Turner brought packages of NBA basketball and college football and basketball to a growing cable audience. He has paid high rights fees, and, combined with the staggering losses he incurred in the wake of other media mis-adventures, the Turner empire's cash flow has been adulterated by a sea of red ink. The coup de grace for Turner perhaps, was his Olympian creation—the 1986 Goodwill Games—considered by most to be more of a narcissistic monument to international understanding than a world-class event. The Goodwill Games turned out to be an over-rated spectacle—a ratings disaster at the hands of an audience which, after months of pre-event hype and hoopla, either tuned out the games after a brief sampling, or never tuned them in in the first place.

In addition to TBS, there are four other active superstations that reach more than one million homes—WGN, WOR, WPIX and KTVT—with several others scheduled to become active by the end of the 1980s. All of them are flagship stations which carry the games of major league baseball teams, a fact which leads to two issues that add gray hair to the heads of team owners, league commissioners, and a host of broadcast and cable industry executives. (They also make countless high-priced copyright and communications lawyers praise the day they decided to go to law school, with sports, television, and cable giving new meaning to the term "full court press.") The first issue is one of copyright—the transmission of protected material without direct compensation to the rights-holder.

Secondly, superstations which broadcast "local" games to cable systems beyond their home market do so for one reason—money. In this case, however, one man's profit is another's belly-ache. The superstation and the cable companies which import the game and retransmit for their subscribers make money. However, team owners whose market is invaded by imported games complain of losses due to lowered gate attendance. They claim that fickle fans often choose to watch an imported game on cable rather than support the home team. Similarly, local TV stations in the same market fear both the loss of audience to competing cable systems and loss of ad revenue. Statistics show that both these fears are unfounded, however, and that superstations have relatively little effect either on home team attendance or on the ratings of home stations. What impacts more on attendance and ratings are the on-field performance of the home teams, their place in the standings, and the use of imaginative promotions. Old-timers days, a menagerie of Philly Phanatics and San Diego Chickens, Dancing Waters, busty-groundskeepers and ball girls, animated scoreboards, and giveaway days (enough bats, caps, seat cushions, and other paraphernalia to make a public television station proud) give little comfort to leagues and teams which feel all but powerless in the face of cable and its superstations. For them, the presence of alien games is a matter of high priority.

If team owners feel that superstations strip them of a certain degree of control, there is another breed of cable service that puts them squarely in the driver's seat. Regional sports networks are the happy compromise which give teams—and fans—the best of all possible worlds. In a retail business such as cable, franchises learn to give customers what they want. The answer, obviously, is home-team games—and more games—and more games. Cable's multi-channel capacity provides the mechanism for televising as many sporting events into local homes as the market will bear. Whether the sports package is on a basic or a pay tier, or on a pay-per-view basis, the relevant questions are simply, "How many games will the subscriber watch and how much is he willing to pay?"

Each regional sports network has a population center and at least one major sport. The Pittsburgh Pirates Cable Network, Blazer Cable (NBA's Portland basketball team), the St. Louis Cardinals Cable Network, and Giantvision (San Francisco) are the smallest regional networks. SportsChannel, a division of Rainbow Programming Enterprises, is the largest regional sports network, encompassing operations in New England, New York, Chicago, Philadelphia, Detroit, and Florida. By 1987, twenty regional sports networks were in operation, some of which pool their programming to expand their reach well beyond local markets. The commercial broadcast networks are the likely victims of this growing practice, which adds one more national sports "presence" to an already crowded spectrum.

The value of regional sports networks increased at a time when the cable industry was undergoing change on two fronts—programming and regulations. When VCRs became as critical to families as automatic coffee-makers and telephone answering machines, TV viewers began renting feature films at a record-setting pace. Rental fees were much lower than the monthly rates subscribers were accustomed to paying for channels such as HBO, Showtime, or Cinemax. Common sense dictates that it is more economical to rent a film of your choice for $2 a day than pay $15 a month for films that the pay services often duplicated several times a month.

This shift in film-viewing habits put a major dent in the marketing and revenue plans for cable systems. They could no longer count on the 300 percent markup they were getting from selling pay services that were in less demand. Sports, whose "liveness" makes them VCR-proof, are a natural alternative for cable systems, particularly in markets with winning teams.

As the programming marketplace was changing, the cable industry was winning a major battle on the regulatory front. In 1984, Congress passed the Cable Communication Policy Act, legislation which put an end to the historic battle between the cable industry and the cities and towns in which cable companies do business. The industry became an unregulated monopoly, and for the first time, cable operators were no longer at the whim of local town officials. The Act assured cable system owners that the franchises they held were renewable as long as they lived up to the terms of the agreement. Now cable companies could feel comfortable investing in more equipment and programming.

In addition, the Act allowed cable operators to raise their rates for basic program services. Regional sports, once the sole province of pay tiers, found their way into basic packages, attracting higher rates for this potentially more exciting, first-run programming. Sports had filled the vacuum caused by the down-turn in the feature film market, offering primarily one-time-only, first-run events, usually in high demand.

Not all of the nation's twenty regional sports services share identical programming or marketing strategies. The types of events that are available vary from region to region, and their relative success is based as much on team performance, stadium attendance, and overall market size as on aggressive marketing. The challenge to regional sports programmers, and to local cable systems carrying the events, is to create a sense of perceived value in the mind of the subscribers. This principle is a basic axiom common to retailing. Satisfy the customer. Make him feel he's getting his money's worth.

Boston is a good example of the sports marketing challenge, blessed (a choice of word probably not shared by many local wives) with two regional services—New England Sports Network (NESN) and SportsChannel New England. Viewers in this highly cable-penetrated area can watch most Red Sox, Celtics, and Bruins games on a combination of these two services. (The NFL League contract does not allow teams like the New England Patriots to enter into local TV agreements except for pre-season games.)

Most Boston-area cable systems offer either NESN or SportsChannel, and many offer both. They are generally on a pay tier and the subscriber receives a reduced rate when he buys both services as a package.

Both NESN and SportsChannel (wholesalers) and the local cable systems (retailers) rely heavily on the appeal of the home teams to attract subscribers. While Boston is an active sports city, the marketing challenge is significant because only 139 games a year among the three professional sports are cablecast. Additionally, most of the non-cable games are shown on local independent TV stations. Each game lasts about three hours, which leaves a lot more time for NESN and SportsChannel to fill.

Subscribers are then left to decide whether or not the variety of college, minor professional and quasi-sports programs that NESN and SportsChannel offer are worth the monthly fee that most subscribers pay for the privilege of receiving the major events. (Even with the competitive nature of cablesports programmers, and the unusual arrangement of having two pay services in one town, both NESN and SportsChannel have increased their number of subscribers, which only seems to prove that, if one chooses to be in cablesports, it doesn't hurt to have the Celtics mystique or the annual Red Sox suicide plunge to offer up to willing and paying fanatics.)

Regional cablesports is no different than other maturing industries. Mergers and acquisitions have become part of the landscape, and many industry observers in the mid-1980s were led to speculate on the precise number of companies that will ultimately survive. Futurologists also question the larger role that the networks might play in regional cable ownership, with CBS already holding about one-third ownership in Home Team Sports (Washington-Baltimore.)

The tremendous profit potential for regional cablesports will lead to more start-up ventures every year as the cable industry matures. But today the battlefields (and bankruptcy courts) are littered with the bodies of well-intentioned entrepreneurs who have tried their hands at cablesports only to have died in the process. Two classic examples from the early 1980s epitomize the old adage that there's no such thing as a sure thing. Both instances show that even the best laid plans of the best minds in the sports business don't always have the right results.

The year is 1981 and the location is the Pacific Northwest. The city is Seattle and the team is the SuperSonics, professional basketball's darling of Puget Sound. They are a city and team which never quite recovered from the shock of nearly winning the NBA title in 1978, losing in the seventh game of the finals. In spite of the downward turn in their on-court fortunes, the Sonics were still one of the most profitable franchises in the league, willing to spend generously to remain competitive in a league that would be dominated for most of the decade by major market entries from Boston, Los Angeles, Philadelphia, and Houston.

The parent company of the SuperSonics, FNI, Inc., is a braintrust which looked to cable as a way of accommodating the overflow crowds that the Sonics regularly attracted to home games at the Kingdome. Perhaps savoring John Lindsay's urban oil-well image a bit too much, FNI saw cable as a way of increasing revenues in an era of escalating operational costs (read "player salaries.")

In the Sonics' favor was Seattle itself, a top-15 market in one of the most densely cabled areas in the country. The mountainous terrain in northwest Washington state is perfectly suited to cable, and is a place where the weather is ideal for watching sports from the comfort of one's home. The scenario seemed almost too perfect to be true: a competitive team; a basketball-hungry audience; turn-away crowds at the arena; and a community that was not only familiar with cable but almost dependent upon it.

The Sonics planned to offer a package of televised games to cable audiences for $120 a year (above and beyond the subscriber's regular monthly basic cable fee). The schedule would include all exhibition and regular season games, except for about seventeen which were telecast over-the-air on local station KIRO-TV. The Sonics also promised these SuperChannel subscribers free installation, insulation from rate increases for two years, and, as a bonus, $120 worth of coupons that could be applied to the price of tickets for games at the Kingdome. The Sonics' break-even target was approximately 12,000 subscribers in the first year (out of the then nearly 250,000 cable households in the Puget Sound area), a target which even the most pessimistic observers felt was attainable. Sonics management even dared to project 20,000 subscribers for the first year of operation. But the experiment barely reached the break-even point in the first year, and showed little growth thereafter.

What went wrong? Why did this experiment, which had all the ingredients for success, not survive? The reasons may be too obvious to be believed, although in retrospect, much was learned, not just by the Sonics, but by other experimenters in cablesports.

First, the venture was new. While the Seattle area was heavily penetrated by cable, there was no tradition of paying extra for sports events, particularly for games still available for free. The KIRO-TV telecasts and CBS's national games both contributed to the subscribers' collective lack of interest in paying for the service.

Then there was the problem with the local cable industry. SuperChannel was to be fed to ten local cable companies, each separately owned and with no history of interconnection. Sonics management saw Super-Channel as a single source feeding ten different faucets. Leaks were bound to occur, mostly in the form of an uncoordinated marketing and promotion effort. When the first trickle of orders came in, the processing went smoothly. But as the basketball season neared and more customers decided to sign on, most of the ten companies—and the Sonics front office—were unable to handle requests adequately. Viacom Cablevision, the biggest of the ten companies, hired two additional employees to handle the rush, and barely succeeded. Both the Supersonics and participating cable companies learned the hard way a fact of cable life that the rest of the industry is still learning—customer service is the heart of cable retailing, and an unhappy subscriber is like a lady scorned. There is seldom a second date.

Finally, there was the Sonics' own inexperience in the cable business. While FNI and the Sonics management were among the best in chalkboarding Xs and Os for selling tickets to the Kingdome, they had no experience in selling, marketing, promoting, and producing games for cable. They were understaffed to handle customer mailings and billings and could not adequately respond to customer requests and complaints that followed the Sonics' first promotional announcements.

The Sonics' ticket giveaway also brought down the wrath of countless customers, many of whom felt cheated by what they considered a misleading promotional stunt. Many customers interpreted the Sonics' promise of $120 worth of ticket discounts as $120 worth of free tickets. The ensuing confusion proved to be a gratuitous headache to an already beleaguered management team.

Needless to say, the Sonics fell woefully short of their goal of attracting 250,000 subscribers by 1985. Within a few years, the white flag of surrender went up and SuperChannel folded, the victim of an idea whose time may not have come, but one which, with better planning, may have survived somewhat longer.

If the Seattle Supersonics were babes in the 1981 cable world, a 1984 partnership rich both in experience and financial backing started another regional sports network. Sports Time, a three-way venture which brought together some of the most experienced sports, advertising, and telecommunications professionals, went the way of the Edsel—a high-priced, overly promoted vehicle that no one wanted. If any cablesports prognosticator were to have predicted that Sports Time would die an inglorious death fewer than six months after its heralded inauguration, you would have suspected him of having ingested a foreign substance. Every imaginable ingredient for a successful cablesports network was there—money, experience in the cable business, attractive and highly promotable major league events, guaranteed cable clearance, and a potential audience with an historic record of unbounded sports enthusiasm. Ready to invest? Three companies did, and today they continue to look for answers as to what went wrong. Follow along and try to find the clues.

Sports Time covered a fifteen-state area primarily in the Midwest, and extended to parts of Colorado, North Carolina, and West Virigina. The network was marketed to nearly 1,000 cable systems in these areas which charged subscribers between $12 and $15 per month, a fee competitive with other pay services.

The roster of events that Sports Time promised was a menu of major professional and college attractions—drawing almost exclusively on local area sports teams—rich enough to make even the most greedy couch potato weep with gratitude. The St. Louis Cardinals, the Kansas City Royals, and the Cincinnati Reds would fill most summer evenings, along with Triple A minor league baseball from the American Association. In the fall and winter, the NBA's Indiana Pacers and Kansas City Kings (which soon relocated to Sacramento) were promised, as were college football and basketball games featuring Big Eight and Big Ten teams, as well as the Missouri Valley, Mid-American, Midwestern City, and Ohio Valley Conferences.

If this lineup were not enough, Sports Time promised to fill the remaining time voids with games from the USFL, the North American and Major Indoor Soccer Leagues, boxing matches, golf, bowling, car racing, tennis, track and field, and a schedule of non-event programming including sports news, interviews, and instructional programs.

The April 1984 network premiere of Sports Time was preceded by an extensive marketing, advertising, and promotional campaign virtually unmatched in the history of sports television. The campaign was targeted at the 18- to 40-year-old males in the $35,000 per-year salary range. The campaign theme? "30 live big league events per month at a cost of only 30 cents a day!"

The Sports Time partners were: 1) Anheuser-Busch, TV's largest sports advertiser, which learned the bitter lesson that this budding world of regional cablesports ownership was not for them. The brewery provided an unmatched track record of sports sponsorship, and in a five-year period in the early 1980s had spent nearly $75 million on cablesports advertising alone. Anheuser-Busch brought advertising revenue to the Sports Time party, and the leverage that a major sports advertiser can apply to teams, leagues, conferences, and cable systems.

2) Multimedia, Inc., the second partner, a media giant whose holdings at the time of the venture included daily and weekly newspapers, radio and TV stations, and a number of cable systems, many of which were in the Sports Time coverage area. In addition, Multimedia was part owner of the Cincinnati Reds and was the largest syndicator of country music programming in the country. Multimedia brought TV production know-how and a large potential audience to the party.

3) Tele-Communications, Inc. (TCI), the largest and most aggressive cable-system owner in the country. In addition to its unmatched understanding of what makes the cable business tick, nearly one-quarter of TCI's subscribers lived in the Sports Time coverage area, a potential audience gold-mine for the network.

After Sports Time died, the three partners asked what went wrong. After all, theirs was one of the most well-financed, experienced triumvirates ever assembled for such a venture. They promised to deliver a potentially exciting product and an impressive audience.

Sports Time's fate was probably sealed by the overabundance of sports events on network television and on ESPN. In addition, the partners miscalculated the amount of money their targeted cable audience would spend to watch games in which other than home teams played. Could a viewer in West Virginia care very much about the Kansas City Royals? Were those games worth $15 a month? How interesting were Big Eight basketball games in North Carolina?

While the world is never short of big spenders willing to invest in one more "sure thing," the short and unfruitful life of Sports Time continues to send a message that reflects the uncertainties of cablesports in general, or even televised sports. While programming is everything, the value is in the eyes of the beholder. As long as viewers, as opposed to advertisers, are expected to pay the bills, the programs had better be good. That means: a) the price has to be right; b) the "store" across the street can't give the same thing away for free; and c) the home team better win consistently, or at least be competitive.

By the late 1980s, cablesports resembles a very good AAA baseball player waiting to break into the majors. Its "stats" are impressive, but not quite good enough to get the full attention of fans and team owners. But most people question, however, how long the old pros—ABC, CBS, and NBC—can continue to fight off their problems of sagging ratings and diminished advertising before cable gains full parity. The key players in professional and collegiate sports—the rights-holders—can see the promising rookie playing a bigger and more permanent role. The NFL, NBA, and Major League Baseball are already into cable, but not in a big way. So is the NCAA. The expense of running professional and amateur sports continues to rise, and cable can help pay the bills. It's only a matter of time.

If one is looking for villains in this scenario, there are none. Decisions in the sports business are made on the basis of corporate self-interest (the NCAA, colleges, and the AAU are corporations, too), and there are now positive signs that show that the real money lies ahead in national and regional pay television. When the time is ripe—when the market is there and more money can be made from moving all games from "free" to "pay" television—it will happen (except for those sports that will continue to benefit from the support of national advertisers that must reach a mass audience which only the broadcast networks can deliver). Also, as long as professional football and baseball are protected from anti-trust regulations, the Super Bowl and the World Series will probably remain on "free" TV to spare these major leagues from the wrath of Congress. Conventional TV and cable will probably co-exist for a while; the NFL package on the networks and ESPN is one example. Future Olympic Games will be shared by the networks and cable programmers. Ultimately, the future of sports on cable rests upon how much fans are willing to pay to watch sports on television, and how much freedom sports owners and leagues will get from the political powers-that-be to make their move from "free" to "pay."

The impetus that may eventually push free television completely over the brink is pay-per-view cable, a mechanism that allows cable subscribers to pay only for the individual events they watch, rather than a monthly fee for a full schedule of programs they may not want. Pay-per-view technology exists and has been relatively successful in a few areas for showing feature films and for one-time-only sporting events like championship boxing. The biggest problem with pay-per-view is that many older cable systems are not technically equipped to provide this service to their customers. Addressible technology, which is expensive to install, allows a cable operator to send a single program down the line on demand to the subscriber's home and bill him at the end of the month. Subscribers who do not choose to pay for a program receive a scrambled signal (or no signal at all on that particular channel.) Neither the technology nor a market for pay-per-view existed during the cable construction boom of the late 1970s, and now pay-per-view programmers are waiting for older cable systems to catch up with the state of the art and the state of the business.

Pay-per-view's potential for raising revenues for sports teams and promoters is staggering to consider. For example, if only *half* of the homes which normally tune in the Super Bowl had to pay $5 to watch the game on cable—their only option—the income would be more than $100 million! That amount of money *for this one event only* would go a long way towards meeting escalating salary demands and other rising costs. Add to this the potential advertising revenue—at the going rate of $1 million-per-minute—and you're talking real money.

Imagine the following scenario. All home games of your favorite NFL team are on pay-per-view, allowing you to pay separately for each game you watch. Would you pay? Would it be worth it? Studies have shown that most football fans would pay a reasonable amount if paying were the only way they could see the games. The question, however, is, "How much is reasonable?" Other studies contend that there are only a few specific major events that will regularly attract a pay-per-view audience. These are the Super Bowl, the World Series, the Kentucky Derby, the

NCAA Final Four Championship game, and an occasional championship boxing match.

While the marketplace will decide the fate of televised sports, the individual fan is left on the bench awaiting the outcome. Sports fans collectively have no more voice in the matter than they did when watching from the sidelines when their home teams moved to riper and richer television markets. They have little or no direct influence on whether the games appear on pay cable or on television. Their sole options are whether or not to watch, and whether or not to pay for watching. The Constitution of the United States has never guaranteed unlimited protection from having sports removed from free television, and the Founding Fathers never guaranteed free televised access to the stadiums of America. Television (including cable), sports and fans are a triangle, and it should be no surprise to anyone which third of the trio is the base supporting the other two legs.

4

PLAYING BY THE RULES
Law and Regulation of TV Sports

IT MAY NOT BE TRUE that television and sports interests take each other to court more often than, say, doctors, but it is abundantly clear that once there they perform with infinitely greater gusto. Their confrontations are often public spectacles of high drama—some real, some contrived for the benefit of public opinion, which always seems to play a major role in these affairs. There is much breast-beating by the aggrieved parties, and warnings of potential catastrophe, should "the other guys" emerge victorious.

The glamour brought to the proceedings does little to mask the unhappiness at being there in the first place, however. The prevailing wisdom in both industries is that the courts are places where several things can happen—most of them bad. The baleful defendants often seem to be dragged in, kicking and screaming, and even the plaintiffs use the courts as a last resort.

Certain frequent participants, however, such as the Los Angeles Raiders' Al Davis, bring a palpable zest to the task. They identify their own organization's financial imperatives as priority number one and seem to relish a good fight, in or out of the courtroom. One can argue whether students of the Al Davis School of Law go to court because they usually win, or that they usually win because they go to court. In any case, batteries of wary lawyers are paid to anticipate the next set of plaintiffs, and fend them off.

Playing by the Rules

Similar personalities and conflicts have always existed in these businesses. In fact, the historical roots of many disputes go back some sixty years, and in some cases the same basic issues have been tested again and again, growing only in expense and complexity. The distinguishing differences have been the avalanche of television money which now beckons the victor; the rise in the number of claimants to that ever increasing treasure; and the dramatic changes in communications technologies, which have made sorting out who owns what, more and more difficult. Aggrieved parties most often seek solace in the comforting arms of the legal system. Satisfaction may be long in coming and difficult to achieve, but many seem to relish the opportunity of enlisting the power and authority of the government on their side. Is there any more delightful prospect than the sight of your competitor cringing before a judge?

The Founding Fathers' legacy is a framework of law and regulation which respects the broadest range of personal, political and religious beliefs even fanaticism. Modern politician/sports-fanatics are frequently in the position of regulating the television sports business. They discharge that responsibility with all the dispassionate objectivity of Super Bowl viewers whose television set suddenly goes blank during the first quarter.

There are, of course, legitimate questions of law and regulation which have been explored in court. The majority of cases cover a fairly narrow range of questions: how do the anti-trust laws apply to sports and television? Who owns the broadcast/cable rights to what sports programming? What technical means can they use to deliver it to a specified paying audience? Or, conversely, under what circumstances can a sports rightsholder impede, limit or forbid television from recording or distributing its event? When is a public event not a public event at all? What property rights are invested in whom at sports events? How many claimants are entitled to a piece of the copyright payments? What is the meaning of the "right of publicity?" As we shall see, the television and sports businesses inherited some of these issues from radio, borrowed a few from entertainment and publishing, and stumbled head first into the remainder. Understanding these issues will help the typical viewer make sense out of otherwise baffling and annoying programming decisions.

To begin to understand the contentious, billion-dollar television sports industry of today, one has to return to a simpler time by a passage that takes us back through the era of innocence, to a time and place where baseball was played by soft-hearted tough guys and jug-eared farm boys in hazy, sun-speckled ball parks filled with apple-cheeked kids in tow of their shirt-sleeved Dads. It was in that time, in those parks, for the entertainment of those kids—in the misty, dreamy morning of big league ball—that the modern era of broadcast sports began. Very soon, there were lawsuits.

71

Pittsburgh radio station KDKA ushered in the era of broadcasting when it went on the air in 1920, mostly to sell Westinghouse's new radios. It carried no live sports events, but its announcers did read baseball scores from the newspapers, and the small audience owning those bulky, balky receivers responded with interest. Within a year, Major League Baseball had authorized the participating teams to sell the broadcast rights to the World Series, for which each was paid a grand total of $1500. These rights were expressly vested in the individual clubs, not the commissioner's office, and there was no provision for sharing the money with other teams, or the commissioner's office.

In other areas, however, franchise owners often seemed to be cooperating when they should have been competing. Critics charged that the major leagues could be regarded as behaving like anti-competitive cartels rather than a collection of robust business competitors. To avert a possibly disastrous showdown in the courts, the baseball establishment rallied fans to help lobby Congress, which granted an exemption from the anti-trust laws—an exemption which still exists. It remains the envy of many a competing sports league or association. Congress had spoken, and two precedents were set that were to be repeated many times: the government had significantly altered the rules for sports in America, and popular support swayed elected politicians to bend the rules for sports.

As the radio industry began to spread throughout the country in the mid-twenties, it was virtually unregulated. Would-be broadcasters could erect a transmitter wherever they desired and begin broadcasting whatever they wished on the frequency of their choosing—even if that interfered with someone else's signal. In short order the airwaves were in chaos. Led by Secretary of Commerce Herbert Hoover, who enjoyed a pre-Depression reputation as the "boy wonder" of the business community (with a social conscience to boot), Congress passed the Federal Radio Act of 1927. The Act, and its successor, the Federal Communications Act of 1934, ordered a raft of changes in the way stations did their business, and in so doing, expressed the Government's right to regulate the industry through the newly established Federal Communications Commission (FCC). Hoover's reasoning was that the airwaves (and, literally, the sky) belonged to the public, and could not be bought by a broadcaster. Instead, the Government, acting as Trustee for the people, would manage the airwaves and lease them to broadcasters under the specifications of a renewable license. The Government had now become actively involved in the regulation of both broadcasting and sports. As it turned out, the FCC had barely settled in when the first angry sports broadcasting outfit appeared on its doorstep.

In September of that year, a Mr. A. E. Newton contracted with several radio stations to feed them a "re-creation" of the World Series between the Tigers and Cardinals. Working from his own home, he got his "running accounts" of the action by listening to the games on someone else's station. Major League Baseball, usually a strong supporter of radio coverage, looked askance at Mr. Newton's efforts for two related reasons. In the first place, someone else had already paid for the rights to broadcast the Series and didn't appreciate the unexpected competition. Second (and, so far as Baseball was concerned, more serious), Newton had neglected to pay for the privilege. Both organizations complained to the FCC and challenged his license renewal. The FCC renewed his license, but he was enjoined from further re-creations without permission of the rights-holder. The decision introduced the notion that a property right existed for broadcast sports. That property was potentially valuable, and in certain circumstances at least, you needed to obtain the owner's permission before using it. A good way to get the owner's permission was suggested: offer to pay for it.

In 1938 another enterprising broadcaster was hauled into court, this time by the Pittsburgh Pirates. They said no rights fee had been paid, and therefore claimed the offender, KQV Broadcasting Company, could not report news (play-by-play) of their games-in-progress. KQV countered with the argument that the games were public events—so public, in fact, that they were clearly visible from neighboring rooftops and a variety of other perches occupied by their announcers. Once again, the decision went to the rights-holder, on the grounds that the Pirates had created the event and were in control of the premises where it was staged. The "news, reports, descriptions or accounts" of the game were the property of the Pirates.

To attend a game you needed to buy a ticket, so it really wasn't public in the sense of being open to all; only those members of the public with tickets gained admission, much as in a theatre. This concept is quite difficult for many people to accept in the 1980s, when huge stadia are sold out for games of tremendous importance to millions of people. Many fans, broadcasters, and journalists believe the games are news events because they are of great interest to the public. In fact, though, they are private events, staged by their owners, albeit on a mammoth scale in massive "theatres."

But what about legitimate news coverage of these events? Could the general public really be excluded at the owners' whim? Another case the same year settled the question. In *Radio Corp. v. Chicago Bears*, the Bears emerged victorious, with a ruling that extended the right-holders' protection to include a "right of publicity" of an event, balanced only by the constitutional doctrine of free speech. In essence, the court said the news media have a constitutional right to report newsworthy aspects (limited highlights, or newspaper accounts), but only after the event was over. As a result of these two decisions in 1938, the seeds of our modern system of high-priced, exclusive broadcast rights were sown. From then on, reporters and broadcasters would have to get permission (broadcast rights or a press pass) from the owners of the event.

It has been stated that the United States is a nation of inventors—of tinkerers, really—people who repeatedly look for new solutions to old problems. In 1955, a gentleman named Martin Fass thought he had come up with just such a solution: how to make money transmitting sports events without having to pay for the right to do so. He listened to radio broadcasts of Giants baseball games and then teletyped the play-by-play to a small network of subscribing stations. The Giants' parent company sued him. In *National Exhibition Co. v. Fass,* he claimed to be an "independent newsgatherer." Besides, he reasoned, earlier decisions had banned unauthorized broadcasting of such accounts, but had said nothing specifically about teletyping them. The court, however, agreed with the Giants that he was just as wrong as A. E. Newton had been.

As recently as 1981, rights-holders were still fighting off this sort of challenge. WSBK-TV, the Boston flagship station for Red Sox games, finally got fed up with seeing extensive highlight clips, taken from its signal, appearing on ESPN. Since ESPN had not paid any rights fee to WSBK nor sought its permission in the matter, Channel 38's parent company followed standard procedure and filed *New Boston Television Corp. v. ESPN.* ESPN defended its actions, saying that the short clips of sports highlights are what constitutes legitimate "news" on an all-sports network. It also claimed that the small amount of footage, run after WSBK's broadcasts were complete, could do little damage to WSBK. ESPN's claims were rejected, and it was instructed not to carry game highlights, even if they came from a signal intercepted "from the air," without the expressed written permission of the original rights-holders. If all ESPN wanted to do was to provide "news" of the games, it could have simply read a description, without using highlights at all. ESPN decided not to appeal, and opted to negotiate a fee structure with WSBK-TV.

Another related suit had been heard in 1977, with echoes of those much earlier disputes about the "news" value of an event and the performer's publicity rights. In this case, the plaintiff, a gentleman by the name of Hugo Zacchini, earned his living as the "Human Cannonball" of a small, traveling circus. Typically, the circus would set up at an outdoor location in cities across America. Mr. Zacchini's performance was short, but loud. When fired from his hydraulic "cannon," he would arch through the air and land in a safety net. Quite frequently, part of his flight was visible from outside the circus grounds, and many people, startled by the BOOM! heralding his high-velocity emergence from the cannon gun-barrel, would turn to see his apogee. This being a somewhat unusual occurrence in most cities, it was not uncommon for local television news crews to record the visible portions of his flight, for inclusion in a newscast. Zacchini would attempt to discourage them, often vehemently.

Mr. Zacchini consistently objected to the videotaping, stating that the news clips, in fact, had recorded a substantial portion of his act without his permission. Consequently, he left a plume of smoke, and a trail of legal protests against stations, across the nation. The matter happened to reach the courts in a suit against a station owned by Scripps-Howard Broadcasting. Zacchini claimed its news crews had filmed all ten seconds of his act, from gun to net. *Zacchini v. Scripps-Howard*, was a resounding victory for Hugo, and cannonballers everywhere, as well as others whose right of publicity was reinforced.

If Hugo Zacchini had a legally protected right to his performance, then surely other attention-getting performances, which, charitably, might be referred to as unique, must enjoy the same. That point, among others, was made in *Giannoulas v. KGB*, which delineated the rights of Ted Giannoulas, better known as the San Diego Chicken.

It seems that Mr. Giannoulas first climbed into the suit as an employee of San Diego radio station KGB, Inc., whose trademarked logo appeared where his breast or white meat would otherwise be. Giannoulas's highjinks as the "KGB Chicken" became a fixture at Padres' games, where he became a crowd favorite. In fact, his popularity grew to the point that he was invited to take his act on the road, sans Padres, and make paid public appearance at various sports arenas. KGB Radio sought to have him enjoined from doing so, claiming that his appearances as "The Chicken" at non-KGB events would cause the station loss of revenue, as a result of understandable public confusion with their "KGB Chicken." What further complicated the matter was that most people referred to this example of poultry in motion as "The San Diego Chicken," not the "KGB Chicken" anyway.

Giannoulas's position was that he had a right to make the appearances as just plain "The Chicken"—a performer distinct from other, admittedly similar fowl. The court found that KGB could indeed control any use of the trademarked "KGB Chicken" but said Giannoulas was entitled to constitutionally protected artistic "free expression" (dressing up in public in a ridiculous chicken suit), and that that constitutional guarantee took precedence over any potential loss of station revenues.

75

Sometimes it seems that news organizations just won't take "no" for an answer. Having been repeatedly rebuffed by the victories of rights-holders in cases which debated the "news values" of sporting events, they continued to assert their interpretation of the situation. In 1981 the Hartford Civic Center hosted a national ice-skating championship. ABC Sports owned the exclusive television rights to the championship, which was scheduled to run for several days, beginning in mid-week. The telecasts were to begin on Saturday's *Wide World of Sports*. A local television station owned by Post-Newsweek Broadcasting sent news camera crews to the Civic Center in mid-week to cover the event as "news," since its presence in Hartford was clearly a good story. The news camera crews were barred from shooting at the arena, however, and Post-Newsweek went to court to test the issue, in *Post-Newsweek Broadcasting v. Traveler's Insurance* (Traveler's being the owner of the building).

The court found that, indeed, where an exclusive television contract has been granted, news coverage of the event can be barred by the property rights-holder, even in an event that runs for several days. The size and scale of the private performance (it is private because they sold tickets) does not affect the definition of "private" for property rights purposes. It was Traveler's property, and they controlled admission. The news crews could have gained admission by purchasing tickets, but ABC owned the exclusive television rights, so the crews could not have brought their cameras in with them. This case was, in effect, the icing on the cake for those rights-holders wishing to assert the most restrictive claims of copyright and property rights.

In theory, anyway, almost any event—no matter how large or public—could be private, and could control news coverage. This theory may have stretched to beyond all credibility when ABC attempted to employ it during televised ceremonies of the Statue of Liberty rededication. Virtually a week of events, the rededication featured President and Mrs. Reagan, about a million spectators, several military units, an international Tall Ships procession and most of New York harbor, including Lady Liberty herself. ABC had bought the rights to certain of the events, and tried to fend off competitors' camera crews; no competing news executives, however, paid the slightest attention to ABC's threats of dire consequences, and ABC threw in the towel after a day or two.

The year 1939 saw the emergence of televised professional football, as NBC carried a game between Philadelphia and Brooklyn. The sets themselves were huge, ungainly affairs, and had just begun to show up in the homes of a few well-to-do families. An infinitesimal audience strained mightily to make out the snowy little gridiron images through the blinding glare of those early screens. These sports nuts were probably the grandparents of middle-of-the-night ESPN "junkies" some fifty years later. Enough must have been watching, however, because in 1940 Mutual Broadcasting paid $2500 dollars for the rights to telecast the NFL Championship Game. Following the model established by Major League Baseball, the rights fee was split between the two teams, bypassing the commissioner's office. For the infant television system, it was a modest beginning, but, as one radio executive of the time would later say, "I wish we'd strangled it [TV sports] in the crib."

During this period, rights-holders were often hesitant about dealing with broadcasters, if they dealt with them at all. Many forbade any broadcasting of their games, on the grounds that broadcasts reduced the sale of admission tickets. Others were more liberal, counting on the publicity generated by broadcasting to increase fan interest and thereby actually boost future gate admissions. Foremost among the latter group was William Wrigley, who one season placed his Cubs' games on no less than seven radio stations; in 1949 all three Chicago television stations carried Cubs games simultaneously. Every game of the season was carried, a club policy still in effect in the days of cable and superstations some forty years later.

The baseball owners eventually came to recognize that this aggressive marketing of some major league broadcasts was having a negative effect on minor league baseball. Attendance was dropping, as more and more people began listening to (and later, watching) faraway major league teams, while the local minor league franchise—heretofore the only game in town—suffered. Ted Turner may have called his superstation Atlanta Braves "America's Team" in the 1980s, but he was some four decades late in identifying the phenomenon. Public and political pressures, particularly from those states whose once prosperous minor league teams were suffering, forced major league owners to adopt Rule 1-D, which prohibited broadcasts into minor league markets. They rescinded the Rule 1-D in 1951, citing a potential anti-trust suit against Major League Baseball (despite its anti-trust exemption). Cynics were prompted to observe that the real reason was their unwillingness to forfeit their hold on the huge percentage of the national audience then represented by minor league markets.

The onset of American participation in World War II, and a freeze ordered by the FCC, delayed work on most commercial television developments, including color television, UHF signals, and cable until 1952. The war years were a busy time for federal regulators, and one of the FCC's actions was to have a profound impact on the future of television sports. In 1941, NBC was forced to divest itself of one of its two TV networks, the so-called Blue Network, which re-emerged as the fledgling ABC. A chronic weakling, ABC struggled along as the fourth network (behind NBC, CBS, and DuMont), and was even considered inferior to some independent producers, such as RKO and Paramount. It was finally rescued from a lingering death by a merger with the much richer Paramount Theaters—a move which would set off its own anti-trust actions some years later. But within ten years, ABC would become a major force in television sports.

When the war came to an end, sports broadcasting took off. Perhaps it was the impact of millions of former servicemen returning to civilian life, or their pent-up interest in sports, or their disposable cash. Whatever the reason, interest soared. In 1946 Larry MacPhail was able to sell the New York Yankees' TV rights to DuMont for the remarkable sum of $75,000. By 1948 the World Series was on national television. As rights fees rose, and the tantalizing potential of significant television revenues was recognized, teams and leagues began maneuvering to carve out and protect what each regarded as its own exclusive piece of the pie.

The year 1953 brought more adjustments to the relationship of television and sports franchises. In short, the rich were starting to get richer, and the poor, poorer, as popular powerful franchises crowded their weaker sisters out of the market for fan allegiance and broadcast revenues. A new and troubling solution was for the weaker franchises to abandon their traditional home in search of more financially rewarding surroundings. The Boston Braves were first, as they decamped for Milwaukee (later, of course, jilted in favor of Atlanta; Seattle was then deserted to restock Milwaukee, and then Seattle was restocked, in an orgy of infidelity). The St. Louis Browns went to Baltimore in 1954, the Athletics left Philadelphia for Kansas City in 1955, and in 1958 a thunderous shock was felt when the Giants and Dodgers collaborated, and bolted New York City for San Francisco and Los Angeles, respectively.

The major reason for the Giants-Dodgers moves was the lure of exclusive TV revenues. The Dodgers' Walter O'Malley was calculating potential Los Angeles Pay-TV revenues as early as 1957. He entered into secret negotiations with Skiatron, a Los Angeles Pay-TV company, for Giants and Dodgers packages which would have doubled the Dodgers' Brooklyn income. Skiatron's legal problems, and ultimately a voter initiative, blocked this plan, and O'Malley had to "settle" for a broadcast TV contract in which he strictly blacked out all Dodgers home games, and still received revenues second only to the mighty Yankees. In none of these decisions were franchise owners impeded by their peers, or by the commissioner's office.

The news about television wasn't quite so good for all franchises, or all sports. In 1949, the Los Angeles Rams drew 205,000 fans to their home games. The next year, they televised home games, and attendance sank to 110,000. In 1951, once more they blacked out home games, and attendance promptly doubled. Apparently needing yet more evidence of their folly, the Rams sold the rights to air all games during the 1952 season, for a fee of $300,000, only to see ticket sales plunge once more. Interestingly enough, a Brookings Institution study many years later concluded that the relationship between the Rams' televising home games and a drop in gate attendance was indirect. Other factors, including the record of both teams, the weather on game day, competing recreational options for fans, stadium facilities and convenience, and promotional campaigns also had to be considered.

In 1952 NFL Commissioner Bert Bell, at the time bereft of any high-priced research, concluded that unlimited television was a threat to the league, and that any action to restrict it should be taken by the league as a unit. He rammed through the annual owners' meeting bylaw amendments which gave him virtual complete control over NFL television. His action raised a storm. The Justice Department filed suit, charging a variety of anti-trust violations. Judge Alan Grim agreed with the NFL's contention that it was a "unique kind of business" which would be harmed by a classical interpretation of anti-trust law, and he upheld the league-wide imposition of blackouts of home games. On the other hand, he rejected Commissioner Bell's attempt to gain sweeping control over the individual franchises' television rights.

In the late fifties the NFL was prohibited, probably in reaction to Bert Bell's earlier attempts, from selling its rights to any one network in a single unified package. However, in 1960, the upstart American Football League shocked the complacent NFL when it did just that, signing on with ABC. Another surprising feature of the contract was the equalized distribution of television revenues to all franchises. In response, the NFL asked for an anti-trust exemption allowing it to sign the same kind of unified package. The AFL, in an eerie precursor of the USFL-NFL anti-trust fight some twenty-five years later, opposed the NFL petition, claiming the NFL would sign contracts with more than one network and so drive the AFL out of business. The NFL disclaimed any hostile intent towards its competitor.

To prove it, the NFL's suave new Commissioner, Pete Rozelle, went to Capitol Hill and assured Congress the purpose of the exemption was to allow the league to sign on with only one network—CBS. However noble the NFL's intentions, marketplace realities virtually dictated that it sign exclusively with CBS. ABC had the AFL, and in the existing NFL contracts CBS was carrying nine teams, while NBC had only two—plus a host of expensive obligations to other sports. The CBS contract was soon signed, and almost immediately, Judge Grim, who had denied Bert Bell's 1952 attempt, ruled this contract an anti-trust violation.

Rozelle's legendary lobbying skills, buttressed by fan support for the NFL's claim that the AFL had been given an unfair advantage, carried the day. Congress quickly passed by voice vote the Sports Broadcasting Act of 1961. The Act extended anti-trust exemptions to professional football, basketball, and hockey for the limited purpose of pooling their individual franchises' broadcast rights while negotiating unified network television contracts. Baseball, of course, already enjoyed a blanket exemption from the anti-trust laws. In return, the four professional leagues agreed not to schedule their games directly opposite Friday-night high-school football or Saturday-afternoon college games.

Although the one-network per league policy was never actually written into the Congressional exemption, the House committee staff report, which accompanied it, stated that it was not intended to exempt any agreement "whose intent or effect" was to exclude a competing league from selling its television rights. This phrase, which was considered to place the professional leagues on "moral notice" regarding multi-network deals, contains the precise language later cited by the USFL in its fight to the death against the NFL.

The leagues quickly used the freedom granted them to negotiate new pooled network contracts of the sort we are now accustomed to. The franchises' pooled rights were vested in the commissioners, who became immensely more important and powerful than their predecessors. By controlling the lucrative television contracts, they and a few owners on the Television Committee had a powerful grip on the league purse strings. NFL Commissioner Rozelle, for example, convinced the most powerful owners (The Giants' Wellington Mara, The Bears' George Halas, The Steelers' Art Rooney, The Rams' Dan Reeves) to accept a policy of equalized distribution of TV revenues among all NFL franchises, regardless of a team's market size. To convince them they would be better off, he promised—and delivered—a much larger contract with CBS. It was an idea borrowed from the AFL-ABC contract, and it was to become Rozelle's chosen instrument of power.

For the first time the Green Bays of the league could now compete with the New York, Chicago, Washington, and Los Angeles teams (with huge regional networks of their own) on a more even footing—and compete they did. In short, the 1961 Act created the modern television package which now subsidizes the professional leagues. It prescribed the power of commissioners who, by controlling the flow of television money, could for the first time control the previously autonomous and autocratic owners.

In 1962 another case, *Blaich v. NFL,* had been heard, and once again the NFL emerged victorious. Blaich had challenged the league's right to black out telecasts of championship (and by inference, regular season) games in the markets of teams playing at home. The league, citing again the sad experience of the Rams a decade earlier, had argued it needed the blackouts to prevent erosion of home ticket sales. As a result of this ruling, and some later modifications (specifically, the 1973 anti-blackout legislation), the current NFL policy mandates blacking out not only the home team's game in its home market (except when sold out 72 hours in advance), but also banning the importation of an out-of-town game into the market of a team playing at home, while the home game is in progress.

The NFL's unique ban on local television contracts enhances Rozelle's clout more than that of any other commissioner, because he controls all of the television money coming to the franchises. Each team receives the same amount (now approximately $16 million per year) regardless of market size. There are no bonuses for consistently fielding a winning team, or penalties for chronic losers. Ed Garvey, former executive director of the NFL Players' Association, habitually referred to this system as "socialism for management." The NFL owners have deeply appreciated the money Rozelle regularly squeezes from the networks, and most of them have supported him against all challenges. A few renegades have occasionally felt he was actually restricting them from cutting an even better deal on their own. Other owners (and, it is said, Rozelle) regard them as ingrates at best, and at worst, deliberate killers of the golden goose. As Rozelle has proven (and Al Davis learned) over many years, a series of billion-dollar contracts will buy a lot of loyalty.

Beginning with the 1961 CBS contract, the NFL prospered as never before: ratings and attendance were both steadily rising, costs seemed under control after the worst days of the AFL-NFL salary war, and cities all across the country were clamoring for expansion teams. When the league indicated that it would expand in 1966, the competition for the coveted franchises increased even further. At about the same time, new rumblings in Congress were heard, with not-too-subtle hints that yet another anti-trust case might be brewing. Pete Rozelle was called on to bring to bear his legendary political lobbying skills to head off the unhappy prospect. With the powerful backing of Senator Russell Long and Congressman Hale Boggs, both from Louisiana, Congress passed, and President Johnson signed, the Football Merger Act, which gave an additional anti-trust exemption to the AFL-NFL merger. Coincidentally, perhaps, an expansion franchise was awarded to New Orleans nine days after the bill was signed into law.

During the late sixties, sports executives become more and more aware of the complex issues raised by their alliance with television. In 1970 Pete Rozelle faced a problem that had been overlooked earlier. When the AFL was merged into the NFL, it carried with it into the merger a television contract with NBC. Rozelle wanted to maximize the revenues he could extract from both CBS (with the NFC games) and NBC (AFC games). The problem was that the CBS/NFC combine enjoyed a two to one advantage over the NBC/AFC pairing in television market size and total audience delivery. With this imbalance, the prospects for the league being able to negotiate ever increasing amounts from NBC seemed at risk. Therefore, Commissioner Rozelle arranged to move Pittsburgh, Baltimore, and Cleveland into the AFC, reducing the CBS advantage to a more reasonable seven to five. In appreciation for their willingness to make the move, all three franchises were paid a large indemnity, handled by the commissioner's office. NBC agreed to pay a higher rights fee.

Blackouts were becoming more and more of a touchy issue every year. The days of NFL teams attendance problems were long forgotten, and in some cities there was a waiting list of several years to get season tickets. Yet the league blackout policy remained unchanged. The NFL stuck to the position won in the courts over many years and many cases: that the games were private events staged for the entertainment of the audience, and that the NFL was under no obligation to make them available to anyone. There was no "right" to see sports events, they said, and certainly no right to see them for free. Besides, if they put the sold-out games on television, there wouldn't be any more sellouts. Elected politicians, however, had come to enjoy the popular support they received when they said that blackouts were not only unfair to those who couldn't buy a ticket but probably un-American as well.

In fact, many Congressmen and Senators seemed strangely emotional about the issue this time. Their strong support swiftly brought forth the 1973 anti-blackout legislation mentioned earlier. It declared that all four professional leagues must lift the network blackout of games sold out 72 hours before their scheduled starting time. In reality, it soon became apparent, the bill only affected the NFL, since sell-outs three days in advance were rare in baseball, and only a theory in hockey and basketball.

The rule was quickly dubbed "the Redskin Rule" because it permitted all those politicians to watch their beloved Redskins games in Washington, D.C., despite the fact that the Redskins were sold out literally years in advance. Many observers believe that, without the support of grumpy Congressmen, forced to watch something else on Sunday afternoons, the rule would never have been dreamed up in the first place. Curiously, the rule expired in 1975, but has been observed by the leagues ever since, probably to avoid again offending the sensibilities of Redskin fans on Capitol Hill.

What had been a fairly simple, straightforward system of unified network broadcast contracts was complicated by the birth and growth of cable television (which the networks and leagues initially regarded as a dire threat), and the growing intensity of network competition for sports programming. In 1968, for example, the FCC (cheered on by professional sports leagues) had asserted its right to regulate cable television in a sports case. *U.S. v. Southwestern Cable* was a result of a San Diego cable system carrying Dodgers games. In the anti-cable regulatory atmosphere of the day, both sports rights-holders and their network friends were vehemently opposed to sports on cable. They said that moving sports to cable would be akin to stealing from the public, and holding at ransom, its precious TV games. There was little doubt about the outcome. The cable carriage of imported Dodgers games was forbidden. Soon after, the FCC issued "anti-siphoning" rules, and, the development of cable sports slowed appreciably.

It wasn't until 1977 that the supply barriers impeding popular cable programming were removed, when Home Box Office, Inc., took the FCC to court and won a verdict overturning the "anti-siphoning" rules. They had precluded cable carriers from competing for the rights to most sporting events. The forbidden list included any "specific" sporting events (such as the World Series) which had appeared on broadcast television in the previous five years; or more than the minimum of "non-specific" events (regular season games) which had appeared in the previous three years. This amounted, of course, to a total ban on HBO and other cable outfits from even negotiating for the rights to all but the most obscure event. Anything desirable certainly had to have been aired on broadcast television in recent years.

The court decision in HBO's favor rescinded these blatantly unfair anti-competitive protections. A decade after the decision, during a period of cable growth and wide public acceptance, it seems hard to believe that these rules were ever enacted in the first place. However, one must realize the immense lobbying power of the broadcasters, the sports interests (who didn't want to be on cable, no matter the rights fee), and their natural allies in the Congress, all of them only too willing to denounce cable as a threat to so-called "free" TV, and to the "right" to see certain sporting events on broadcast television.

At long last the tide had turned, and the *HBO* decision gave cable the right to acquire attractive sports programming. At first, few cable operators had the money to compete for major sports events, and they ended up with many minor ones. Over the course of several years, though, they became a more and more serious competitor, and as their balance sheets turned more positive, they could compete successfully for almost any sport.

The pace and breadth of technological change in the television industry could no longer be ignored or suppressed. Cable television systems were springing up around the country, communications satellites were hovering overhead, and a funny kind of hybrid local television station, the "superstation," was being talked about. These new technologies made it possible, and cost-efficient, to send signals to, and receive signals from, virtually anywhere in the United States. Frequently, cable systems were "importing" distant signals by simply plucking them out of the air with a dish antenna, and then re-transmitting them to their own local audience. This was all done without the permission of the company whose signal was being re-transmitted, and without payment in kind. The cable industry asserted that the signals were in the public domain, because they were made for dissemination to the general public and were traveling through the public's airwaves. Not so, countered the owners (principally movie distributors and sports organizations). According to them, these were copyrighted materials intended for a specific audience at a specific price; they demanded compensation for the unauthorized infringement of their copyrights.

At about the same time, Congress acted to fill a void created in copyright law by several recent court decisions. It enacted the Federal Copyright Act of 1976, which established a new regulatory body, the Copyright Royalty Tribunal (CRT), to act as a sort of collection agency and middleman. The CRT is supposed to collect a small royalty fee from cable operators for every non-local re-transmission. After collecting all these fees in a kitty, the CRT invites any claimant that believes its copyright had been infringed upon, to request payment of an appropriate amount from the funds collected by the CRT. While a noble gesture, the CRT's salutary effect has been minimal, principally because the amount claimed by copyright holders dwarfs the available amount many times over. For example, in 1978 less than $1 million was available to all sports organizations nationwide, at a time when claims exceeded $100 million; by 1985, available funds had risen only to approximately $3 million. The overwhelming percentage of royalty fees was reserved for the Motion Picture Association of America and the National Association of Broadcasters.

Many leading sports executives condemned the Government for stepping in, as well as for the CRT's lack of funds. Baseball Commissioner Bowie Kuhn insisted that the Government had no right to "expropriate" Major League Baseball's property or copyright, no matter what compensation scheme it came up with. Kuhn never changed his views on the subject, nor has MLB abandoned that position. Kuhn also attacked the cable and superstation operators, including the superstation teams in MLB. He warned they were damaging the flagship stations of all the other teams. A settlement of sorts was ultimately negotiated. Under its terms, the five superstation teams—Mets, Yankees, Cubs, Braves, and Rangers—contribute annual fees totaling about $15 million, to be distributed among the other clubs. Kuhn and his successor, Peter Ueberroth, continue to remind the superstation teams that unforeseen legislative changes might someday force them to change their behavior.

Another result of this latest in the long string of disputes over copyrights and who controls them was the significantly more aggressive assertion of those rights by their owners. Broadcasters were careful to announce prominently, and often, print on the TV picture, their famous claim (. . . no pictures, descriptions and accounts of this game . . . may be used without the express written permission. . . .). Don Meredith used to sing it in a jocular fashion on Monday Night Football, but ABC's lawyers were dead serious.

As for the teams, they had their lawyers sharpen the language printed in tiny letters on the back of every admissions ticket, because that, too, was a copyright claim. For example, the Boston Red Sox tickets stated that the ticket-holder granted to the Red Sox and their opposing team full rights to use the ticket-holder's "image or likeness incidental to any live or recorded video display or other transmission or other reproduction in whole or in part of the event" to which he is admitted. The ticket-holder further agreed not to "transfer or aid in transmitting any description, account, picture or reproduction" of the game. Thus, the Red Sox used the ticket to claim copyright in whatever might be recorded during Fenway Park games, and protect themselves further by sharing an on-air copyright with their local TV station (which applied to the broadcasts).

The purchase price of big events continued to rise dramatically through the late seventies and early eighties. Broadcast and cable networks were now competing feverishly. The resultant cash flow began to enrich league and team coffers, with the owners the prime beneficiaries. Player salaries soon were also rising, often by astronomical amounts. However, a belief took hold among the various players' associations that their members were entitled to share in the additional revenues raised by the cable retransmission of their performances during the game. In other words, the associations said, we want a share of any royalties paid to the league or team, since it is our performance cable companies are paying the fee to transmit.

In the NBA, Paul Silas, then president of the NBA Players Association, filed *Silas v. Manhattan Cable;* in baseball it was *Rogers v. Kuhn.* The

NBA suit was postponed and later dropped. Instead, the Players Association and the league agreed to disagree on this matter, and tried to negotiate an acceptable solution in collective bargaining. *Rogers v. Kuhn* was superseded by a related suit between the Baltimore Orioles and baseball's Players Association. The Orioles won a ruling that the players had assigned their individual rights to the team when they signed their contracts, and that the team did not have to share the revenues with them.

The year 1984 brought yet another dispute over exactly which party or parties owned the rights to the "performance" of a professional sports event. In baseball, the clubs had long since staked out their own property right claim and had fought the Players Association claim that the players should share in any copyright royalties generated by the retransmission of their games. Now the flagship television stations of several teams were arguing that *they* should be entitled to some of the profits. They believed their copyrighted television version of individual games was, in fact, a "performance" quite different from that being viewed by spectators at the ball park. After all, the telecasts had announcers, camera angles, special effects, even commercials; none of these was available on a regular basis to the ball-park spectator.

The CRT agreed and issued the *Joint Authorship* ruling, which held that flagship stations could rightly claim 50 percent of any copyright royalty fees the CRT might distribute for any particular game. To qualify, the station had to present a version of the game which was significantly different from that seen at the park (which is almost taken for granted). Further, since copyrights only cover tangible, physical works, the broadcasts had to be "fixed" on a tangible medium (much like a book or magazine is "fixed" on paper). Videotape qualifies nicely as a fixed medium, so all a station had to do in meeting this requirement was to record its own broadcast, which had long been standard procedure, anyway. In most cases, the royalty fees turned out to be negligible, but local stations still insisted on their fifty-fifty split.

Rights-holders had become somewhat touchy about having to share the copyright income. They were downright angry when that income was threatened. The New York Mets had signed an exclusive contract with WOR-TV to carry their games locally. The Eastern Microwave Co. (EMI), a satellite relay carrier, began selling the re-transmitted WOR broadcasts in their entirety—including commercials—to cable systems around the country. EMI did not pay WOR or Doubleday Sports (the Mets) copyright fees, and the local cable systems paid only the inexpensive compulsory CRT fee. Doubleday and WOR tried to cut off the Eastern Microwave re-transmissions. It was only a matter of time (and not much time, at that) before *Eastern Microwave v. Doubleday Sports* landed in court.

Playing by the Rules

The Mets and WOR testified they regarded WOR as a "involuntary" superstation—that it had deliberately not transmitted its signal nationally, but that EMI was doing so without permission. The appellate decision went in EMI's favor, with the court ruling that so long as EMI made no alterations whatever to the program, and did not initiate any programming of its own, it could re-transmit the WOR signal without obtaining permission. Cable systems using the feed should make the small payment to the Copyright Royalty Tribunal, in lieu of negotiating a payment directly with the rights-holders. If WOR or Doubleday Sports (or both) felt this was a copyright infringement, they could apply to the CRT to recover some share of the revenue.

By 1983, dissatisfaction with the CRT had risen to a new level. Motion picture studios, professional sports leagues, and other major rights-holders felt they still weren't receiving fair compensation from the limited pool of revenue contributed by re-transmitters. They joined forces and as "Joint Claimants" petitioned the CRT to demand better royalty treatment and to address the problems that importation of distant signals were causing for local TV stations that owned the rights to sports events. Their efforts didn't really accomplish very much in terms of increasing the total size of the available royalty pool. However, the CRT did adopt a new fee structure that had a dramatic impact on the number of superstations most cable systems were willing to import.

A sliding scale of payments made importing more than two superstations financially prohibitive (in many cases raising the cable systems' royalty obligations by a factor of ten). Most cable operators cut back to carrying two superstations, and in a bitter irony for long-suffering Cubs fans, the superstation most often dropped was WGN. This took place shortly before the 1984 season, which saw the Cubs stage a spectacular run for the pennant, their first in years. In what some devoted fans saw as a Cosmic Joke, or simply another indignity heaped on their suffering, the Cubs had been nationally available when they were awful, but now, just when success seemed within their grasp, they went off the air in many cities. The team fizzled in August (right on schedule), but the inevitable collapse was witnessed by relatively few of the faithful outside the Chicago area. Perhaps it was more dignified that way; interment was certainly more private. In all, almost nineteen million Americans lost at least some distant signals as a result of the decision cable operators dubbed "Black Thursday."

While professional sports leagues and franchises had been almost constantly involved in litigation to protect their piece of the growing television pie, amateur sports had managed to avoid the unseemly public squabbles over money. It was always of great importance to amateur sports organizations, especially the National Collegiate Athletic Association (NCAA), to maintain an image of squeaky clean amateurs competing for the joy of sport, and of colleges and universities offering athletic programs as a well-rounded adjunct to the main priority of education. Everyone knew this idealized image had long since ceased to exist in many major intercollegiate athletic programs (if it ever truly existed at all), but most were reluctant to talk about it. The NCAA maintained a public posture which included the image of student-athletes, harmony between big schools and small, and between revenue-producing sports (principally football and basketball) and the non-revenue sports. All member schools supposedly subscribed to the same code of ethics and policies. Inside the organization, though, cracks were showing in that façade of unity and shared purpose.

As NCAA football grew in stature as a television sport, and as rights fees rose, many of the big football powers became disenchanted with the NCAA's policies regarding television. These policies limited the number of times each team could appear on network TV each year, mandated that the network broadcast a certain number of Division II and Division III games, distributed revenues earned by the big schools to all members and conferences (including those that never appeared on network television), and vested in the NCAA central office the power to issue sanctions against schools caught violating certain rules—using banishment from television as one of several penalties.

In addition, a number of the major football powers came to believe that they could make much more money in rights fees by selling their individual rights to broadcast and cable television. Why, they wondered, should they have to surrender their property right to the NCAA, especially when the NCAA returned less money to them than they believed they could make on their own? This argument is very similar to the one raised by individual NFL franchises in challenging first Bert Bell and then Pete Rozelle. The difference was that NCAA Executive Director Walter Byers wouldn't (and couldn't, really) buy the loyalty of the football powerhouses by throwing ever increasing rights fees at their feet.

The Universities of Georgia and Oklahoma, acting with the backing of several sister institutions, finally challenged the NCAA's right to negotiate a unified, pooled TV contract. In the suit they pointed out the Sports Broadcasting Act of 1961 had permitted only professional leagues to do so. For the NCAA to supersede their individual copyrights, they charged, was an anti-trust violation. The court agreed, and in *Board of Regents v. NCAA* it dissolved the NCAA's control over the individual school's cpoyrights. Judge Burciaga's opinion said the NCAA had acted as a "classic cartel."

A new entity representing the major football schools, the College Football Association (CFA), emerged during the dispute. Immediately after hearing the court's decision, many of its members announced the availability of their television rights, and waited for the money to flow in. Ironically, so many of them flooded the market with available games, that supply far exceeded demand, and the networks were able to cut the prices they paid virtually in half. Some CFA members ruefully concluded they had won a glorious victory, one that gave them all the right to reduce their football income quickly.

There may have been some philosophic principles at stake in the billion-dollar anti-trust suit that marked the death rattle of the United States Football League, but most people agreed it was about money, plain and simple. Money had always been the lure which encouraged a score of challengers to the sleek and wealthy NFL. The USFL was only the latest, and most audacious pretender. For three years, it had played a spring schedule, and its games were carried by both ABC and ESPN (earning excellent profits for the networks). In fact, it was widely regarded as a "television league" from its inception, because the television contracts were signed before some teams had names, coaches, players, or playing fields. There is little doubt that the television money kept the league afloat in the early years and provided a sort of "instant credibility" with sponsors, potential draft choices, and fans.

When the league decided to shift to a fall schedule and head-to-head competition with the NFL, the networks (with the exception of ESPN) showed very little interest in purchasing the rights. The USFL soon brought suit against the NFL and the three broadcast networks on the grounds that they had engaged in anti-competitive activities whose "intent or effect" was to destroy the younger league. The three networks had each refused to offer the USFL a contract for its proposed fall schedule. Thus, the USFL claimed, they had engaged in an "involuntary conspiracy." By contracting with all three networks simultaneously, the NFL had violated the moral notice" of the Sports Broadcasting Act of 1961, and it was also guilty of trying to monopolize the pro football business, the USFL said.

In 1986 the jury found that the NFL was indeed guilty of trying to monopolize the professional football industry through market domination. However, it also found that the USFL had created most of its problems itself, and the jurors cited a litany of management errors. In addition, the NFL and the networks were found innocent of using network television to illegally monopolize the market. After all, the jury reasoned, the networks had made concrete proposals to continue carrying the spring schedule, which the league spurned in moving to the fall: whose fault was that? Further, ESPN had offered to carry the fall schedule, and at the time the NFL was refusing to make a cable contract. So, in a sense, although broadcast television may have been monopolized by the NFL in the fall, *all* network television was not.

The USFL shortly appealed the decision, and asked that the NFL be forced to make its American and National Conferences negotiate their own, separate network contacts—thus leaving one broadcast network available to the USFL in the fall. Federal Appeals Judge Leisure, in his denial of the USFL motions, noted that, although the NFL may have been found guilty of causing harm to the USFL by its anti-competitive practices, it had not been shown to have caused harm to the public or the marketplace. In anti-trust cases, demonstrated harm to the market and the public is considered a most important element. Finally, citing the NCAA's illegal use of television restrictions as sanctions for non-television offenses, Judge Leisure noted it would be improper to apply a television penalty when the NFL had been found innocent of illegal activity vis-à-vis the networks.

In the end the USFL was awarded the nominal sum of one dollar (the amount was trebled, as in the case in anti-trust awards). Despite many brave statements by some owners and Commissioner Harry Usher, the league soon sank without a trace. It was only a matter of days, however, before at least two new professional football leagues announced their future intention of competing with the NFL for a piece of the huge pro football market. The next year the NFL broke with its previous practice and signed a multi-year cable contract with ESPN, to take effect in 1987. Since the league now has contracts with all three broadcast networks *plus* ESPN, the next challenger may fare better—in court, if not on the field.

It can be stated with some certainty that legal and regulatory disputes will continue apace in television and sports. While no one can predict with complete confidence the flashpoints of future disagreements, some areas seem more likely than others to provide the fireworks. New leagues will continue their attempts to crash the party. Relations between league commissioners and their franchise owners, and clashes concerning the powers allocated to the commissioners by the owners, seem inevitable. If the rights paid for pooled network television contracts stop rising, or even decline, franchise owners are likely to fight for their independence in making broadcast and cable contracts without restrictions or equalized distribution of revenues.

The shortfall in rights fees may be made up through the sale of expansion franchises, or the accelerated turnover in ownership of established ones. The proliferation of new communications technologies, including distribution systems, and satellite dishes will produce a new round of legal complications. Players and their representative will insist on receiving a greater share of television revenues. Franchises owned by television companies, or affiliated with superstations, will increase in number and will form self-interest groups within leagues, often in direct conflict with the non-television teams. Invasions of television markets by other teams will increase, as may the number of market-hopping franchises. Politicians will continue, through legislation and government regulatory agencies, to exert themselves for the benefit of various constituencies. Other issues are sure to arise, perhaps in altogether new contexts no one can anticipate. One thing we can be sure of: the attorneys will be busy.

5

HONEY SHOTS AND HEROES

"Two-and-a-half to air, guys."
"Coming up on two minutes to air."
"About a minute-and-forty-five to air."
"A minute and twenty five."
"Y tape is next."
"All right, let's all calm down." (Voice of director)
"Have a good ball game, everyone." (Voice of director)
"Forty-five seconds to tape."
"Thirty seconds; we're in black; remote's in."
"Twenty seconds to Y tape, Andy."
"Fifteen to Y tape."
"Stand by."
"Ten-nine-eight-seven-six-five-four-three-two-one. . . ."
. . . and another Saturday afternoon NBC Game of the Week begins.

What followed the countdown was nearly five hours of base-ball from Fenway Park on a day that started early in the morning and ended fifteen innings later in mid-evening for nearly fifty members of the NBC production team. This Game of the Week between the Tigers and Red Sox was the network's secondary game, and thus would be sent to only a small percentage of the network's affiliates. The day's primary game, between the Cincinnati Reds and the Houston Astros, would be seen by most of the country. Regardless of the amount of coverage, the production from Boston demanded—and got—the same energy, attention, and professional pride that all network sports events receive fifty-two weekends a year.

For logistical reasons alone, producing a game from a remote location calls for a totally coordinated effort from the entire production team. In addition to their creative endurance, this fifteen-inning marathon also tested the physical endurance of all concerned. As the game progressed, there was little time—even during commercial breaks—for anything nutritional other than an occasional nibble of a hot dog or a sip of omnipresent cold coffee or warm soda. A trip to the bathroom was a luxury, and only some members of the production team were lucky enough to have back-ups. If the producer, director, and several others involved in the telecast were to add "iron stomach and bladder" to their résumés, it would accurately describe their capacity for endurance, which reached Olympian proportions during the course of the unusually long afternoon. To paraphrase the Bangles' hit song of the early eighties, this was "just another manic Saturday," a weekend sports experience that all three networks replicate all year long.

This Fenway Park production was choreographed by a production team led by producer John Filipelli and director Andy Rosenberg, two young network veterans. In addition to baseball, Filipelli has produced network football, track and field, boxing, and segments for NBC's anthology series "Sports World." He seemed accustomed to the routine of having to call home from the remote truck to say that he has missed the last flight out of Boston and will call whenever the game ends and when he has had time to make new arrangements.

Announcer Tony Kubek was not quite as fortunate. He had planned to fly to Toronto immediately after the telecast for his regular announcing duties with the Blue Jays, but he was also short-circuited by the extra-innings game. Any alternate travel plans were either inconvenient or inconceivable. While Kubek's on-air demeanor from the Fenway Park announce booth was characteristically cool, much rustling went on behind-the-scenes in the NBC remote truck. The producer had his staff call the Boston hotel room to recheck Kubek into the room he had vacated earlier in the day, and to reserve the announcer a seat on the earliest available Sunday morning flight to Toronto.

The director of the telecast was Andy Rosenberg, whose network directing credits in addition to baseball include golf, football, and college basketball. Once the game starts, virtually total creative control falls into his hands. His air of perennial youthfulness and boyish good looks—picture Michael J. Fox in the director's chair—belie a steely toughness that can call a too-aggressive graphics coordinator to task when the occasion warrants, or let anyone else involved in the production know who's in charge of the program's on-air look. Rosenberg's comments throughout this chapter provide a behind-the-scenes feel for producing and directing network sports:

> Production people are weekend warriors. For a job that seems extraordinarily glamorous, it's far from it. As a director, you're generally on the road about forty-five weekends a year. Ten weekends at home would be a lot. You can't go out Saturday nights with friends because you're always away. When you add kids into the mix who have gotten too old to travel with you, you're at home when they go to school, and you're away when they have the weekends off. The whole family has to be flexible, because your family life becomes very different from someone who works at a Monday through Friday job.

Any television viewer who has heard the opening announcement that a game is coming "Live from the Astrodome!" or "Live from Mile High Stadium!" has heard one of life's great misstatements. There is nothing live about televised sports except the electronic transmission, and most likely many segments inserted into live televised games are pre-recorded on videotape. Moreover, anyone who has ever seen a major league game should have a chance to watch one from the control room of a network remote truck to appreciate the difficulty of capturing an event for television.

In the ball park, the spectator chooses what to watch—the shortstop creeping in behind the runner at second, the third base coach giving the batter signals, the pretty blonde two rows in front. From the control room, the line monitor feeds a single picture which the director uses to tell the story.

The crowd noise behind a seventh inning home-team rally excites spectators sitting in the grandstand. On television, the same drama is reduced to a series of pictures and sounds assembled in a meaningful sequence. Conversely, television can often make a dull game more exciting because the producer, director, and announcers can divert the audience's attention by using a variety of live and pre-taped information to sustain interest where none exists at the stadium.

What makes the television experience different is that the TV event involves camera panning and cutting, and a selection of shots composed for a 19-inch screen. What viewers see and hear on television is the director's vision compressed through five or six cameras (many more are used for major events like the Super Bowl), sweetened with visual electronic effects, and paced by a half-hour or more of commercial interruptions.

While each network has its own style and philosophy for producing and directing sports, the net result of their work is superior, and network sports producers and directors are simply the best in the TV business. Witness Frank Chirkinian's muted coverage of golf at the sedentary Masters Golf Tournament in Augusta, Georgia; Bob Fishman's cool restraint when the NCAA Basketball Championships finalize in spontaneous and unrestrained on-court rejoicing; Chet Forte's crisp direction which gave Miami Dolphins' games the look of Miami Vice because Monday Night Football was expected to meet the demands of prime-time entertainment; or Harry Coyle's uncanny feel for baseball's rhythm and tempo in choreographing World Series coverage since 1947.

By comparison, one look at virtually any local station's coverage of sports reveals how good the networks are, for often they have no more equipment at their disposal than most stations. Basketball is a good example. In general, a floor camera positioned under the basket is used primarily for reaction shots or closeups of players at the free throw line. It is seldom, if ever, used for play-by-play action because the cut from the side camera to the radical angle underneath will disorient viewers. Yet countless times, local directors cut to the under-the-basket camera for action, giving TV viewers a shot of ten pairs of satin-clad derrières passing before the camera until the side shot is restored or the whistle blows to rescue viewers from optical confusion.

In general, the quality of most network sports leaves little to complain about, although when TV misses an opportunity, particularly in a major televised game, critics are quick to point out the error. In the 1987 Super Bowl, for example, CBS neglected to show a critical replay of a Denver Bronco pass completion which may have changed the complexion of the game, even though the network had fourteen cameras and ten replay machines at its disposal. Production gaffes like this are fodder for the new breed of columnist who only covers TV sports. Many of them turned this error of judgment into something cataclysmic in their post-game analysis, even though the game eventually turned into a rout.

While network sports executives pride themselves on the superior "look" of their sports productions, they hold their collective breaths when they consider how the changing financial landscape around them is affecting their product. In responding to competition from cable and a soft advertising market, new ownership at ABC, CBS, and NBC has contributed to the tense business climate by demanding tighter operational controls and leaner and more fiscally prudent production budgets.

One network executive put into perspective the new era of fiscal prudency as it affects sports productions:

> We really have not cut back on facilities like cameras or tape machines, nor have we cut back on production or engineering staff. What we've

really tried to do is cut the fat out of budgets that grew fat in the late 1960's up until 1984. Then, our sales guys were just order-takers, there wasn't much selling to do. They could just literally bring in as much money as was needed for income, and we didn't track our production costs as carefully as we have in recent years.

A lot of people who have been here for a long time are not as concerned about money as we [network management] are now. Production people were accustomed basically to getting their way. They could rationalize the expense if they needed another camera, and they could usually get it. But they haven't understood the tremendous change taking place in the industry. We are trying to become more efficient in cutting the fat without cutting the meat.

To face the budget challenge, the networks have tried to protect the quality of their sports productions while reducing overhead costs. One answer has been to "buy" packages of games from qualified independent sports producers, a practice which one network executive has called "the wave of the future." As an example, ABC contracted in 1987 with International Management Group (IMG) to produce five golf tournaments live from different locations. IMG had to work within the limits of ABC's union restrictions, but they were able to produce the events more economically because of fewer limitations and less overhead.

In 1987, CBS produced its CFA football package under agreement with independent producers working in conjunction with the network's producing teams. This kind of cooperative arrangement is not without risk, particularly in the area of labor relations.

To a considerable degree, the key to networks using outside packagers successfully lies in the willingness of technical unions to accept the changing sports marketplace. Jurisdiction is at the heart of the matter as the networks begin to consider the wider use of outside productions as a means of reducing expenses and increasing profits. CBS technicians are members of the International Brotherhood of Electrical Workers (IBEW), while ABC and NBC are under an agreement with the National Association of Broadcast Employees and Technicians (NABET). These two unions have jurisdiction over all in-house network productions, and while each network's contract varies to a degree, they are fundamentally alike in wage scales and in defining the number of non-union technicians participating in programs produced specifically for the network.

For example, IBEW and NABET mandate the number of local technicians a network may hire to supplement its crews working on productions at remote locations. The quota is usually governed by the distance the stadium is located from any of the network-owned-and-operated stations which are also parties to the network's union agreement. The farther away the game site, the more non-network technicians the network may hire. This issue is critical in light of the number of events the networks originate away from their home locations in New York and Los Angeles.

Unlike network news programs or talk shows, sports events are more complex. They require specialists experienced in working on live productions, often under difficult conditions. The complex logistics of feeding television signals from remote locations is one aspect of televised sports that distinguishes these programs from studio productions. On locations, the networks rely heavily on union technicians experienced in arranging and coordinating satellite or microwave feeds. This technical skill is mastered only after many years of working on sports telecasts that often require ingenious solutions to get the signal back to the network.

Successful sports coverage also depends on the quick, almost reflexive, reactions of experienced camera people who understand the nuances of the game they're covering, and who can anticipate action on the field. As NBC learned bitterly during a contract dispute with NABET in 1987 when technicians were on strike, the networks are hard pressed when they face the necessity of filling camera positions competently with untrained personnel.

There are several other instances when technical unions have gone on strike against the networks. The results in these cases, however, were more than faulty camera work. One which most affected sports coverage occurred in 1972 when IBEW technicians walked out of CBS in a primary economic strike over wages, benefits, and job security. During the course of the strike, network phone lines between Shea Stadium and CBS's Manhattan studios were cut, canceling the Jets–Redskins game. That same day, phone lines carrying the Packers–San Francisco 49ers' game from Green Bay were severed and the network was forced to cancel the second half of its broadcast. Following the Shea Stadium incident, three IBEW technicians were arrested and convicted.

In its 1987 strike against NBC, NABET brought pressure against the network in a less confrontational way. The union urged members of the NFL and the Major League Baseball Players Associations to boycott NBC *and its affiliates* by refusing to appear for on-air interviews on pre-game shows or nightly sportscasts. The boycott met with mixed reactions from most of the players, however, and the absence of those few who did observe it went generally unnoticed.

But unions are only one of the many headaches that networks now face, and union technicians are only one part—albeit an expensive one—of a network production budget.

The various line items in network budgets are divided between variable and fixed expenses—referred to as "above-the-line" and "below-the line" costs. Expense items that are incurred specifically as part of a particular event—rights fees, travel expenses, talent fees, the package of NFL Films that ABC buys to run during half-time of Monday Night Football, and specialized services such as statistical information provided by outside agencies—are generally considered to be above-the-line costs, and therefore subject to close scrutiny. Above-the-line items are more likely to get the axe in hard times. Almost all technical or production charges—personnel, studios and equipment, mobile units—are considered below-the-line costs and are incurred by the network whether or not the event takes place and regardless of its cost to produce. Each of the networks differs widely in how it charges items in both above- and below-line categories.

Battles in budget-making are a way of life in every business, and TV sports is no exception. In network sports the battle lines are usually drawn between the creative team—the producer and director—and the sports division's comptroller. There is probably no TV director or producer worth his or her salt who doesn't ABSOLUTELY NEED two more cameras, several thousand more feet of cable run, a mobile van that is more state of the art than the one they have, a few aerial shots, and the newest special effects generator to make the next production a smash. "Just give us those, and next Saturday's show will really be something special!" they plead.

The step-by-step budgeting process starts once the sports division's acquisitions team conceives of a program. Working with budget comptrollers, they decide on each of the likely cost factors involved in the program. They then meet with sales planners to project likely revenues the event will generate. If the network is planning to buy rights to an event that will not take place for several years, adjustments for inflation, future mandated labor increases, and any other costs that may arise over time are factored into budget projections. At this point, profit-and-loss projections are then forecast, and if favorable, the project is accepted. If not, it dies.

Once the event gets closer to reality, budget estimating continues as production, technical, and creative personnel join with a unit manager—the business person assigned to the project—to refine their estimates and bring them into line with network expectations. These refinements may involve such items as the scheduling of technical crews so that overtime costs can be reduced, or saving money by eliminating certain pieces of equipment that the director feels would improve the look of the show but would send the production over budget.

Clearly, projections are affected by the location where the event originates and by the type of sport involved. For example, network budgeters prefer that all games originate from the Meadowlands in New Jersey, close to New York City, where no travel time, air fare, car rentals, and minimum overtime and per diem expenses are involved. A game in Denver, however, is totally different, when a one afternoon pick-up becomes a four-day event—two days of travel add dearly to the network's costs.

Budgets can also soar based on the nature of the sport itself. "Skiing's a bitch," attests one network finance officer, citing the differences between outdoor and indoor events. "Skiing is impossible because of the length of the cable runs. Obviously, indoor events are easier to set up because you don't deal with the weather, but of course, you do have lighting problems. Certain arenas are much more difficult than others in which to mount first-class productions."

Networks often insure themselves against some of the risks involved in sports production. For example, when ABC televises the Indianapolis 500, some of its crew put life and limb in jeopardy, their cameras situated in cherry-pickers located close to the track. In 1987, one spectator who was killed during the race was watching from a spot not too far from the ABC camera position. Many other televised events require that production technicians have the endurance of a decathalon entrant, the daring of a stunt pilot, and the agility of a mountain goat. To network sports producers and directors, these he-men are the difference between a good and a great program. To budget-makers, they are actuarial risks.

Networks also take out insurance policies against rainouts. However, several years ago, ABC decided to save money and forgo producing a backup game because the primary game involved the Dodgers playing at Chavez Ravine. However, the network took out a substantial insurance-policy "just in case." ABC was actually banking on perfect weather in Los Angeles—and got it—much to the pleasure of its insurance company.

ABC's insurance policy paid off in 1986, however, when rain postponed its Sunday telecast of the Indy 500, and race promoters rescheduled it for the next day. The Monday telecast meant that the network had to pre-empt its profitable soap operas, but the lost revenues were protected by insurance.

But budgets and money matters aside, the production quality of the telecast is what ultimately makes the difference to TV viewers. Once the go-ahead is given to produce an event, a miniature army, in a tour de force of teamwork, begins to create the end product. Without this teamwork, the results can be anything from frayed nerves and a shoddy production to shattered careers. The experience of producing sports has properly been called "a cumulative art." In the stress of live televised sports, there is no time on game day for hurt feelings or long-winded explanations of why things are done in a certain way.

From the perspective of the mobile van, the director is clearly the leader of the pack. Part psychologist and part diplomat, the director works closest with the producer who has the ultimate responsibility for making sure that the game gets to the network from the stadium.

During the telecast, both depend on the eyes and ears of the camera crew and the announcers, as well as the combined expertise of their technical staff. What appears to be an effortless telecast at home is actually the result of the director and producers assimilating information from eight to ten monitors and several audio sources, and condensing them into a single story. How important is teamwork? When a cameraman does not respond instinctively and fails to follow a runner trying to go from first to third on a hit-and-run, or stay with the quarterback when he fakes a hand-off at the goal line and bootlegs around end for a touchdown, the moment is lost and the production suffers.

While the networks generally try to keep the same team of on-air announcers together for a full season, producer-director teams often vary. From the director's perspective, pairing the producer, director, and talent for a whole season has its advantages and disadvantages. Andy Rosenberg comments:

> The most you may work with the same pair of talent is six to eight times a year during the season. My personal contention is that we should work together more as a team since you can actually work up something as the season goes along. I find that as the director shuffles in and out, he eventually ends up getting shuffled with somebody who has worked with some other director a few times before. If it's your first time working with that particular pair of announcers, perhaps their habits are a little different than other announcers you've been working with.
>
> You find yourself adjusting, perhaps holding back on how much you want to assert your ideas and thoughts into the structure of the telecast because the announcers have developed a pattern which you, as the director, don't want to disrupt.
>
> But it works both ways. What we gain by working with different producers and talent is that as director, you don't get stale by doing the same thing every week. There is an infusion of different approaches to covering a game. For good or for bad, it's nice to see some different ways to think about the same thing.

Many sports producers and directors find the challenge of adjusting to the rhythm of different sports is even greater than having to work with different producing teams over the course of a season. Each sport has a unique rhythm, pace, and tempo to which the producing teams must adjust. From the point of view of television coverage, football and baseball are spurts of stop-and-go action followed by a minute or so to regroup and plan the next sequence of shots. These stoppages conveniently allow for replays without disrupting action. TV viewers find nothing more offensive than the injudicious use of replays, which may be very appealing and instructive—but seldom at the expense of live action. On the other hand, boxing and hockey offer continuous action until the bell rings or the whistle blows. Then, there is time for replays or commercials.

In addition to the different rhythms, the different design of playing areas impacts on television coverage. For example, football and basketball provide directors an ideal coverage area, because the field of play is rectangular and is in the same 3 : 4 aspect ratio of the television screen. A wide shot can thus take in the whole area at one time. Baseball, on the other hand, is played on fields of varying dimensions. The distances from home plate to the farthest reaches of the outfield differ, as do the areas in foul territory. Different grandstand configurations create nooks and crannies that are often difficult to cover adequately with cameras.

In terms of following game action, a football or basketball is big enough to be seen on television while play progresses. However, a baseball is smaller and harder to follow in flight against a pale sky or a grandstand filled with shirt-sleeved spectators. While the shape of a hockey rink makes for good television coverage, cameras can barely follow a moving puck.

TV sports professionals accept these differences as part of the telecast, however, and meet the challenge by doing an extraordinary amount of homework. Their preparation actually begins several weeks—and often months—before the event itself and carries up through game day. Early in the process, the director and several engineering and production supervisors conduct a technical survey at the remote location where the event is to take place.

Depending on how familiar the director and engineers are with the stadium, the survey may actually take place as much as a year in advance of the event. If the network has never produced a telecast from a particular location, the producing team needs as much time as possible to scout camera and announce booth locations. Because some older stadiums lack adequate facilities in which to park the remote vehicles, the engineers are particularly concerned about access to the stadium. Any restricted areas might necessitate unduly long cable runs to some camera locations.

Although the size and shape of playing fields are identical—a football field is always 100 yards long and end-zones are always 10 yards deep—directors worry about the shape of the stadium. Andy Rosenberg comments on the difference this makes to a director:

You have to work around the way the stadium has been built. For example, the announcer's position at the Coliseum in Los Angeles is somewhere in the clouds, up near Heaven. The same is true in Tampa Bay. As for camera positions, there are stadiums like the one in Buffalo where the main camera positions are all nice and low to the ground and well-placed. The Fiesta Bowl is an example of where the position we use for our main camera is not on the fifty-yard line. It's not dead center because there are seats there and there is no aisle at the center of the field. Our choice is either to go very high with the camera or come down, slightly off center by about five yards. It's not as distracting from there as being way up high looking down on the players. Ideally for the team, it sells all the seats so you can't remove any of them for your cameras. If it's a very major game, you might spend the money to buy them out but the team doesn't want you to do that on a regular basis. They want their fans there. Our basic "meat and potatoes" game consists of five cameras. We primarily use three cameras that are somewhere up in the stadium parallel to the sideline. One is ideally at the fifty yard line and the other two are to the left and right, anywhere between the 20 and 35 yard lines. This all depends on the shape of the stadium.

When we used to televise the Jets games from Shea Stadium, one of the side cameras was on about the 10 yard line, which is further to the goal line than where we would normally set a camera. The idea is to be as close to the line of scrimmage as possible with your play-by-play camera, so if you're at about the 50, 25 and 15 yard lines, you're never more than about 15 yards away from the ball.

You then have an end zone camera, either to the left or right depending on the stadium and whether or not one side is open-ended. In Cincinnati, the end-zone camera is not dead center so that when you're watching a field goal, it's sometimes a little difficult to tell when the ball is very close to the goal post whether or not the kick is good.

A fifth camera is located in a vehicle which moves along the sideline.

For his sideline camera placement, the director actually has only one half of the stadium to use if he is to observe the 180 degree rule. Regarding camera placement, the "180 degree rule" dictates that the director place his cameras along or behind only one of the sidelines, thus effectively alllowing him to use only one half of the stadium (not including the locations behind the end zones). Imagine that the action on the screen is moving from left to right. As long as all sideline cameras are positioned on one side of the field, the director is free to use as many shots as he wants to follow the action. Were he to cut to a camera located on the opposite sideline, a reverse angle shot would result and appear to make any continuous action seem to go in the opposite direction (right to left). This would surely disorient the viewer. A few years ago, ABC Sports purposely incorporated the use of reverse angle shots to highlight action in replays, presumably to give viewers another perspective on the play.

The following is a week in the life of a typical sports production, in this case a professional football game. The producer and director generally begin serious preparation for the weekend on Monday or Tuesday preceding the telecast. (Remember that during the season, they have just finished their last game on Sunday.) On Monday, the producer usually checks several Monday morning newspapers thoroughly for the past weekend's results, paying particular attention to the cities whose teams will play in the following Sunday's game. This gives him a feel for what to expect:

Who were yesterday's heroes and what story lines might develop?

Was the injury to the quarterback serious enough to keep him out of action next Sunday?

How experienced is his replacement?

Will the all-pro offensive guard be at full strength after coming off the injured reserve list?

Are the stories about a coach being fired if his team loses anything more than rumor?

This research will probably be used in the following Sunday's opening 50-second "tease." If not then, viewers are assured of hearing these stories sometime during the first quarter. Some producers start producing video portions of the tease during the week, while others wait until the weekend when they can work more closely with the announcers.

The rest of the week is spent checking technical details with engineers and technicians. They review the "package" again—how many cameras, lens extenders, replay machines, graphics generators, and other auxiliary equipment will be available. Between Tuesday and Thursday the producer will probably call both teams' publicity staffs to probe for any inside stories and to learn when team meetings and practices are likely to be held on Friday and Saturday.

Friday is usually travel day for the production team and also the day when the remote truck heads for the location site. The more precise countdown towards Sunday's telecast begins on Saturday, when production and technical crews begin to set up the equipment. Saturdays are more relaxed than Sunday for the producer and director, who spend their time watching the teams go through the motions of practice sessions, talking to coaches and players, and making any necessary adjustments in the opening tease. Finishing touches will come on Sunday.

The Saturday meeting involving the producer, director, and the announcers is important for finalizing story lines for the game and discussing the best way to present them. Director Andy Rosenberg comments:

> What probably separates network telecasts in general from local telecasts is that you're on only once a week and you're trying to make each game a special event in its own way. It's not like the home fan watching his team all week long on his local station. The story line is important in making the game something special. Basically, you want to find some sort of thread to create initial interest. It can be anything from a newsworthy event to something historical.
>
> As the game goes along, you try to maintain the story. Then at halftime, we try to review what we talked about in the opening tease to see if what we said earlier has held course. If it hasn't, we try to explain why it hasn't.
>
> There are a lot of professionals involved in the telecast and our job is to make the game a little more enjoyable to watch. You can't pretend that every game you do is like the Super Bowl, but you can do your best to bring the viewer some insights that he might not otherwise have.

On Sunday morning, the countdown continues as the producer, director, announcers, technical crew, and stage managers review production details. Cameras are checked to see that tally lights are operational. Phone lines for communication between the control room, stadium camera positions, and the announce booth are checked. Announce booth and stadium microphones are tested. Videotape machines are readied, and occasionally, material to be used in the telecast is pre-taped. Communications with network control are readied to ensure that any highlights fed from the remote location to network for inclusion in either the pre-game show or during the game itself will go smoothly.

To the network, the most important part of the game is the commercials, and therefore phone lines between the remote site and the network control room remain operational throughout the game. On cue, the network inserts commercials as each game around the country progresses. A missed commercial means thousands of lost dollars.

Then, precisely at 12:59:50 p.m. (Eastern time), the associate director begins the ten-second countdown, and another live remote goes on the air.

During the season, the weekly routine of network sports producers and directors seldom varies, but they approach each game as though it's their very first and try to make every game something special. The preparation pays off when the director, cameramen, and announcers are able to capture those very moments that make watching the game at home a little more enjoyable—the tension of the two-minute drill when the field-goal kicker waits on the sidelines for his chance to become hero or goat;

the rejoicing of crowds in the stands; closeups of players agonizing over defeat or personal injury; and the reaction of the losing coach, often more interesting than that of the winner.

State-of-the-art technology has made watching sports on television more than just a series of pictures and sounds. Slow-motion replays from every angle capture the grace of a Dominique Wilkins slam dunk: time-lapse shots follow the precise arc of golf balls in flight; electronically generated chalk boards make a John Madden or a Billy Cunningham coaches without portfolio from the comfort of their announce booths; wireless microphones go into referees' huddles, while wireless cameras go into all parts of stadiums in search of the perfect "honey shot," television jargon for pictures of pretty cheerleaders and prettier fans. From the viewer's perspective, however, the game is still what matters, and the test of a sports director is how effectively he or she uses the technology.

If a poll were taken among directors, athletes, officials, and viewers about which innovation in sports production has provided the most blessings, the result would probably be unanimous for the instant replay. The replay was devised and first used in 1963 by CBS director Tony Verna in an Army-Navy football game. It can be fairly argued that the replay was one of the primary factors that propelled professional football into one of television's most popular sports, capturing and reshowing offensive and defensive intricacies of a sport recognized generally for its brutishness.

From its humble technological origins, designed to give TV viewers a second look at exciting action, instant replay has evolved into a maligned cyclopian witness to critical and disputed plays. When properly used, the replay shows how and why things happen on the field. If the action is dramatic enough, replays show the action again. But instant replays depend on directorial judgment which often leads to human error. Was the action dramatic enough to warrant a replay? Do replays obliterate live action? Do they replace live shots that show the real emotions of fans and players?

In reviewing NBC's coverage of a 1987 NFL playoff game for the *Boston Globe,* Jack Craig, dean of TV sports columnists, wrote,

> NBC used so many replays during the Browns-Broncos game that the audience often received less information, not more. Repetitive and unrevealing replays filled the screen and required analyst Merlin Olsen to state the obvious, which in turn prevented play-by-play man Dick Enberg from updating the situation.

When the Broncos intercepted a Bernie Kosar pass in the first quarter, so many replays were squeezed in that Enberg got the microphone back only in time for the snap of the ball. Enberg never did identify the line of scrimmage.

There were so many replays forced upon the audience, especially in the late stages, that the building drama between plays was drained; the audience was forced to watch what it already had seen instead of speculating on what was to come.

Craig properly zeroed in on the likely root of the problem when he wrote that "the bigger the game, the better the chances of replays overrunning the screen, because there is more equipment and more personnel to use it."

Networks have increasingly fallen victim to their own technology, as game officials become more dependent on network replays as an extention of the officiating process. While only the NFL, horse-racing, and NCAA basketball have official policies about using TV instant replays as a means to settle disputes, other sports such as track and field and golf have dragged network cameras into the middle of officiating disputes, much to the producers' chagrin. Their dismay is probably justified. While a single picture may be worth a thousand words, TV camera angles are often not worth two cents in trying to judge whether or not a player has stepped out of bounds in the end zone, or slid under a tag while being called out at second base. The seventh game of the 1987 World Series between the St. Louis Cardinals and the Minnesota Twins was a modern classic in terms of controversial events which subsequent replays revealed were apparently missed by the umpires. The three plays—one involving a runner called out at home plate and two other plays at first base—may well have affected the dramatic outcome of the Series.

But on balance, TV replays probably add more to viewers' enjoyment than they detract. The same can also be said for other visual advances, which, when judiciously used, make network sports viewing unsurpassably enjoyable and informative. For example, the remote-controlled camera placed next to the driver in the car at the Daytona 500 provides an extraordinary perspective of the speed and imminent danger of auto racing. The Action-Track superimposes a series of still pictures showing the form of professional golfers teeing off, and gives home-bound duffers a graphic look at how tee shots are really meant to happen; and the Quantel compresses into one quadrant of the screen a picture of the runner poised to tag up at third, while the rest of the screen is filled with the center fielder setting himself for the catch and throw home.

The Quantel was used in what may have been a television "first" in the last days of the 1987 pennant races. On the last weekend of the season, when the outcomes of both the American and the National League races were in doubt, NBC showed two games simultaneously by compressing the video of one into the lower-right quadrant of the screen. Meanwhile, the other game in progress filled the remaining three quadrants. Obviously, only one audio source could be used, which was supplied by the announcers doing the primary game.

Electronic chalkboards—telestrators—have elevated the role of announcers doing color commentary. John Madden, Bob Griese, and Tommy Heinsohn are among the most skilled in using this sophisticated device which allows commentators to use a light-pen to draw arrows and circles (the coaches' Xs and Os) over replays of game action. The Dubner is another complex device which allows technicians to explain game action through electronic animation. But the success of these devices is again dependent on the skill of the announcer and the timing and discretion of the director in using the technology artfully.

Graphics that superimpose information in the lower third of the screen challenge both the speed-reading skills of the audience and the imagination of production associates who prepare such statistics. ("Dave Winfield is batting over .400 in night games played in July and August when the humidity has been over 75%. He's hitting .275 in all other games except rain-delayed games played in May and June.") While some networks buy statistical information from syndicated services, many rely on their own production staff to gather data. Prior to a weekend baseball game, a production associate will prepare the basic information ranging from players' names and batting averages to performance records in various game situations. The information is stored electronically and called up on cue during the course of the game. Stats are changed and updated as the game progresses, and totally new information is created as the situation warrants. ("That's the third time in his career that Reggie has thrown a bucket of Gatorade at the bat rack.")

During the game, statistical information appears on screen at the director's discretion. He either calls for a graphic to be ready on his next cue, or the production associate "sells it" to him during a game situation. ("I've got the number of times Mike Schmidt has driven in base runners when there have been two outs. Let me know if you want it!") There is usually very little time for the director to decide what graphic to use and when to call for it. His attention is generally focused on eight or more camera and videotape monitors, and so he relies totally on the accuracy of the information and the spelling skills of the production associate. The general rule of thumb is that a missed stat is always better than a wrong one.

One of the most overlooked aspects of sports production is not what's seen but what's heard—or better yet, what's *not* heard. Top TV sports directors are as concerned about the audio portion of their telecasts as the video, and they often spend as much time planning for the sound as they do for the picture. Every sport has its own audio challenges, whether in capturing crowd noises in the stands or the sound of a golf ball plunking into the hole. The director's aim is to bring as much field color as possible to each telecast, to simulate a live presence. In football, hand-held microphones roam the sidelines, strategically placed about seven to ten yards ahead of the play, to hear the quarterback calling signals, the fury of linemen blocking, and the sound of running backs being met by near devastation.

In baseball coverage, microphones point towards home plate to catch the crack of the bat, while others are aimed towards first base to catch the sound of the ball when it's caught.

In basketball, a microphone is often taped to the basket struts to capture the swish of the ball as it goes through the net, and the sound of bodies bashing together for rebounds under the boards.

The ever-present courtside microphones used in covering tennis matches provide valuable ambient sound that adds flavor to the television coverage, but on occasion, have led to some embarrassing moments. In the 1987 U.S. Tennis Open, John McEnroe let loose with one of his patented tirades directed at the linesmen and the referee, and both the network producing team and viewers at home were treated to more invective than they bargained for.

Several years ago, NBC tried an announcer-less football game, using only field microphones to capture crowd noises, while the director superimposed statistical information that the announcers would ordinarily have provided. The experiment met with less than critical acclaim, not so much because home viewers couldn't live without the dulcet tones of the million-dollar mouths in the booth, but because the TV experience is simply different than being at the game. There is no way that microphones can replicate the swelling of the crowd's roar during a rally, or the cackle of vendors hawking their wares in the stands. For all of the production excellence that networks and money can provide, the experience of sports on TV is sterile compared with being at the ball park.

But what about the ultimate sound that makes the game at home different from being at the ball park? A word here about the voices from the announce booth.

There are many theories about what makes a good sports announcer. Marty Glickman, éminence grise of sportscasters, has suggested certain qualifications which he feels are essential for becoming a network-calibre announcer. Glickman has coached NBC and Madison Square Garden Network announcers since the late 1970s, and during his lengthy broadcasting career did play-by-play of New York Giants football for thirty years as well as New York Knicks basketball and college sports. He suggests three qualities for success: succinctness, self-discipline, and awareness of the action. In an interview, Glickman said, "Too often, announcers say too much and run the risk of spoiling the game for viewers. It's the discipline of being quiet, the discipline of letting the picture speak for itself. The viewer has to be allowed to enjoy the moment the way everyone else is enjoying it."

In both radio and television, the announcer is the human link between the broadcast and the listeners. Unlike radio, however, which is an announcer's medium, television belongs to the director. The announcer is simply another (high-priced) member of the crew. In radio, the announcer is more critical, because he—not the camera—provides the word pictures, which allows the radio announcer more room for error. An anecdote from the early 1950s illustrates the point.

Bill Stern was one of radio's most popular network sportscasters. He had a smooth-as-silk voice and a rapid-fire delivery that were ideal for the medium. One Saturday afternoon, Stern was announcing a college football game. Towards the end of the game, a runner broke free at the line of scrimmage and headed down the sidelines towards a sure touchdown and an upset victory. Stern was his usual brilliant self in capturing the drama of the moment as only this master of the announce booth could. He was barely distracted by his spotter pounding the table beside him, pointing frantically at the depth chart. While Stern's description of the action was dramatic, it lacked one minor detail: he had misidentified the man carrying the ball on the way to glory.

Undaunted, Stern did what any golden-tongued radio announcer would do in the same situation. He invented a play. As the runner neared the five-yard line, Stern nary skipped a beat in announcing that the runner lateraled the ball to a halfback whom he said had been trailing the play. By the time the ball went into the end-zone, the correct runner had scored the touchdown.

A week or so later, Stern was in New York's famous 21 Club when he ran into Ted Husing, another giant in radio sportscasting.

"Hey, Ted, I've just been over to NBC and I need some advice. They asked me if I was interested in announcing some horse-races for the television network. What do you think?"

"I think you ought to turn this one down, Bill," Husing replied.

"Why?" Stern asked.

"Because on television, you can't lateral a horse."

As any regular sports viewers will attest, it appears that there are a few certain criteria to become a network sportscaster: race, gender, age—and length of name. Almost every network sports announcer is a white male, age somewhere between thirty and mid-fifties. While occasionally a MER-lin, a BILL-y, a TOE-ny, or even a HOW-ard will make the grade, it's more likely that the edge will go to every Tom, Dick, and Brent. For every on-air sportscaster of two syllables, there are a half-dozen named Al, Bob, Curt, Dick, Frank, John, Len, Joe, Keith, Pat, and Vin.

Men of color only do color commentary and seldom play-by-play. Ahmad Rashad, James Brown, Irv Cross, and very few others are relegated to pre-game and half-time shows, even though professional sports has produced a substantial number of articulate black athletes, presumably qualified to be the lead announcer. And while Phyllis George may have set back by a century the women's quest for equality, several qualified female ex-athletes—Billie Jean King, Donna DeVarona, Nancy Lieberman, and others—do color commentary for golf, tennis, and Olympic events in which women athletes are competing.

In mid-1987, NBC made a concerted effort to bring women into more prominent roles by grooming two female sportscasters for network duties. Gayle Sierens, a WXFL-TV (Tampa) news anchor, was tutored by Marty Glickman in preparation for announcing NFL games. NBC also hired Gayle Gardner away from ESPN, where she was a sports news anchor. The network groomed Gardner to be studio host and anchor during NBC's 1988 Summer Olympics from Seoul, Korea.

The issue of how effective "jocks" are in the booth is one on which writers who fill TV sports columns thrive. A usual criticism centers on the real or perceived biases that they may have for their former teams—Bob Griese doing Miami Dolphins games for NBC and Tom Heinsohn's Boston Celtics games on CBS were among the most widely criticized over the years.

The answer to whether ex-athletes can be good on-air talent is similar to the answer that one-time St. John's basketball coach Joe Lapchick gave when asked if one of his players was helped by making the sign of the Cross before attempting a free throw: "Yes, particularly if he takes a deep breath, bends his knees, keeps his elbow straight, and follows through with his wrist."

For every Joe Namath and O. J. Simpson, who were widely criticized for their performances on Monday Night Football, there are the Frank Giffords, Pat Summeralls, and Merlin Olsens whose work is generally acclaimed. These men seem to possess the attributes that Marty Glickman preached: succinctness, self-discipline, and game awareness, all far more important to their success in the booth than their earlier on-field heroics.

While the gift of insight is not the sole purview of ex-athletes, clearly, former players bring perspectives to a game that non-players generally would ignore. An observation by Tony Kubek that Roger Clemens warms up before a game by throwing a ball in the outfield to a catcher, periodically increasing the distance to stretch his arm muscles, is a nuance that only a former athlete can deliver. The same is true of ex-Philadelphia 76'er and Chicago Bulls coach Doug Collins describing a coaching maneuver that misfired, costing the Detroit Pistons an NBA playoff game; or Tim McCarver criticizing a New York Met for failing to execute a hit-and-run play or not hitting the cut-off man in a throw from the outfield.

While sometimes objective journalism is hard to achieve, fans are generally more concerned with accuracy and the announcers' knowledge of the sport. A good working relationship between the director and the announcers is essential to the telecast. In a well-directed telecast, there is a balance between the director leading the announcers with pictures, and the announcers leading the director with their commentary. Because the director is limited to the vision of five or more camera monitors, he is heavily reliant on the eyes of the announcers to scan the field and suggest action that may be happening away from the play.

Because part of their job is to make the game more entertaining, announcers often want to tell a story about one of the players. During the commercial, they might ask the director to come out of the commercial with a particular shot of the player instead of the usual wide shot.

From the perspective of most announcers, the faster the game action, the easier it is for them to work. Vin Scully, the master of creating word pictures that enhance the visual quality of most telecasts, has said that "the slower the sport and the more gaps between the action, the more difficult the sport is to do. You have plenty of time to hang yourself if you don't know what you're talking about." Scully cites football among the easier sports to broadcast and golf perhaps the most difficult.

A common but mistaken assumption is that announcers make a difference in network ratings. Nothing could be further from the truth. Every study shows that people watch sports because of the teams involved, not because of who is doing play-by-play announcing or color commentary. (On the other hand, informal research conducted in 1983 showed that many people who were unhapy with Howard Cosell watched ABC's Monday Night Football while turning off the sound and listening to Jack Buck and Hank Stram broadcast the game on CBS Radio.)

There is an axiom in TV sports that says a good director can often make a bad game better to watch, but a bad director can only make a good game bad. With all the preparation, team-work, and experience that go into producing television sports, the difference between a good and a bad telecast is ultimately the creative expression of the TV director. What TV sportsviewing all comes down to is whether or not viewers have enjoyed the game. NBC's Andy Rosenberg summarizes the rapport that links the person in the director's chair with the viewer occupying the comfortable couch at home:

> One of the marks of a good telecast is if the viewer feels comfortable watching the game, because things come up on the screen when he wants to see them. When he wants to see a shot of the line-backer, he doesn't strain. It's there. Watching a baseball game, when he wants to see the grit of the batter's teeth before he swings, the shot is there. It's almost as if you could do an instant poll to let each viewer direct the game, they would call for the shots and they'd be there. In a good telecast, the viewer is never rocketed out of his seat in surprise.
>
> To be a good director, you have to be a sports fan. You have to grow to understand whatever sport it is you're televising. It helps a lot if you enjoy the sport so that you bring your enthusiasm and your interest to it. If you don't know a sport you can do a mechanical job, but you can never do a terrific job.

6

MONEY TALKS

IT SHOULD COME as no surprise to even the most idealistic reader that the television sports business is thoroughly imbued with the profit motive. What may be surprising, however, is the range of techniques used to calculate or define "profit," and the networks' careful assessment of a more important measurement: the "total return" generated by their investment in sports programs. At some point each decision whether to bid on the rights to certain programming must be stripped to its basic essentials: can the total cost (including rights fees, production, promotion, the "pre-emptive impact" of displacing other programming, and miscellaneous expenses) of the program in question be justified by the "total return" (advertising and/or subscriber revenues, audience sampling, promotional benefits to other programs, public image, denial of programming to competitors, good-will with important rights-holders, the "inside track" for future rights)? Can the network afford to pay the price? Can it afford not to? These questions form the basis of that most unpredictable and delicate moment when money changes hands and contractual commitments are made: the purchase and sale of television rights to sporting events.

The bargaining leading up to an agreement is often characterized by considerable huffing and puffing on both sides; as in any complex and ultimately expensive negotiation, there is much posturing and pouting, some threatening displays, even a bit of chicanery here and there. Over the years the negotiations have occasionally been enlivened by dirty tricks, clever charades, and the sheer force of individual personalities. At other times, they have resembled nothing so much as a grimy pawn shop, in which desperate owners attempt to peddle their wares for whatever meager commitment the disinterested networks might offer. Unpopular sports, weak leagues, or fledgling operations are about as likely to receive significant payments as obscure emerging nations foreign aid. At the other extreme, hard-nosed, sophisticated owners of extremely popular programming have sometimes turned the tables on the networks, virtually dictating a competitive free-for-all in which the bidding frenzy has driven rights fees through the roof. More generally, the bargaining positions of both sides are influenced by larger "outside" forces which may constrain the maneuvering room of the parties, or add an element of intransigence or submissiveness to their bargaining positions; these negotiations do not take place in a vacuum. The only constant is that money not only talks, it screams.

Network negotiators must calculate their bid after studying the overall state of the economy, forecasts of future inflation, the networks' own financial situation, existing commitments to other sports programs, competitive programming and counter-programming strategies, the cyclical popularity of certain sports, and the level of support offered the sports division by network management. When they estimate the value of the event, they must also consider the length of the proposed contract, the relative uniqueness of the event and the exclusivity of its rights, the ratings track record of the programming, advertiser interest, production costs, scheduling needs and conflicts, and other factors. They want to come to the bargaining table armed with relevant statistics and information which not only buttress their arguments but also indicate to the rights-holders that the network has other, less expensive alternatives, which would achieve its goals quite nicely, thank you. They do not want to arrive hat (or checkbook) in hand.

The rights-holders facing them across the bargaining table must ask themselves equally challenging questions, and must be prepared to counter any objections raised by the other side. Is money, or exposure and promotion (or some combination of them), the key element of a proposed contract? Are they better off settling for less cash in exchange for greater exposure and promotion? Are they willing to balance their desire for maximum programming and exposure against the networks' fears of oversaturation of the airwaves? The rights-holders' own financial calculations are crucial: how much money can they reasonably expect in rights fees without making the package unaffordable? It is not in the long-term interests of most rights-holders to make things so difficult for the networks that profits are tiny or nonexistent; that serves only to discourage attractive bids next time around. Can the rights-holders enter the negotiations from the virtually unassailable position of having pre-sold their event to sponsors or advertisers? The most important bargaining chip that can be held by the rights-holders, however, is the realistic threat of selling the rights to a competitor. The rights-holders must stimulate and nurture the interest of more than one network, so they enter negotiation with at least the prospect of alternative suitors.

Underlying all the research and preparation, all the pretense and posturing, is the shared assumption that, in the larger sense, both sides need each other, and that a deal will eventually be struck. Major sports cannot long exist without television, and those negotiating know this. The television business cannot continue its customary programming practices and audience delivery, nor can advertisers reach their target demographics, without sports, and this, too, is known to the negotiators on both sides. Further, both seller and buyer usually understand that short-term interests must be sacrificed for benefit of the overall, long-term relationship. There will always be a next time another round of negotiations—at which mistakes can be rectified, imbalances in current contracts adjusted, and options reassessed. The only questions resolved by the intricate, sometimes stormy courtship preceding the inevitable agreement, is, therefore, not whether, but HOW MUCH?

Some sports, such as soccer and ice hockey, which simply do not fare well on network television, are consigned to the tender mercies of regional and local television. There is little interest or action at the network bargaining tables when they are offered for sale. Others, including tennis and golf, continue to exist on network television, supported mainly by their upscale demographics and the need of certain advertisers to reach a small elite audience; more and more frequently their tournaments are pre-sold to sponsors who place them on television as part of an overall marketing strategy. A third category of sports events includes such ugly ducklings as bowling, professional wrestling, and auto racing, all as dependably profitable as they are unfashionable: no one claims to watch them, few production personnel brag about working on them, yet their ratings remain stable and their advertisers loyal. Others, most notably boxing, are subject to wide swings in network interest, premised to a great extent on the emergence and availability of high-profile American fighters such as Muhammad Ali, Sugar Ray Leonard, Marvin Hagler, and Mike Tyson. Both professional and college basketball exist on television solely for their playoffs, which put them in the black. The dynamics of rights negotiations may best be illustrated by the biggest and most valuable perennial properties: baseball and football (both professional and college). The evolution of their television contracts left a landscape littered with the bleached bones of faint-hearted negotiators.

Through the years, the outcome of these rights negotiations has depended to a great extent upon the relative power of three oft-competing parties at the table. The complex interplay between leagues and networks has been matched by that between individual franchise owners and the commissioners (at the intercollegiate level, the parallel structures are the individual NCAA member schools and the Executive Director). As the total amount of broadcast revenues available to rights-holders has risen, so has the dependence of franchises on those revenues and the tension between sellers and buyers. More strikingly, however, an examination of the historical record reveals that the role of the commissioners—indeed, their very survival in the job—has come to be defined by the manner and extent to which they centralize control over broadcast revenues. Whatever their success in dealing with other issues, such as scheduling, player discipline, or labor negotiations, the commissioners, who serve at the pleasure of the franchises, are judged most severely on their performance in handling television. One may even estimate the staying power, standing, and stature of an individual commissioner by quantifying the percentage of total broadcast revenues which flows through, and is distributed by, his office: the more he controls, the "stronger" he is. Surprisingly, in the more than fifty years since broadcast sports hit the airwaves, only one commissioner, Alvin "Pete" Rozelle, has become master of the system (and hence the owners), and, when he leaves the scene, his kind may never be tolerated again.

As befits its stature as the first—and for many years, only—"national" professional sport, Major League Baseball was midwife to the broadcast sports industry. "America's Pastime" is the oldest, and in many ways, most traditional major broadcast sports organization in the country. Many of the franchises have been held for years by families of great wealth and conservatism, dedicated to the old-fashioned notion that they could do with their property pretty much as they pleased, and no one—least of all an employee of theirs like the commissioner—was going to tell them what to do. As the value of broadcast contracts has grown, many of them have come to view the commissioner as at best a competitor for those revenues, and at worst an impediment to receiving them at all. Operating like little fiefdoms, these franchises were alternately suspicious of broadcasting and selfish in enjoying its benefits; the former can be traced, particularly in the early days, to ignorance and the relatively small sums at stake, the latter continues to attract adherents among the most savvy and sophisticated owners.

Money Talks

In 1921, baseball authorized the sale of the radio rights to the World
Series for the total sum of $3,000, to be split between the competing
teams. Like much other early radio programming, the purpose of baseball broadcasts was to provide entertainment which would sell radio
sets. Even David Sarnoff of RCA noted that his fledgling NBC network
needed baseball to "sell enough sets to go on producing other kinds of
programming." Throughout the mid-twenties, more and more sets were
sold; by 1927 more than 35 million listeners could receive at least one
of more than 600 stations then on the air, and the World Series broadcasts grew in popularity. However, the regular season games fared less
well, and many franchises ignored or forbade them, on the grounds they
would damage ticket sales. Even then, it should be acknowledged, some
owners went their own way, and embraced broadcasting wholeheartedly.
William Wrigley was a strong advocate of broadcasting: the more the
merrier, he felt. For years, he declined to charge stations a fee for the
games, and as many as seven carried Cubs' games simultaneously. This
general policy of carrying the Cubs' full schedule would survive protes-
tations from the commissioner and other owners as late as 1949, when
all three Chicago television stations carried the games, and again in
1987, when the entire schedule was still being carried on Superstation
WGN-TV.

As listenership continued to rise, a few brave companies began to
buy advertising during the games, but this generated insignificant revenues. In 1935, however, the Gillette company, under the prodding of
young advertising maven A. Craig Smith, took the plunge and began sponsoring entire broadcasts of major sports events, usually boxing matches.
It did this not by buying individual ads but by purchasing the broadcast
rights to the entire event, and then finding a station to carry it. Smith
was soon attracted to the World Series, which he secured for Gillette
with surprising ease. As sole sponsor, Gillette in fact owned the rights to
the World Series and the All-Star Game until 1965; NBC-TV and Radio
were only allowed to carry the games. By 1939, when most owners were
so fearful of radio's effect on attendance that all three New York teams
barred broadcasts of home games, Smith paid $203,000 for the exclusive
World Series rights, which he placed on the Mutual Network. Of that
amount, approximately half went to the owners and the rest to production costs and administrative overhead. Emboldened by his success,
Smith and Gillette developed in 1941 "The Gillette Cavalcade of Sports,"
which ran until 1964, carrying in that time some 600 boxing matches, as
well as hundreds of other programs. Until the mid-fifties, they virtually
hand-raised the broadcast sports industry, buying enough air time to
develop reliable audiences for sports programs, and convincing a lot of

wary broadcast executives that sports would be an important element in their overall programming mix. It is widely accepted that Smith and Gillette were indispensable actors in first subsidizing radio sports, and then underwriting the transition to television.

The new medium approached baseball very tentatively, and there was hesitation and mixed feelings on both sides. Some television executives were afraid of competing with the popularity and advertising clout of radio. However, the game did offer the prospect of steady, dependable, reasonably inexpensive programming during the summer doldrums. Many team owners resisted television as they had radio and closed it out of several major markets. There were very few stations operating in the heartland of the country, where baseball loyalties (including the then-flourishing minor leagues) were strongest, so audience was limited there, too. Besides, the two major leagues were operating for a time under Rule 1-D, which prohibited major league broadcasts into minor league markets; faced with the potential of an anti-trust action, and the reality of their own desire to reach those audiences, the owners rescinded the rule in 1951. A few brave souls took the plunge at the local level, most notably Larry MacPhail, who began televising about one Dodgers home game per week in 1940. World War II halted the project, but in 1946, Mac-Phail, then running the Yankees, sold their local rights to DuMont for $75,000.

In 1947, Gillette paid $30,000 to co-sponsor (with Ford Motor Company) the Yankees-Dodgers World Series, which was jointly telecast by CBS, NBC, and DuMont to an audience of approximately three million viewers. At the time, Ford was Gillette's only significant rival in sports sponsorship: it owned the rights to Madison Square Garden boxing and four baseball franchises. By the next year, Gillette was able to secure the sole television sponsorship of the Series for $175,000. That this was a rock-bottom price was made evident in 1949, when the cost escalated to $800,000 for the nationwide rights; Craig Smith was satisfied, however, by the knowledge that the telecasts now reached some ten million households, and his research showed that they were selling tens of millions of his company's razor blades.

By 1950, Commissioner A. B. "Happy" Chandler was able sell the rights to the 1951-56 World Series for $6 million. Research indicated that upwards of 50 million viewers were now watching. Chandler, who had only been in office since 1944, undoubtedly felt he had accomplished a significant advance in baseball's fortunes. The owners, once again rebelling against any increase in the commissioner's powers, or usurpation of their own, promptly fired him—for being too independent—a maneuver they would resort to in similar situations some years later. In fact, one of the motivations underlying their displeasure was their own individual interests in expanding their unilateral radio and television networks as they pleased, without any provisions for revenue-sharing. Their premise was that baseball fans were intensely loyal to individual teams and players, not necessarily to the overall structure of MLB, and it was the absolute right of owners to protect and profit from that loyalty.

Edgar Scherick was perhaps second only to Craig Smith as a visionary in the development of television sports. Like Smith an advertising man (as were so many of the pioneers of broadcast sports), working out of small offices at the firm of Dancer Fitzgerald & Sample in New York, he began by acquiring rights for sponsors—most notably Falstaff Brewing. He was later to leave Dancer Fitzgerald for an ultimately frustrating tour at CBS, and finally to set up his own production and marketing company, Sports Programming, Inc., and begin packaging sports rights for ABC. Scherick's little company grew in importance to the point that he virtually controlled all sports at ABC, at a time when he wasn't even an employee of the network. SPI eventually formed the kernel of what would become ABC Sports.

In 1953, Scherick proposed a television "Game of the Week" to Falstaff Breweries, and they bought the idea, agreeing to sponsor the games on the young and struggling ABC network. When he tried to sell the idea to the baseball moguls, however, only three teams were willing to sell him their rights, and the rest pushed through a rule blacking out the games in all Major League Baseball cities. Knowing that he had a sponsor and a network already lined up, Scherick ignored the opposition, and proceeded with his audacious plan; he hired Dizzy Dean as on-air talent (his crazy-like-a-fox "country boy" mangling of the language provided an enormously popular entertainment value that previous baseball broadcasts had lacked), spent money on publicity and promotion, and began the series in June 1953. By the end of that inaugural season, Dean and the Game of the Week were getting a 51 share on Saturday afternoons, in spite of the MLB blackout. By 1954, the Dodgers and Giants relented, and permitted the ABC production team to enter their ball parks; they were soon followed by the rest of the teams, who felt they, too, had to get on the bandwagon of popularity generated by these telecasts. In the long run, perhaps the most important effect of Dean's broadcasts was to interest viewers in watching games which did not involve their local or favorite team. He helped make possible the later emergence of "national" teams.

Chandler's successor as commissioner was Ford Frick, who in 1954 proposed an alternate plan for a nationally televised, regular season "Game of the Week." According to this plan, Frick would negotiate a pooled rights agreement in behalf of all the major league owners, who would share the resulting revenues. However, when some eyebrows were raised at the Justice Department, the plan was quietly dropped, as few owners had the stomach to take any action that might end up in court and call into question baseball's unique anti-trust exemption. The collapse of the Frick plan only accelerated the trend towards unilateral action, and more clubs began to go their own way, aggressively pursuing local, regional, and national contracts. In addition to the many local stations affiliated with teams, CBS carried national games both Saturday and Sunday, and NBC had a weekly competitor. By 1958, some 800 games were available on television annually.

Another young advertising man had become involved producing Dodgers and Giants games, and by 1955 he had a problem. Tom Villante of BBD&O (who would continue his association with MLB for many years, and eventually become the Commissioner's chief media adviser) could not afford to pay the high cost of leasing long-distance telephone lines from the monopolistic A.T.&T., and he was looking for relief. He was introduced to Dick Bailey, an ABC technical operations specialist, who showed him the cost-efficiency of a consortium or pool of teams sharing the lines, each feeding its games on a somewhat different schedule. To Villante's surprise, Bailey volunteered his own services as middleman, buying the A.T.&.T. lines and leasing them to the participating teams on a pre-arranged schedule he devised. Bailey soon quit ABC and set up his own company, Sports Network, Inc., to handle the logistics.

The growing competition among francises for broadcast revenues spurred the first wave of migrations to new markets. From 1953 to 1958 the Boston Braves moved to Milwaukee, the St. Louis Browns to Baltimore, the Philadelphia Athletics to Kansas City; and then the Dodgers and Giants jointly forsook New York for the West Coast. Not only did the movement of major league teams devastate some remaining strongholds of minor league ball, it spread the franchises over great distances, thereby increasing dramatically the cost of transmitting broadcasts. Dick Bailey and SNI suddenly became more important than ever to sponsors, local stations, and networks alike. Edgar Scherick, feeling the pinch, proposed that he and Bailey work together: Scherick's SPI would provide the programming (at first, Big Ten basketball) and sponsors, Bailey's SNI the telephone lines. To the confusion of many people, including their customers, the two similarly named outfits began working together on a variety of projects. In the long run, both did well. ABC Television Network president Tom Moore decided to build an in-house sports division and bought out SPI in 1961; and Howard Hughes paid $18 million in 1968 for SNI, which he renamed the Hughes Sports Network.

Tom Moore was unlike most other senior network executives in at least two respects. He was a southern gentleman of considerable personal charm and ease, rarely given to the tantrums and histrionics often displayed by his peers. And he was interested in sports, which he saw as one of several means to hasten the time of ABC's financial stability. The network, chronically cash-poor, had still not overcome the handicap imposed on it by its recent and unglamorous birth as NBC's sacrificial lamb, when RCA was forced to spin off one of its two networks, and it chose the Blue. Saddled with fewer and weaker affiliates, unable to compete for expensive programming, and discounted by major advertisers and sponsors, ABC needed attention-getting, popular, reasonably inexpensive programming. None of the other senior executives at ABC wanted to oversee sports (things were still pretty much run by Scherick), not even the head of News, the traditional home of sports coverage at CBS and NBC, so it fell to Moore almost by default.

As the 1959 baseball season drew to a close, there arose the possibility of a National League playoff to determine the pennant. NBC, which as usual controlled the World Series rights, had no provision in its contract for playoffs or extra games. Moore sensed an opportunity for his struggling outfit, and he called the Dodgers' Walter O'Malley to ask about the rights to Dodgers playoff games. O'Malley, whose keen nose for television money had led him to Los Angeles in the first place and who was pushing for night games on network television, was ready with an answer: the best-of-three playoff would cost $125,000 per game, but O'Malley would have to offer it to NBC first. Tom Gallery at NBC refused to bid on the two games scheduled to begin at 5 p.m., Los Angeles time, because they would have necessitated pre-empting NBC's popular prime-time lineup. Tom Moore's prime-time lineup would hardly be missed, so he was delighted to buy the playoff—whether it went two or three games—for $300,000. O'Malley was equally happy, having obtained the extra cash, as well as his cherished prime time games. At the last moment, though, National League president Warren Giles (perhaps working at the behest of NBC) intervened and declared there would be no evening games. Tom Moore was convinced he would lose the games back to NBC, but to his great surprise and pleasure O'Malley stuck to the deal and delivered the playoff to ABC.

ABC's commitment to sports was now apparent, and its willingness to compete aggressively for rights helped stimulate further price increases. Major League Baseball's network rights rose from $3.25 million in 1960 to $16 million within ten years, despite the fact that ratings remained essentially flat throughout the period, and in the face of enormous growth in the popularity of the NFL. What was worse, so far as some baseball advertisers were concerned, the NFL's demographics were more attractive. Their research revealed that the televised baseball of the fifties—Dizzy Dean's down-home show—had left it in the early sixties with an audience that tended to be older, more rural, less well educated, and less wealthy than that attracted to the NFL on CBS. That research, coupled with the staggering number of commercial availabilities in all those hundreds of televised games, tended to diminish advertiser demand for baseball spots. Some new, more "modern" owners had come into baseball through franchise shifts and expansion, including a few associated with the television business; they attempted to solidify MLB's position relative to college and pro football, increase the ratings, and improve the demographics. Prodded by mavericks including Charles O. Finley, they instituted many cosmetic changes—exploding scoreboards, colorful uniforms—and a few aimed at making the game more appealing for television—the lower pitching mound, smaller strike zone, and in 1973, the American League designated hitter. However, the prevailing Old Guard among MLB owners seemed at a loss in responding to the mounting challenges, so the owners did in 1965 what they had always done in moments of uncertainty: they changed commissioners.

Ford Frick was seventy years old and had held the job since 1951, during which period he had seen it change considerably. Dealing with the owners had never been a particularly enjoyable experience, but that was now complicated by the task of confronting a newly energized Players Association under Marvin Miller's professional leadership, as well as competing with the razzle-dazzle NFL led by its "boy wonder" Commissioner Pete Rozelle. After nearly thirty-one years in various baseball administrative posts, he wanted to retire. In his stead, the owners selected a virtual unknown, retired Air Force General William (Spike) Eckert. He possessed no relevant experience whatsoever, particularly since his military command background would be useless in baseball: the commissioner didn't get to command anyone, least of all the owners who paid his salary. Looked at with a certain illogic, Eckert's selection made perfect sense, as he would be commissioner in name only, keeping the chair warm while the owners ran the show. The experience was, unsurprisingly, a most unhappy one for Eckert, and he resigned the job under fire in 1968.

Having forced Eckert out, the owners were unable to agree on a successor, despite months of meetings and dozens of inconclusive ballots. Finally, a compromise choice emerged, and the weary owners broke the deadlock by appointing Bowie Kuhn, a successful attorney with a background in sports (he had been cut from his high school basketball team by coach Red Auerbach) who had previously done considerable legal work for baseball. Imposing in intellect as well as appearance, Kuhn was the first man steeped in the requirements of the modern position. He understood labor relations, legal issues, marketing, and television; he also understood the limits and uses of power in that office. His determination to test those limits was quickly signaled. Within two years, he had established the office of Director of Radio and Television at MLB headquarters (reporting to the commissioner), moved some World Series games to prime time, and stretched the season for the benefit of television by adding an additional October weekend. The owners reacted cautiously to these initial moves, because network rights fees continued to increase, and their own private preserves seemed unaffected. Commissioner Kuhn committed himself to a sustained, personal effort designed to improve the network television situation.

In 1975 he targeted ABC with a proposal for Monday Night Baseball. The idea was based on the sound premise that ABC wanted to break NBC's baseball monopoly. MLB clearly stood to benefit from a competition between the networks, and it need look no further than the rival NFL to see what network competition had done for rights fees: Rozelle had the three of them fighting like scorpions in a bottle. In addition, Roone Arledge had made such a success out of ABC Monday Night Football, it seemed a logical programming extension to provide Monday Night Baseball when football was out of season. Interestingly, the idea of Monday Night Baseball was not entirely new, having had an unsuccessful three-game tryout on NBC in 1966. Arledge agreed the new concept made some sense, but he insisted any package must include the rights to some All-Star playoff, and World Series games. He also insisted on his right to select the announcers for the telecasts, and his intention to choose Howard Cosell, who had developed a reputation for boosting the NFL and knocking baseball. Whether Kuhn made Arledge pay extra for his prerogatives, or Arledge sweetened the deal to overcome Kuhn's deep reservations about Cosell, is a matter of interpretation. When the contract was signed, however, it provided for ABC to alternate postseason playoffs and the World Series with NBC; Cosell was assigned the Monday Night Baseball games; and Kuhn delivered $92.8 million in new rights fees to the owners. And although few people gave him credit for doing so, he set in motion competitive forces which would produce truly staggering sums in just a few years.

The development of cable television continued apace during the seventies, and the increasingly common link between cable and sports seemed a natural one. The emergence of "superstations," with their power to invade the home markets of teams throughout the nation, troubled Kuhn. It also deeply troubled the networks, since they were losing their monopoly on the national distribution of games. When the flamboyant Ted Turner bought the Atlanta Braves in 1976, the owners approved the transaction, despite the commissioner's misgivings about Turner's intention to turn local station WTBS into a nationally distributed superstation. Kuhn knew the issue would not resolve itself, and that a troubling precedent had been set. He also knew that his opposition to the growing number of superstation teams would cost him their support, and perhaps that of other owners who wanted him to keep hands off their television arrangements. In 1981 he opposed the Tribune Company's proposal to purchase the Cubs from the Wrigley family, citing Tribune's ownership of Superstation WGN in Chicago and the Yankees' flagship WPIX-TV in New York. The purchase was approved, but only after Kuhn received assurances from the new owners that they would comply with all of MLB's broadcasting policies, and not contest baseball's (and the networks') official position, as stated in Congressional hearings, concerning copyright payments and the obligations of superstations.

That same year, an opportunity arose for the growing number of anti-Kuhn owners to flex their muscles. As a result of the fierce battle for market domination between Miller Brewing and Anheuser-Busch—the so-called Beer Wars—A/B found itself outbid for the beer category in MLB network games. Smarting from the defeat, and foreclosed from such an important sales vehicle, the Cardinals' Gussie Busch leaned on Kuhn to pressure ABC and NBC into eliminating Miller's hard-won exclusivity. Kuhn declined, and thereby lost another vote. Busch and Turner formed an alliance whose purpose was to deliver the MLB package to Superstation WTBS; the bid failed, but the two men never repaired their split with Kuhn. Later that same year, Kuhn had to foil a plan by A/B to create and sponsor a package of 52 Cardinals and Yankees games, to be carried nationally on ESPN. The plan would, he was certain, constitute a violation of the ABC and NBC contracts he was charged with enforcing.

In 1983, NBC made an attempt to recapture its former position as the exclusive network of Major League Baseball. Considering the ever-growing problem of the superstations, satellite delivery systems, and cable, true exclusivity was probably wishful thinking. Added to Roone Arledge's intense, almost obsessive competitive instincts, the thought of driving ABC out of baseball must have been doomed to futility and failure. In any event, NBC made a pre-emptive bid of $550 million for six years to renew its part of the MLB package, and offered a flat $1 billion to buy back its former exclusivity, should ABC fail to pay its share. Whether this strategy was based on NBC's honest evaluation of the future advertising revenues available to support network baseball, or it was, as some suggest, a clever ploy intended to impoverish ABC just prior to the bidding for the Seoul Olympics, NBC simply miscalculated. ABC accepted the challenge, and agreed to pay $575 million for its share of the package.

The resulting total of $1.2 bilion in rights fees meant $4 million per club annually—double the previous amount. Ironically, this contract, which was the high-water mark of Kuhn's tenure, was also his last significant act as commissioner. To achieve the huge payout, the contract had been modeled to a great extent on the NFL's: it favored the networks by eliminating any local telecasts opposite network games, and it called for the abandonment of the USA network's Thursday night package; these two provisions propped up network advertising rates by reducing the total amount of national commercial inventory available for sale. What was worse, in the eyes of the disaffected owners, it seemed to link the growth in rights fees to the increased centralization of power under the commissioner. Although some teams still earned more money from local contracts than they did as a result of the network deal, their owners were more suspicious than ever that Kuhn's future course might lead further in the direction of the NFL model, possibly including restraints on their sacred local television revenues.

The advent of free-agency threatened to unbalance the competitiveness of the leagues, as star players made themselves available to the highest bidder—usually a team sitting atop immense local television and cable revenues. Kuhn, troubled by the implications of the revenue disparity among franchises, had begun discussing a system of modified revenue-sharing, somewhat similar to the NFL's. Of course, to many baseball owners it was anathema because it embodied two things they didn't want: a limit on local television and an all-powerful commissioner who controlled the purse-strings. The growing anti-Kuhn sentiment was led by those owners most closely associated with media ownership or superstations (they felt most threatened by any infringement on their prerogatives to maximize television income.) Although they were in the minority, the dissidents controlled just enough votes to foreclose his reappointment as commissioner, and he was unceremoniously dumped in 1983.

Peter Ueberroth, flushed with the success of planning the Los Angeles Summer Olympics of 1984, was named the next Baseball Commissioner. A man of unquestioned media and marketing skills, he seemed baseball's long-sought answer to Pete Rozelle, and was swept into office on a wave of favorable publicity and expressions of cooperation and good-will from the owners. Almost immediately, however, he had to begin confronting two intractable problems, both legacies of the Kuhn years. First was the inescapable fact that the billion-dollar 1983 contract was proving a disaster for NBC and ABC. The former was losing money, and the latter was abandoning ship, cutting back on telecasts and openly wishing the contract would expire sooner. Future negotiations will assuredly be tougher, with the vivid prospect of actual reductions in rights payments. The second problem facing Ueberroth was the rambunctious and growing group of media-related owners (Gaylord Broadcasting had just tried to buy the Texas Rangers) and the problems of cable and superstations they represented. In short, the new commissioner had inherited a fifty-year-old tradition of hostility towards authority, in an era when the economic survival of MLB, based as it is on television, seemed to demand it.

Successive baseball commissioners learned the hard way that, the more they seized the reins of power, the more they acted like a real commissioner, the more likely they sowed the seeds of their own destruction. The independent-minded entrepreneurs who owned professional franchises would not tolerate what they regarded as the usurpation of their properly selfish business prerogatives. Amateur sports, on the other hand, could be distinguished from such crass behavior by their dedication to the maintenance of organizations like the National Collegiate Athletic Association (NCAA), which stood to protect the idealism of amateur sports, and represented the common interests of its member schools. In reality, though, the NCAA would be profoundly shaken by a long-simmering dispute in many ways resembling baseball's. Its root causes could be traced to familiar issues—the control of television rights and revenues, and the centralization of authority—which troubled the organization for thirty years before boiling over into open revolt.

College football had always enjoyed a special status among American sports, representing as it did the squeaky-clean image of student athletes, harmless good fun, and educational tradition. For many years it was the only football game in town, facing little opposition from other fall sports, including various early attempts at professional football. It is difficult for many present-day fans to understand that professional football, especially the NFL, labored under a severe image problem in comparison with the NCAA games; pro ball was considered unseemly, full of questionable characters, shakily financed, unimaginative, and dull. It could not compete against the NCAA for attendance, hoopla, news coverage, or fan support until the late fifties, when their relative positions began to reverse. Just as important, the NCAA version held sway over an audience much more to the liking of sponsors and advertisers, who were drawn to upscale demographics.

College football was first televised in 1939 (Princeton versus Columbia), and the broadcasts grew steadily in popularity—particularly among the fans and alumni of the "prestige" schools. There was little regulation or oversight by any governing body, and each school was virtually free to make whatever television arrangements it desired. As early as 1948, however, the first rumblings were heard inside the NCAA, as some members expressed concern that television was diminishing ticket sales and gate attendance. These worries were buttressed by a public opinion survey which indicated that 50 percent of those responding felt watching a game on television was equal or superior to seeing it at the stadium. By 1950 the University of Pennsylvania and Notre Dame had signed national television contracts—with ABC and DuMont respectively—and many other schools had local or regional packages. Some Saturdays, viewers might be able to watch as many as eight different games. In response to the deluge, the Big Ten banned television, hoping to protect the gate, and the NCAA formed a television committee to recommend policies. To this point, their actions paralleled to a remarkable degree those of their brethren in professional baseball. Despite all the endorsements of the amateur ideal, the members were acting more and more like businessmen. This growing internal tension between lofty idealism and hard nosed reality was to bedevil the NCAA until the late seventies, when major football powers rose in organized revolt, formed the College Football Association (CFA), and in 1982 threw off what they regarded as the shackles of commercial restraint.

The television committee commissioned a survey by the National Opinion Research Center (NORC), which reported that television tended to diminish attendance by nearly 40 percent. In response, the NCAA began to limit the number of games on television and to restrain each school's appearances. It signed a $700,000 sponsorship with Westinghouse (which chose to air the games on NBC), stipulating no more than seven games per season in each region of the country, and limiting each team to one network appearance per year. The selective blackouts and other restrictions had a quite predictable effect: they aroused the animosity of several constituencies which considered themselves injured by the new rules. Fans of big-time schools were outraged that they could not see their favorites often enough, and the schools felt unfairly deprived of potential income. Advertisers claimed the greatly reduced inventory of commercial availabilities drove up prices and unjustly favored Westinghouse. Broadcasters (other than NBC, of course) felt shut out of popular programming, and politicians rose in indignation to decry this disenfranchisement of the voting public's "right" to see football on television. All these arguments would echo through the dispute as it built up steam over the next thirty years.

The defense of these television policies fell most heavily on the shoulders of the new Executive Director, Walter Byers. Appointed in 1952, Byers was granted powers which would have seemed extraordinary to most baseball commissioners, and he was to use them with a clever ruthlessness for three decades. He needed a broad mandate, because in addition to the fractious television issue the NCAA faced a related, potentially more damaging problem: the erosion of its public image. A series of point-shaving scandals and academic indiscretions, first in basketball and later football, rocked colleges and universities; charges of "professionalism" clouded the athletic programs at several major powers. Byers had to fend off calls for government investigations of the scandals on one hand and calls for anti-trust actions against the television policy on the other. He effectively rallied the political clout of the member schools, and waged a successful long-term effort to convince the Congress that the NCAA could clean up its own act and that the television policy was the lesser of two evils, considering the "damage" unrestricted television would do.

Things were less sanguine behind the scenes at the NCAA. The two original network teams, Notre Dame and Pennsylvania, fought the restrictions from the beginning. Notre Dame called them "groundless," citing the fact that they had sold out all their home games for the previous three years despite televising them. Penn simply announced they would ignore the NCAA and proceed with televising all the games called for in their $75,000 ABC contract. The NCAA, led by Byers, reacted by suspending Penn and demanding its opponents drop the Quakers from their schedules; enough of them complied to force Penn into backing down. After many angry words and loud protestations, the NCAA had won its battle, but the heartbeat of an embryonic CFA could be heard faintly beating.

In 1955 another precursor of the CFA emerged. The Big Ten was limited to one national game under the $1.3 million network contract, at a time when the conference was receiving outside offers of a million dollars for a full schedule of its games. Politicians readily seized the politically popular issue, and in seven states they introduced legislation compelling the state universities to televise all their games. Perhaps shedding crocodile tears, the affected schools prepared to obey the mandates of their governments, which were "forcing" them to accept all that extra television money. This time, the NCAA backed away from a confrontation, and it installed a mixed regional-national plan permitting a maximum of three appearances per year. This system was to remain in place for seventeen years, until some of the same arguments and opponents brought it down in federal courts. Its adoption ushered in a period of relative peace within the organization, and sustained increases in rights fees for the televised schools, NBC's payments increased from $700,000 in 1952 to $3 million in 1960, most of which went to the participating big schools. Teams not appearing on television not only saw a tiny fraction of the money; their attendance was probably damaged by the availability of nationally attractive television games. They protested and called for some form of revenue sharing, only to be ridiculed as "socialistic" by the major powers. Eventually, to keep the peace, Byers was able to force the reluctant networks to accept a few "marginal" games per year involving smaller schools.

Tom Moore and Edgar Scherick were joining forces with Craig Smith at about the same time: a very formidable combination of talent and money which would alter the balance of television sports. ABC landed the Gillette account, worth some $8.5 million, and decided to use a portion of this war chest to go after NCAA football. An outright bidding war with the incumbent NBC was out of the question, because NBC probably had more money in petty cash than anything ABC or Gillette could afford. Moreover, the cozy relationship which had developed over the years between Byers's NCAA and NBC meant any competing bid would have to be significantly better than NBC's to succeed, and that NBC would, in all probability, be given every chance to match it. Accordingly, Scherick and Moore came up with an ingenious subterfuge to finesse the rights away from NBC. The plan succeeded, becoming a legendary milestone in the rise of ABC Sports.

The NCAA announced it would award its television rights after opening sealed bids from prospective buyers. Scherick guessed correctly that the supremely confident NBC representatives, led by Tom Gallery, would arrive at the meeting with two bids, sealed in separate envelopes. If they recognized a competing high-bidder in the room, they were to lay down their own high bid, but if no such competitor showed up, the low bid was called for. Scherick designated an unknown ABC accountant named Stanley Frankel, who was selected because he was the sort of person no one would notice in a crowd, to carry ABC's one and only bid into the meeting. Frankel was instructed to blend into the drapery until NBC had placed its bid on the table; he carried off the assignment perfectly. NBC's low bid was placed before the NCAA poobahs, and both sides began to congratulate each other about extending their happy relationship. At that moment, Stan Frankel emerged from obscurity for one shining moment, and placed the upstart ABC's winning $3 million bid on the table—to the shock and dismay of the NCAA as much as NBC. The committee retired hurriedly to a back-room conference, but emerged shortly with the grim news that ABC's victory would stand.

The next major problem facing the Scherick/ABC team was that of affiliates and program clearance: put simply, the network came up short on both counts. ABC had perhaps 20 percent less national clearance than NBC or CBS, and too many of the affiliates were on the UHF band (to say they were on the "UHF Dial" only highlighted their problem, as many American television sets of the day did not even have a UHF dial), which meant inferior reception where it was available at all. Finally, too many of the affiliates were located in small markets. Advertisers exacted a "penalty" when buying time on ABC, discounting the ABC advertising rates to account for the lower audience figures. ABC could not do much in the short term to improve the state of its affiliates, so Moore and Scherick set about getting clearance from NBC and CBS affiliates, particularly those in the South, where college football was king. Their pitch was so successful that some of the stations were willing to clear other ABC programming as well in order to get the NCAA games.

Scherick now set about assembling a production team to handle the games, as neither he nor ABC had a competent staff on hand. Remarkably, he was able to select and train as fine a group of young producers and directors as ever entered the business; they included Chet Simmons, Chuck Howard, and Jim Spence, all of whom would go on to hold senior executive positions at the networks. And as Producer of the NCAA games, he hired a twenty-nine-year-old unknown who had previously produced an NBC children's program: Roone Arledge. The young man had caught Scherick's eye with an audition tape entitled "For Men Only," which revealed the bare bones of the anthology format later perfected for "Wide World of Sports," and a number of innovative and attention-getting production techniques, which enlivened the program. Working for a salary of $10,000, Arledge soon began applying those now-familiar production techniques to the NCAA games: double the usual number of cameras, crowd and sideline shots, multiple microphones, more aggressive on-air talent (he insisted, over the objections of Byers, on the right to select the announcers), promotion, and a sense of "taking the game to the fan." To say that this approach contrasted sharply with the conservative, almost passive coverage by NBC and CBS is an understatement. Arledge's first telecast aired September 17, 1960, a turning point in the history of television sports. It would be an exaggeration to say the sponsors shared Scherick's enthusiasm for Arledge's blossoming talents. In fact, they objected vigorously to the notion that a green "kid" was producing, and were mollified only when Scherick, assured them (untruthfully) that he, not Arledge, was producer of the telecasts. The NCAA, which had never wanted ABC in the first place, also refused to be impressed, and in 1962 delivered its rights to CBS for $5.1 million.

NBC recaptured the prize in 1964–65, offering $6.52 million annually. The cost of rights continued to escalate during the decade, eventually reaching $12 million in 1970. Money talked, and with all three networks bidding against each other, the days of sneaking accountants into the room were over; ABC would have to pay top dollar from now on if it wanted to compete. By 1964, both NBC and CBS were deeply committed to pro football packages. Not only did this diminish their bankrolls, it filled their weekends with football, straining their production capacity in the process. More ominously, their pro contracts offended the sensibilities of Walter Byers, who regarded professional football not only as a rival but as an unhealthy influence on the football scene. To him, it represented everything that was wrong with professional athletics, and he was not prepared to rub shoulders with it by sharing a network. Of course, NCAA football had its own share of ethical, legal, and public relations problems—then, as now—but to Byers, the hired hands playing pro ball were a nothing less than a threat to decency, idealism, and The American Way.

Arledge, angling to regain the NCAA contract, sweetened his bid by promising Byers that, if ABC got the exclusive rights, it would stay out of pro football. This was a somewhat disingenuous promise, as ABC had already carried the American Football League in 1961–62. Nevertheless, he successfully appealed to Byers's vanity by implying that, while NCAA football would always take a back seat to the professional game on CBS and NBC, it would be number one at ABC. Arledge's combination of guile and largesse proved persuasive, and ABC got the contract. Although he violated his promise in 1970, when ABC introduced Monday Night Football, ABC would retain the exclusive rights until 1982. However, soothing Byers's anger at the betrayal would add to the cost of renewals in the years after 1970.

Byers was not above playing a little hardball himself, for he was a very tough, almost imperious bargainer, even by network standards. Few ABC executives relished the prospect of baiting the old bear in his Shawnee Mission, Kansas, lair, or confronting him across the bargaining table. Sometimes, however, a confrontation could not be avoided. In 1968, ABC had lost nearly $1.8 million on the NCAA package. By 1970 the shortfall had become $4.5 million. Despite this, Byers continually demanded—and received—annual increases averaging a million dollars per year. ABC wasn't alone in bearing the burden of increased college football costs: in 1960 NBC had paid the Rose Bowl $500,000, which grew to $7 million in 1983. Even minor bowls were getting $500,000 each. Byers approached the 1970–71 renewal negotiations determined to push rights fees even higher, even though he knew ABC's NCAA schedule had been losing money in recent years. He also wanted to spread the gravy around to other NCAA sports besides football. His demands included an additional twenty-six weeks of non-football NCAA event coverage during the winter and spring: much of it, including many intercollegiate championships in such sports as swimming and diving, track and field, gymnastics and wrestling, would become staple features on Wide World of Sports.

When negotiations commenced, ABC indicated it wanted a post-season championship added to the package. Long a cherished dream of network sports, such a playoff system would attract very high ratings, extend the season, and produce sufficient additional advertising income to make the entire NCAA package profitable. When the NCAA refused, ABC suddenly sprung the news of its accord with the NFL. Byers, betrayed and angry, responded by lifting the unofficial ban the NCAA had placed on NBC four years earlier for the same offense of cozying up to pro ball (in NBC's case, the AFL). NBC seized the invitation to bid and offered a remarkable turnabout: it proposed that a clause be inserted in the contract prohibiting any network already carrying pro football from holding the NCAA rights. Since NBC held the AFL rights, this proposal meant either that it was willing to abandon pro football for the NCAA, or it was a colossal bluff. In any event, the NCAA attorneys quickly recognized it for what it was—a clear anti-trust problem—and declined to include it. NBC was also willing to offer a considerable increase in payments, which would either secure the rights, or at the very least drive ABC costs still higher.

There is no indication that Byers and NBC collaborated to put the squeeze on ABC, but both certainly enjoyed watching the leverage being applied. The NCAA set its "take it or leave it" asking price at $12 million, which was a lot of money in light of the outlays ABC had just committed to the NFL, and considering that the network had been losing money on the NCAA while paying much less. Arledge balked (or bluffed, depending on whose version you believe) and talked about dropping the NCAA. However, when the affiliates heard of this prospect, they objected, unwilling to lose all those lucrative local commercial slots they inserted in the games. Arledge relented, but he devised a plan under which the affiliates would be paid lower station compensation fees to carry the games. They would be forced to back their words with action, and carry some part of the network's burden. The lowered station compensation reduced ABC's expenses enough to permit meeting Byers's figure.

ABC had long been saddled with the NCAA's insistence upon televising as many of the 138 "major" football powers as possible, while also granting some exposure to small schools, which ABC offered on a regional basis. For the network, this was a no-win situation. The regional game would, of course, pre-empt the national game in some part of the country, and most football fans were outraged to see, for example, Harvard-Dartmouth instead of Notre Dame-Southern California. Ratings for the regional games were often lower, costing both the network and its affiliates advertising revenue. In addition, it was a public relations disaster for ABC, which was the object of ridicule from newspapers, local commentators, and the average fan; few of whom took the time to understand that it was the NCAA not ABC, which insisted on the policy. By 1971, however, the NCAA, perhaps sensitive to ABC's predicament, began to soften its position somewhat. Although it would not give in to the network's desire to televise only the most attractive teams all the time, it did let them appear more often. ABC was given the right to select its game just twelve days before kickoff, and to insert an additional minute of commercials in each game. Otherwise, the main aspects of the NCAA television policy remained in place, as they had since Penn and Notre Dame first disputed them.

The NCAA's efforts at conciliation were too little, too late for the football powers, who in 1976 formed the CFA to organize and represent their interests within the larger organization. Months of fruitless discussions followed, as the small but financially important CFA locked horns with the numerically larger non-television schools, while the NCAA and Byers tried to keep the lid on an increasingly volatile situation. About the only thing he could do to was to deliver more and more ABC money, hoping to enlarge the size of the pie being shared among so many members. In 1977, it would cost ABC $120 million for a four-year pact, which was about as high as it could go, considering production costs and advertising revenues. When the agreement expired, the NCAA again sought to demonstrate its ability to bring in money—and perhaps, as well, to foreclose the possibility of a CFA breakaway by locking up several networks at once—by splitting the package among ABC, CBS, and WTBS for an annual total of $74.3 million. At the same time, the NCAA offered more concessions: each team could now appear six times, the networks got five additional commercial minutes (for a total of 26), and teams whose conference didn't appear in a television game were cut out of any revenue sharing. It was, at best, a holding action, and it could not succeed for very long. The CFA's pent-up grievances and impatience with the incremental pace of change had built sufficient momentum to land them in Federal Court, seeking their independence from the NCAA.

Despite numerous close calls with potential anti-trust actions through the years, the NCAA had neglected to get a written waiver like baseball's, or to lobby for inclusion in the 1961 Sports Broadcast Act, which it saw as necessary only for professional sports, that were, after all businesses. It clung to the naive belief (or perhaps self-delusion) that the

NCAA was not a business, per se, despite practices which year by year clearly had become more business-like. The distinction was an important matter of principle to Byers and his organization, and it accounted for much of their hostility towards professional football. It also blinded them to their own evolution into a monopoly. They were stunned when Judge Burciaga fund the NCAA to be a "classic cartel" and stripped it of its power to involuntarily control the television rights of member schools. His ruling, later upheld by the Supreme Court, effectively deregulated the college football business, and schools scrambled to set up their own packages in the free marketplace.

The realities of that marketplace provided a rude awakening for the victorious litigants. There were plenty of interested television producers out there waiting to buy the rights to games. Unfortunately, the sellers vastly outnumbered the buyers, and in the competition for air time the price of rights plummeted. The lucky teams took what amounted to a 50 percent cut in rights fees. The unlucky ones disappeared from television altogether. In the aftermath of the long fight, amidst the wreckage of both his centralized system and the CFA's comparative free-for-all, Walter Byers stepped down, and quietly left the scene. He had held sway over television policies for some thirty years. Ironically, his tenure would likely be matched by only one man—Pete Rozelle, who presided over professional football's eclipse of the NCAA game and raised centralized control to a high art.

Professional football's image problems were such that for many years it ranked fourth in popularity among major sports, behind baseball, college football, and even boxing. Until the mid-fifties, teams rarely made money, and in the first thirty-five years of the NFL's existence, some forty franchises had come and gone. The initial, tentative steps toward television followed the now-familiar pattern of individual franchises pursuing their own policies. As early as 1948, the Chicago Bears televised six home games but earned a total profit of less than a thousand dollars on the venture. Three years later the Bears and Chicago Cardinals formed an 11-city ad hoc network, with the Chicago ABC station as its flagship. Things went so badly they had to pay stations in Louisville and St. Louis to carry the games, and the teams ended up losing money. Even the peripatetic Edgar Scherick couldn't breathe life into the network—he convinced Falstaff to put up $2000 per week in sponsorship (the network covered the core of Falstaff's prime marketing area), but ABC was too weak and disinterested to pursue the idea. For that matter, the entire NFL made only $50,000 from television in 1951.

CBS and NBC ignored the league, so DuMont was left to carry the games: five in 1951, rising to twelve in 1954. DuMont was also able to purchase the rights to the league championship game from 1951 to 1953 for only $95,000 per year. The televised games began to grow in popularity, so that by 1954 they averaged nearly a 37 share (there were many fewer TV household then), and NBC and CBS started paying attention. The following year CBS, bankrolled by Falstaff, bought a regular season schedule for a million dollars, and NBC took the championship game. All these contracts were negotiated directly with the participating teams, and there was no revenue sharing. Even so, according to NFL Commissioner Bert Bell, broadcast revenues from all sources (radio and, television, both local and network) amounted to only 15 percent of the franchises' revenues during the early fifties. It was a time of relative innocence for television and the NFL; the former was gingerly experimenting with sports, mostly at the behest of outsiders like Craig Smith and Edgar Scherick, and the latter was still being run like a sleepy suburban country club, under the genial leadership of Bert Bell.

The central office of the National Football League actually consisted of two rooms in a country club just outside Philadelphia, which was adequate space, considering that Commissioner Bell and a secretary were the only two employees of the head office. Most important decisions were made on the telephone, or in meetings with the small group of influential franchise owners. This key group consisted of families which shared common ethnic, social, and business backgrounds, and which held each other in high esteem. The names are now familiar: Halas, Mara, Rooney, and Marshall, among them. Their approach to policy-making was, compared with baseball, refreshingly collegial, and they tried to work out problems amongst themselves, or in conjunction with Bell. Perhaps the difficult rocky road the league had traveled convinced them that they didn't have all the answers. Whatever the reason, the NFL owners favored a commissioner with a solid business background, and they seemed more willing to cede authority to him. This tendency would suit perfectly his energetic successor.

It is widely believed that 1958 marked a turning point for the fortunes of the league. The dramatic, sudden-death championship between the Colts and the Giants was a television triumph; some 30 million viewers saw Alan "The Horse" Ameche's winning plunge. More importantly, the game went a long way towards convincing the skeptical New York advertising community that the league should be taken seriously as a business venture. One other, little-noticed event that year marked the NFL's growing accommodation with television advertising. Commissioner Bell institutionalized the infamous "TV time-out," whch had been experimentally introduced in 1955. From now on, the advertisers knew their interests would be protected by the league, and the precedent of "staging" the games for the benefit of television had been set (the other classic artificial interruption, the "two-minute warning" would debut in a 1969 AFL game). The suddenly bright prospects for NFL prosperity encouraged a new wave of applicants for expansion franchises, but there was little disposition among the incumbent owners to proceed very quickly in that direction. Impatient in their eagerness to acquire franchises in rapidly growing areas of the country, the disappointed applicants decided to form their own league.

The American Football League was born in 1960 out of frustration. Its organizers and owners included a few men of extraordinary wealth, such as Lamar Hunt and Bud Adams, both scions of Texas oil families, who had been denied NFL franchises, and were willing to underwrite a competitive venture. They had to dig deeply into their ample financial reserves, because the AFL lost more than $3 million its first year, and several franchises were shaky, to put it mildly. Other owners were badly undercapitalized, their resources stretched to the breaking point by the investment and operating expenses of the venture. Attendance was low, the quality of play mediocre, and the league had no recognizable "star" players. In addition, the NFL reacted harshly, dangling the prospect of its own, much more valuable expansion franchises to keep important cities away from the AFL. This predatory policy—which would be used again in the 1970s against the World Football League, and in the 1980s against the United States Football League—proved successful. The NFL awarded franchises to Dallas—thereby driving Hunt's Dallas Texans to Kansas City—and to Minneapolis, thus foreclosing the proposed AFL franchise there. To be taken seriously, and to provide desperately needed public exposure, the AFL simply had to have a television contract. It also needed the money just to survive.

The networks hadn't exactly rushed after the AFL rights. CBS, well entrenched with the comparatively mighty NFL, wasn't interested, nor was NBC, and DuMont was weakening as a national network. That left Tom Moore's ABC, which, although chronically short of cash, was busily giving life to Ed Sherick's dreams of a major network sports division. Still working out of his dingy SPI offices across town, Scherick was known to be on the prowl for ABC, a sort of unofficial stalking-horse for Moore. The two men agreed to meet with the AFL's designated representative, the mercurial Harry Wismer, to discuss a possible rights purchase. One hopes that Moore and Scherick had an appreciation of good theatre (they must have, to have concocted the Stan Frankel impersonation of a potted plant), because what transpired at that meeting was nothing less than a tragicomic tour de force, starring the erstwhile AFL negotiator as himself.

They should have known something unusual was going to happen when Wismer gave them specific instructions to follow a complicated and circuitous route to his apartment, including deliberate doubling-back and seemingly aimless wandering; he even talked about their wearing disguises to the meeting. As they were shortly to learn, Wismer was full of vaguely paranoid conspiratorial theories and tended towards unpredictable behavior. Thoroughly nonplussed, Moore and Sherick followed the instructions, made it safely to the apartment, and got down to business, offering to pay $800,000 per year for the AFL rights. When he heard that low figure, Wismer flew into a histrionic rage, declared the meeting adjourned, and stormed out. Unfortunately, his dramatic performance had two flaws: he was storming out of his own apartment, and he went through the wrong door, ending up for the next ten minutes in a hallway closet.

Not long thereafter, he was replaced by Music Corporation of America president David "Sonny" Werblin, who enjoyed a good reputation in the entertainment industry, and could speak the language of television when bargaining in behalf of the owners. Werblin convinced Moore to raise his bid to $1.7 million annually, over five years, and the deal was signed. ABC got the inexpensive programming it was seeking, and the AFL got a life-line, albeit a fragile one. The teams continued to run up deficits, the league as a whole was awash in red ink, but ABC managed to profit over the life of the contract. Interestingly, this pattern would be repeated twenty years later by ABC and the USFL. The ABC money really wasn't enough to make a difference to the owners, because after being evenly divided among them, each received only about $170,000 per year. The NFL was unimpressed by the size of the contract, but Pete Rozelle, who had just taken over from Bert Bell following the latter's heart attack, instantly recognized the significance of its formulation.

Wismer and Werblin had been authorized by the owners to pool the franchises' individual rights for the purposes of negotiating a unified, league-wide contract. At the urging of Lamar Hunt, the other owners had further agreed to the equalized distribution of network revenues—revenue sharing. In theory, anyway, this system would better provide for franchises in small markets (or those otherwise undercapitalized) to compete on an even footing with the rich and powerful ones, including Hunt's own. It also placed more responsibility in the hands of the Commissioner, who now had the important function of handling relations with television. Rozelle, on the other hand, had inherited a league in which each team controlled its own rights, and many had built sizable regional networks. The Giants, on DuMont, owned New England, the Redskins the Southeast, and the Rams the West Coast. CBS held the rights to all but four teams, at a cost of $1.5 million. Chicago, which still had two teams, was blacked out most of the time, since most Sundays either the Bears or Cardinals were playing at home. Some team had no television package at all. The scrambled situation had to be straightened out for Rozelle to strike a network deal structured like the AFL's.

Rozelle had to hit the ground running, and in 1960 much of his time, prodigious energy, and powers of persuasion were devoted to the problems and potential of television. His professional background in public relations and management with the Los Angeles Rams had convinced him of the key role the mass media would play in the "selling" of the league, and he made the care and feeding of the media and key politicians a major emphasis of his management strategy. His skills would develop to the point that only the legendary Arledge was thought to match him in creativity and toughness at the negotiating table. It is not unusual even today to hear other major figures in the industry wistfully wish they could, just once, overhear the private negotiations between Arledge and Rozelle: one said it would probably remind him if King Kong versus Godzilla. That they emerged the two heavyweights of the business is beyond question, and when they grappled for position, each trying to maneuver the other into a position so competitive it would restrain his demands, they dominated the landscape. Sparks sometimes flew, but out of their relationship came many of the most original, creative, and expensive ways to package and present television sports. The contracts thus arrived at often set the standard for everyone else's, and were the starting point, or frame of reference, for many competitors' own negotiations.

The NFL has a standing Television Committee, which is charged with developing television policy in conjunction with the commissioner. In the Rozelle era the committee has often taken a back seat to the commissioner, although the final authority remains in their hands, and a vote of all franchise owners must be obtained before policies are implemented or contracts signed. The commissioner's dominance of the process and his high-profile management style make it easier to describe the history of rights negotiations on his watch in personal terms, to say, "Rozelle" when, strictly speaking, it means "Rozelle, with the agreement of the Television Committee and support of other owners," took a certain bargaining position, or made certain demands. This is not to indicate that he often acted unilaterally, but there was rarely any disagreement from his owners, who were usually only too happy to unleash him on the networks, and watch him shake the money tree.

The commissioner began by contacting major CBS affiliates, encouraging them to clear a proposed network schedule of games. This would make it easier for the network and advertisers to realize the profits they needed to undertake the venture. He reminded the NFL owners to conform to "league think" and to take actions for the collective benefit of all, including pooling their rights. He explained the advertisers' reluctance resulting from the effective blackout of Chicago, the nation's second-largest market, and got the owners to support the Cardinals' transfer to St. Louis. Part of the $500,000 the team received came from the other owners, part from CBS, which saw a major impediment to its proposed football network removed. Rozelle soon got his wish, and CBS signed a unified, national contract with the NFL, guaranteeing each franchise about twice as much as their AFL counterparts were getting.

The joy in league headquarters (now moved to a modern office in Manhattan) was short-lived, however. The unified contracts soon attracted the notice of Federal Judge Alan Grim, who ruled them to be in violation of the anti-trust statutes. Rozelle's immediate task became the lobbying of Congress for legislative relief. Although representatives of other sports leagues joined the effort, Rozelle was by far the most aggressive and effective spokesman—he had to be, since the NFL was the prime target of Judge Grim's ruling, and stood to lose the most from it. Baseball already enjoyed a special anti-trust exemption, and the notion of the NHL or NBA being offered lucrative network contracts was distant, at best. The AFL seemed to enjoy the court's sympathy, perhaps because of its underdog status, or because its success would reduce the NFL's hegemony over pro football, and thus was a mixed blessing, in anti-trust terms. His efforts were rewarded by the passage of the 1961 Sports Broadcasting Act, which permitted the pooling of rights for the purposes he desired. Following the passage of the Act, CBS signed a renewal agreement, which cost it more than $4.0 million, double the previous amount. The lure of exclusivity, and the power of Rozelle to bargain in behalf of all the franchises, had already been demonstrated.

Nielsen ratings for the NFL rose some 50 percent between 1961 and 1963, and all three networks decided to bid on the NFL rights beginning in 1964. CBS wanted to retain its profitable investment, NBC was attempting to wrest it away, and ABC had grown weary of the AFL's slow, uneven progress towards mediocrity and popularity. NBC offered $13.2 million per year but was nudged out by CBS's final bid of $14.1 million to retain the NFL for each of two years, a figure that exceeded the owners' fondest expectations. Given the razor-thin margin of CBS's victory, NBC bitterly suspected someone must have tipped off CBS to the NBC figure, allowing it to raise its own numbers accordingly. What really made them suspicious, however, was that fact that even poor-boy ABC had topped NBC's bid—something they could not believe would have happened without some "inside" information. While CBS may have been tipped off, it was willing to go that high because it correctly interpreted the omission in the contract of any prohibition against doubleheaders to mean that they would be permitted. The Sunday doubleheaders could double the network's potential income. This contract, shared as it was among all the franchises, is often cited as the savior of the Green Bay franchise, whose continued existence in so small a market would otherwise have been impossible; shortly thereafter, the Packers began their long domination of the league.

The fallout from these negotiations was widespread and important. Rozelle, always seeking to engage as much bidding competition among as many networks as possible, began discussions with ABC about Friday night football. ABC showed some interest in the idea, but apparently was dissuaded by its friends at the NCAA, who were outraged by the infringement on Friday-night high-school football which had been offered some protection in the 1961 Sports Broadcasting Act. Besides, the NCAA still saw the high schools as its natural allies against pro football, and was eager to support their interests. Also in 1964, Sonny Werblin reappeared on the AFL scene, this time buying the nearly bankrupt New York Titans from Harry Wismer, and signaling his intention to strengthen the all-important New York franchise, now renamed the Jets. Werblin also recognized the need for a major influx of television money, and he soon found willing partners. NBC's Robert Kintner and Carl Lindemann, still steaming over the recent NFL negotiations, shocked nearly everyone by agreeing to a five-year, $42 million contract with the AFL. Their anger was not cooled much by the rumor that their secret bid had been shown to Tom Moore by AFL Commissioner Joe Foss (perhaps out of loyalty to the AFL's orginal network). Everybody seemed to be getting "insider" information except NBC, and for many years a feeling would persist at the network that the deck was stacked against them. Foss would certainly have been pleased if a bidding war could be stimulated between the two, but ABC declined, saying that at those prices it would lose $5 million annually. Once the NBC contract was signed, the war between the networks and their client leagues would henceforth be a more even match. NBC, by guaranteeing the AFL long-term national exposure as well as an influx of cash, enabled the league to sign many of the brightest collegiate stars; Werblin himself went after Alabama quarterback Joe Namath, signed him to a record pro-football contract—and the rest, as they say, is history.

By 1967, there appeared no realistic prospect of a bidding war for the NFL rights. ABC had made its major commitment to the NCAA, NBC was committed to the AFL, and that left CBS alone as a prospective network. Always searching for ways to increase competition and thereby drive up rights, Rozelle began talking of the NFL establishing its own network to carry the games. Ironically, some of the money which would be used to fund such a venture would come from previous CBS rights payments. The possibility—threat, really—of an NFL Network would thereafter remain a sharp arrow in Rozelle's quiver. Using it, Rozelle could, effectively, bid for his own rights, daring the networks to call it a bluff. The structure of the hypothetical NFL Network has undergone revision through the years, and these days it is usually described as a pay-cable venture. He did offer CBS a carrot along with the stick: permission to broadcast an out-of-town game into the market of a blacked-out team playing at home. The combination of incentives and threats proved sufficient to induce a two-year bid of $18.8 million annually, plus an additional $2 million each for the two championship games.

Having paid the piper, CBS was especially shocked a few months later, when the two leagues announced their intention to merge and to play a new, "Super" championship game—CBS's $2 million championships, though already paid for, were immediately reduced in value. The merger received the blessings of the government, embodied in the Football Merger Act. The first Super Bowl (that name didn't really attach itself to the event, nor sprout Roman numerals for a couple of years) was actually televised by both CBS and NBC, since each had its own league's contract; after that, they began alternating coverage. Interestingly, they (later to include ABC) spare no expense in producing the telecasts, despite the fact there really has been no competition for the rights to Super Bowls since the rotation sytem was put in place. The game became, like the Olympics, a contest of production skills and budgetary overkill, to some degree designed to impress peers and colleagues at the other networks.

With NBC and CBS now safely on board the NFL express, Rozelle perceived the need to balance more evenly the relative value of the two networks' investments. NBC had not profited from the AFL contract and had lost over a million dollars in 1968. It had included additional revenue-producing commercials by inventing the two-minute warning, but that didn't solve the real problem, which was one of market size. NBC brought into the NFL smaller television markets than those allied with the NFC and CBS, and suffered a permanent "ADI discount" (Area of Dominant Influence is the Nielsen Ratings term for an individual local market). Advertisers would discount NBC's rates as a result of its reduced national audience delivery, thus dooming NBC to perpetually lower income. Rozelle solved the problem by convincing the owners that three major market NFC franchises—Baltimore, Pittsburgh, and Cleveland—should switch conferences to even things out somewhat for NBC. In exchange, he indicated, teams would enjoy an additional $1.5 million in TV revenues from the newly strengthened NBC. One unexpected snag in the partitioning of the league was that Chrysler (the major sponsor closely identified with the old AFL teams) and Ford (in the same position vis-à-vis the original NFL franchises) resisted the "mixing" of franchises, which they felt would dilute the audience identification so important to their marketing plans. Rozelle's exquisite political skills soon brought everyone around to the idea, and the "league think" policy triumphed again.

Rozelle's power and reputation were now soaring. His clever manipulation of the networks and the rapid increase in television revenues, had the owners in his thrall. They gave him full rein, and their Television Committee could only admire how everything he touched seem to turn to gold. They would not be disappointed, for his boldest stroke was yet to come. Rozelle had begun experimenting with prime-time games in 1966, as he saw the need to cultivate additional revenue sources. That year, he had persuaded CBS to broadcast four pre-season and one regular-season game, with inconclusive results. However, two games in 1968 and two the next year had averaged a strong audience share. Following the merger, he once again turned his attention to the project.

To his dismay, none of the networks jumped at the chance. NBC, to whom he first took the idea as part of the strategy of overcoming the "ADI discount," was not interested in pre-empting its Monday entertainment lineup, particularly Tonight Show host Johnny Carson, who threatened to quit if his program were shortened to accommodate football. CBS was unwilling to interrupt its strong Monday prime time, which included "I Love Lucy." Roone Arledge at ABC was interested, but by this time the sports-oriented Tom Moore had been replaced by Elton Rule, and ABC, too, demurred. At this stage Rozelle trotted out another of his favorite gambits—a new, competitive bidder. Hughes Sports Network (which bought out Dick Bailey's SNI) had mounted in 1962 an effort to secure the NFL championship game. On that occasion, it actually outbid both NBC and CBS, but Rozelle, alarmed at the prospect of losing the game to a network without permanent affiliates, arranged to reopen the bidding. Alerted to the danger, CBS had obligingly dug deeper into its pockets to secure the rights. Now, however, Rozelle was once again only too glad to use Hughes as a prod. ABC, with the weakest prime-time ratings, was the most easily cowed, especially by indications it received from some of its major affiliates that they were prepared to jump ship and carry the games if Hughes got the rights. Rozelle's invocation of the possible defections gave Arledge enough ammunition to persuade network management to reconsider, and make an offer. Hughes, apparently fated to be the bridesmaid, once again outbid ABC, but Rozelle awarded the initial package of 13 games to Arledge for $8 million, citing the stronger affiliates and better exposure the network offered.

"ABC Monday Night Football" made its debut September 21, 1970, with Broadway Joe Namath and the New York Jets as star attractions. The program became a runaway success, thanks in great part to Roone Arledge's "full court press" when it came to production techniques. Applying some concepts he had been tinkering with since his proposed "For Men Only," he broke all the conventions of traditional coverage, and ended up with a format most distinguished by the fact that it *didn't* appeal to men only. As part of a prime-time lineup, it would have to appeal to much broader demographics than Sunday football: younger, more female, better educated, less habitual sports junkies. He filled the announce booth with outrageous characters, shamelessly used them to promote the network, added "story lines" and the "up close and personal" approach to the athletes, designed jazzy halftime packages to replace marching bands, and threw his best producers and directors into the effort. His happiness at the public reaction could only be matched by Rozelle's, who now knew he had all three networks hooked on the NFL. From now on, there would be at least three-way competition for rights.

The splashy success of "ABC Monday Night Football" did lead to some resentment at CBS and NBC. No doubt regretting their own decisions to refuse the concept, they complained that Rozelle was favoring ABC with better team match-ups and more promotion. The griping was worst at CBS, where President Robert Wood was said to have threatened not to renew CBS's option unless the favoritism stopped. Rozelle, in a nearly unassailable position, and feeling his oats, called Wood's bluff (an unthinkable gesture just a few years earlier) and CBS backed down. It did not, however, entirely abandon the notion that it was the victim of a particular prejudice: always to pay the most, yet rarely the recipient of any favoritism. Subsequent CBS/NFL negotiations would grow increasingly testy, periodically punctuated by contingency planning for a CBS withdrawal. In 1974, though, CBS joined the other two networks in signing a four-year, $269 million pact worth a total of $2.5 million annually to each club.

In 1974 another challenger rose to peck away at the NFL monolith. The World Football League in many ways resembled the early days of the AFL, and many observers felt this was no accident, and that the

WFL existed to force an eventual merger with the senior league, thus effectively becoming NFL expansion franchises through the side door. The reaction among NFL owners was predictably reminiscent of the old days too. They accelerated a vote which expanded the NFL to Tampa and Seattle, thus pre-empting any WFL move to those cities, and dropped unsubtle hints that a host of other likely cities were being considered for future NFL expansion. The WFL ultimately failed utterly, collapsing after three years of head-to-head competition with the NFL. It did manage to cost the NFL dearly, however, as its raided star players, including Larry Csonka, Paul Warfield, and Jim Kiick of the Miami Dolphins, touching off a hugely expensive salary war in the process.

The WFL's decision to play a fall schedule eliminated whatever slight network interest might have existed for an alternative to the NFL, and only the *ad hoc* TVS network would carry the games. The approximately $100,000 annual rights fee the teams received was just about enough to pay their water-boys in the inflated atmosphere of the time. The lessons of the NFL would be repeated even more painfully by the USFL, which may be surprising, given the fact both leagues involved some of the same investors and entrepreneurs.

By 1976 the WFL was in ashes. Soon thereafter, the NFL Television Committee, consisting of Rozelle, San Diego's Gene Klein, and Cleveland's Art Modell, laid plans for what would become a four-year agreement, beginning in 1978, worth $646 million. For the first time, each team's broadcast revenues, now up to $5.5 million, exceeded its gate receipts. In return for the raise, the league adopted a sixteen-game schedule, added a "wild card" to the playoff system, and okayed four non-Monday prime-time games. The contract also gave the NFL the right to add two additional prime-time games each year, which would have obligated the networks to pay an additional $3 million per game, but perhaps fearing overdoing a good thing, the NFL didn't exercise the option. This display of caution or conservatism would shortly seem unfounded, as the NFL, like Major League Baseball, was about to negotiate a television contract on an order of magnitude beyond anything that had preceded it.

The year 1981 had been the NFL's best ever for combined ratings. Both ABC and CBS scored all-time highs during the regular season; ABC rose 4 percent, and CBS was up 14 percent, making an estimated $30 million profit, and NBC 4 percent. More than 110,000,000 viewers had watched the San Francisco '49ers and Cincinnati Bengals in Super Bowl XVI. Normally, negotiations for the next contract would have preceded receipt of the ratings results from the final year of the previous contract. However, Rozelle and the NFL were so preoccupied fighting the Raiders' Al Davis's suits against the league for opposing his move from Oakland to

Los Angeles that the contract bargaining had to be delayed. By the time they were under way, the powerhouse 1981 ratings were in, much to Rozelle's delight. Partly on the strength of those results, he determined to get $2 billion from the networks. However accustomed they had become to paying enormous sums of money, they may have recalled the words of the late Senator Everett Dirksen, who used to say, "A billion here, a billion there, and pretty soon you're talking about some real money," and were not thrilled at the prospect. To stimulate some cooperation, hints were dropped that maybe the time was finally right for an NFL cable network.

ABC was brought to terms first, induced by the long-sought opportunity to join the Super Bowl rotation. NBC fell into line for approximately $700 million, and CBS—always the hardest bargainer because Rozelle always exacted his own "ADI penalty" by charging it more than NBC—blinked, swallowed hard, and came up with $720 million. After the dust had settled, word leaked out that Rozelle had increased the pressure on CBS by agreeing to transfer CBS's package to NBC, and NBC's to ABC (in effect, letting them "trade up"), should CBS actually choose to walk away. Faced with the choice of developing an entirely new Sunday program schedule or paying, CBS paid. The $2.15 billion total package was a blockbuster, and soon a budget-buster as well.

Professional football was riding high, and the audience's appetite for it seemed insatiable. The worrisome cost of the new contract was beginning to make network people nervous, and more than a few cautioned that the good times couldn't last forever. At about this time, the networks were contacted by representatives of a new venture, the United States Football League, which proposed to begin playing a spring schedule in 1983. In some respects, it was the old WFL idea all over again, except shifted to the spring in a frank admission that a fall schedule would be suicidal. All the networks were approached with the idea, but only at ABC did it receive an expression of interest. The network was looking for an inexpensive spring sports package to counteract the NBA on CBS, NCAA basketball on CBS and NBC, and early baseball. Besides, it *was* pro football, and it just might give the network some trump cards to play with Rozelle in the future. If the league were a failure, so what; the costs were minimal and could be written off; if the idea took off and succeeded, as the owners and investors believed, ABC would own the rights to a very effective counterweight to any NFL hardball. There was no question who held the upper hand between the USFL and ABC, since the league concept was predicated on a television contract, and it could not exist without it—it was the ultimate made-for-television event. And ABC knew it was the only candidate for a spring schedule, aside from

ESPN, which was desperate for any national professional league programming.

ABC agreed to terms which gave it the 1983 and 1984 seasons for a total of $22 million, with options on the following two years at $14 million and $18 million, respectively. The contract called for one national Sunday game on the network. ESPN paid $4 million for 1983 and $7 million in 1984, proportionally high numbers considering the small size of the ESPN audience in those days, and when compared with ABC's rights fee. It must be understood, however, that ESPN was acquiring the USFL games precisely to build an audience, not just to entertain an existing one, as was the case at ABC. In addition, ESPN was carrying two games per week, Saturday and Monday nights, so it had twice as much commercial inventory to sell, although advertisers didn't exactly queue up at the door. The league, promising to keep costs low by avoiding ruinous bidding wars for players, got its first season under way in fairly good shape, but the wheels soon fell off. Promises were broken, and the bidding war began; ownership and franchise locations changed; there was bad blood between owners and players, owners and the commissioner (Chet Simmons, who had signed the contract as president of ESPN); and the results on the field were, at best, spotty. The league, shaky to begin with, soon would make about every mistake possible in finance, management, and marketing, and the wobbling turned to Jell-O.

Nevertheless, ABC made a profit of between $9 million and $12 million on the first season, an astonishing rate of return given the size of the rights fee. It averaged a 6 rating, under ordinary circumstances disastrous, but ABC had only promised advertisers an average rating of 5, so it was 20 percent ahead of the game. Both the USFL and ABC projected the network's 1984 profits to be in the same range, based to some degree on a 10 percent hike in advertising rates. ESPN did less well, but immediate profits were not its initial goal in the first season. While the made-for-television league was profiting television, its own investors were getting socked, as the franchises lost an average $2.5 million in 1983, more than two and one half times the amount their own projections had anticipated.

The 1984 season went about the same way: ever increasing losses for the USFL owners, while ABC and ESPN enjoyed the fruits of their original low rights fee payments. Ratings were slowly trending lower, but remained within the range acceptable to the two networks. The championship got a 9.7 rating and a 19 share, compared with the previous year's 11.9 and 23. ABC invoked its option for 1985 at the original bargain-basement price of $14 million, which caused howls from the cash-starved USFL. The league's frustration was not eased when a television industry survey by McKinsey & Co., raised the estimate of ABC's profit in 1983 to $15 million, $16 million in 1984, and projected $21 million in 1985 and $25 million in 1986. In all their talks, the ABC negotiators remained absolutely obdurate, refusing to up the ante to bail out the league. They rather peremptorily held fast to the position that they would do what was good for ABC, and that the contract, as signed, would be enforced. Despairing of ever getting a better deal from ABC before they drowned in red ink, a vociferous group of owners began lobbying for a move to the fall. With a salary war raging, and losses mounting, the move to a fall schedule was all that was necessary to duplicate the late, unlamented WFL.

ESPN had not signed for any option years in the original contract, so it had to renegotiate after the first two seasons. The desperate need for increased revenues, plus the opportunity of bringing in new bidders to compete with ESPN, soon found the USFL closeted with Ted Turner and his superstation WTBS. Turner, who had tried unsuccessfully to buy several of the networks, including ESPN (ABC then owned 15 percent of ESPN, and held a right-of-first-refusal on any sale of the cable network, which Turner felt it had used to block his buy-out), apparently figured this was a good way of getting even with ESPN, while also acquiring additional sports programming for his superstation. He offered $62 million over three years, which the league gave ESPN three weeks to match; it did, with a $70 million proposal. For a short while, it appeared that a lifeline had been found, but the league was self-destructing over the issue of a fall schedule. ABC indicated that under no circumstances would it televise a fall schedule. To make matters worse, it was invoking a contract provision calling for a 20 percent rebate if the USFL didn't have franchises active in sufficient major television markets; the sum demanded was $7 million, and the league refused to pay. ABC decided to simply withhold that amount from its 1985 scheduled rights payment, and the league sued the network (it lost). Relations were very rapidly going from bad to worse.

The 1985 season began relatively well, as attendance averaged nearly 30,000, and television ratings hovered near 8—due in large part to curiosity over Heisman Trophy winner Doug Flutie's pro debut. Ominously, affiliates in only seventy of the top 100 ADIs even bothered to clear the game. Ratings for subsequent games quickly fell to the 3–4 range, where they remained. Some time in the middle of the season, the decision was made to move to the fall schedule, which hardly did wonders for the mood of the folks at ABC. What really spoiled the soup was the USFL's announcement that it was filing a multi-billion dollar antitrust suit against the NFL and all three networks. The $7 million suit was a nuisance, but this one struck at the network's heart and was a direct attack on the huge NFL contract. The anti-trust trial would drag on for many months after the final USFL playoff games, which were disasters: Oakland-Memphis got a 2.9 rating, Baltimore-Birmingham a 3.4. Television's experiment with the USFL was dead long before the jury awarded the league one dollar for its efforts. The NFL would remain the only football game in town, at least so far as the networks were concerned, and Rozelle could breathe a bit easier.

Soon after the $2.15 billion NFL contract had been signed, the ratings for 1982 were calculated, and they showed an across-the-board reversal of the previous year's excellent performance; regular season packages declined by an average 5 percent, with CBS and ABC suffering the steepest drop in ratings and share. The Monday night package, perhaps showing an early indication of the overall decline in network share of prime-time audiences (as more and more homes were watching cable, independent stations, and VCRs), dropped from a 37 share to 31. Confronted with the obvious slippage so soon after signing the networks to the Two Billion Dollar Deal, the commissioner used a familiar device to ease the strain on his partners in television and advertising; providing yet another minute of commercial time in each game. For their part, all three networks began intensive new promotional campaigns for the upcoming season, and earnestly hoped the ratings decline was a phenomenon—an aberration—which would correct itself, and ratings would resume their upward march. However, the deterioration continued through 1984–85, as ABC's share fell to an average 28, and CBS's cumulative plunge now totaled some three full ratings points and nearly 20 percent of its 1981 average share. These results would have been sufficiently depressing under the previous contract terms, but at $720 million plus production costs and other expenses CBS considered them downright morbid. By 1986 all three networks were sulking as they approached yet another round of NFL talks, and the word on the street was they were prepared to hold the line against any increase, and would probably demand a meaningful rollback to a level that the advertising community indicated it was willing to support. Since television now accounted for 60 percent of all NFL revenues, any cut in rights fees would inflict real pain.

Rozelle was confronted with the realization that the all-important leverage had shifted in favor of the networks. He understood the ratings results all too well, and knew that some fundamental shifts in audience behavior and viewing patterns were under way, unlikely to be reversed any time soon. The entire history of NFL television negotiations in the Rozelle era could be characterized by one strategy: always maintain leverage over the networks by manipulating them into competitive situations, thereby creating more options for the league than the networks could resort to in a crunch. This time, the situation was ripe finally to employ an option he had only hinted at before: cable television. An astute reading of the network ratings data and consultation with advertising executives revealed that more and more viewers, particularly upscale ones, were watching ESPN, by now effectively controlled by ABC. If it made sense for ABC to pursue its audience into cable by purchasing ESPN, why shouldn't the NFL do the same? By allowing ESPN to bid for part of the package, not only did Rozelle add some badly needed revenues to the kitty, but another competitor joined the fray. Interestingly, now that the cable "threat" was becoming a reality, it could never again be used hypothetically, so a new one was encouraged to appear just offstage. The new Fox Network assumed the "spoiler" role previously played by Hughes, the NFL Network, ABC, and cable, with talk of it wooing away affiliates by purchasing the football package. Fox was not content with the "spoiler" role, complaining to the Federal Trade Commission that it hadn't been afforded equal opportunity to bid and win.

In March 1987 the current three-year contract totaling $1.428 billion was signed, which allowed ABC, NBC, and CBS to reduce their payments, and included ESPN for the first time. CBS averages $152 million per year (down 6%), NBC $121 million (down 14%), ABC $121 million (down 20%), and ESPN $51.1 million. ABC got the biggest rate cut because it gave up its non-Monday prime-time games to its cable subsidiary, ESPN. Each broadcast network is paying an additional $17 million to televise one Super Bowl, and CBS and NBC pay $4 million each season to televise the conference championship games. The total package, even with ESPN joining the club, is $12 million per year lower than the 1986 levels, with each team receiving about $500,000 less in network revenues than under the previous contract.

The National Football League Players Association strike early in the 1987 season made the financial picture even murkier, although nearly all observers agreed it would not help the NFL's standing at the networks. "Replacement" games drew a fraction of the accustomed NFL audience, and several advertisers, including major American auto manufacturers (usually mainstays of the NFL), yanked their commercials. Others demanded—and got—massive reductions in the cost of an advertising slot in the games. By the time the strike was settled, enough damage had been done that the NFL agreed to rebate to the three broadcast networks a total of $60 million in compensation. ESPN, which carried only the last eight weeks of the regular season, was not affected by the strike and received no rebate.

No one at ESPN was complaining, however. The cable network's ambitious and expensive entry into the NFL had turned out to be a rousing success. The 1987 ratings averaged 12.5, well above the 9 that President Bill Grimes had predicted to affiliates and advertisers. The half-season of Sunday night games featured exciting match-ups of teams manned by familiar regular players, with playoff spots frequently at issue. ESPN was able to sell the local broadcast rights to television stations in the competing teams' home towns, thereby adding more than $5 million in income. In fact, ESPN's success led to some rather petty grousing by officials of the broadcast networks that it had been unfairly favored by the NFL in assigning teams to the Sunday night schedule. ABC, NBC, and CBS had reason to be envious. the NFL package helped boost little ESPN to a projected 1987 profit of approximately $60 million, at a time when they were all struggling to break even.

The Washington Redskins' 42–10 romp over the Denver Broncos in Super Bowl XXII brought the 1987–88 NFL season to a close. At ABC, which had paid some $17 million for the broadcast rights, the game was a source of both pride and concern. It was a technical and artistic success for the network, which displayed its organizational brilliance by producing the World Series, Super Bowl, and Calgary Winter Olympics within a span of four months.

Whither the future of professional football on television? When the current NFL contract expires in 1991, all bets are off. As Chapter 11 reveals, no one can be sure what will happen. It is conceivable that the latest upstart league, Arena Football on ESPN, will enjoy the eventual success of the AFL, rather than the ignominy of the WFL and USFL, thus providing a counterweight to the NFL's implacable demands. Just as likely, the NFL will cultivate its own options, including pay cable, independent networks, pay-per-view, international distribution, and network ownership. Roone Arledge has already been moved off center stage at ABC by the new owner, Capital Cities, and so will unlikely play a major role in subsequent negotiations. His alter ego, Commissioner Rozelle, may also relinquish the controls, capping off a career which exceeded Walter Byers in length, as well as in satisfaction, brought by triumphant results. His successor would be wise to consider the possibility that, as network revenues level off or decline, the temptation for owners to go their own way will grow. The new commissioner need only consult his peers at MLB or the NCAA to grasp the implications of such a development.

7

THE THRILL OF VICTORY,
THE AGONY OF
WRIST-WRESTLING

"Only a kaleidoscope could shift so adeptly from the annually-awaited All-Madden team and Super Bowl Preview to the grueling course of the World Triathalon Championships—from a Daytona 500 Preview, to our special 1987 Year-in-Review. . . . our anthology focuses on such a variety of sports—from the beautiful to the bruising, the graceful to the aggressive—one might prove the perfect complement to your advertising campaign . . . integrating your corporate presence right into the heart of the event . . . meeting your larger audience expressly where your interests lie. Look into our kaleidoscope as it captures the color, the dynamic diversity, the powerful images of a swiftly changing championship scene —CBS SPORTS SATURDAY/SUNDAY 1987."

This glowing tribute from the CBS sales promotion offices was aimed at drumming up advertiser interest in yet another series in a long line of TV sports anthology programs. Fathered by ABC's Wide World of Sports," anthologies like CBS Sports Saturday/Sunday are standard weekend fare for the three networks, and are as much a staple of the sports fan's diet as potato chips and beer, although probably not as nutritious. Challenge sports, an offspring of sports anthologies, is another breed of made-for-television program, more commonly referred to as "trash sports." If anthologies aren't particularly filling, challenge sports are about as tasty as a ballpark hotdog.

151

Both of these programming forms fall somewhere under the broad definition of "sport" found in *Webster's New Collegiate Dictionary:* a source of diversion; a physical activity engaged in for pleasure; a jest; a mockery; a derision; a laughingstock. Critics of made-for-TV sports have had little trouble in finding ample inspiration in at least several of these meanings.

In the total picture of television sports, anthologies and challenge programs stand apart from network talk shows—Howard Cosell's Sports-Beat on ABC, or NBC's Sports Pros . . . & Cons—or syndicated programs—Greatest Sports Legends, or This Week in Major League Baseball. Semi-serious sports like wrestling and roller derby, once the sole province of independent TV stations, are now staple fare on several basic cable channels. These, along with ESPN's odd assortment of contrivances such as arena football and karate matches, have a place in the electronic sports world, but for some reason, critics seem to devote much less attention to them than to network anthologies and challenge sports.

The low esteem in which anthologies and challenge sports—particularly the latter—are held belies just how important they are to the networks from an economic standpoint. Well produced and relatively inexpensive, they attract an audience that is comparable in size with more traditional sports programs. They have a long shelf life and are convenient for replacing low-rated programs or fitting in between seasons when there are few live programs available.

Despite their economic importance, these made-for-TV programs regularly draw the wrath of the TV sports press corps. For some reason, these are singled out as the bane of twentieth-century living, and are often discussed with a sense of disdain usually reserved for plastic flamingos on lawns. Any programmatic value that these programs may have for network sports divisions and independent producers (who profit greatly from them) is usually described by sports pundits through gritted teeth. A *Sports Illustrated* writer once went so far as to brand them "as mindless pieces of treacle as can be imagined."

From time to time, pioneers in the made-for-TV sports business come to the defense of their creations. Barry Frank, for example, a former ABC and CBS Sports executive instrumental in bringing The Superstars to television, once said, "As long as some guy who's putting out widgets all week on an assembly line enjoys the program, I don't particularly care what the critics say."

Eddie Einhorn, part owner of the Chicago White Sox and whose network producing-credentials include the CBS Sports Spectacular, echoes Frank's sentiments: "The ratings tell us that people want the human interest stuff. They don't want to watch hard-grind sports all the time. A guy lifting a barbell—that's boring. But the same guy lifting a refrigerator, a car, barrels of water, that's human interest."

Einhorn's entry into anthology programming is a rags-to-riches story that would have made P. T. Barnum proud. In the late 1960s, Einhorn paid $1000 for rights to televise from Madison Square Garden an unheralded college basketball game between Bradley and St. Bonaventure. He intended only to transmit the game to the two home cities—Peoria and Buffalo. Einhorn pocketed $400 from his $1000 investment (plus production costs) and was soon on his way to becoming one of the first and most prominent packagers of college basketball.

Through TVS, Einhorn's newly formed independent production company, he began buying rights to the games of a number of secondary college basketball conferences. Barely succeeding in his company's formative years, Einhorn struck oil when Shell Oil expressed interest in sponsoring college basketball. Once fueled by Shell's involvement, Einhorn turned TVS, a losing proposition, into one of the country's largest independent sports networks. He subsequently bought the TV rights to the games of such major independent basketball powers as Notre Dame and Marquette.

TVS and Einhorn's success was a case of perfect timing. In the late 1960s and early '70s, television sports audiences began to tire of the perfection and complexion of the NBA, and turned instead to college basketball, which offered a more rousing and unpredictable brand of play. In 1973, the ever opportunistic Einhorn parlayed TVS' ratings and timing success into a literal fortune, selling the company for $5 million.

In 1978, CBS hired Einhorn to resuscitate its Sports Spectacular, at a time when only pro football was consistently drawing a larger audience than anthology series. Among Einhorn's contributions was the Cheerleader Classic, a five-week package in which cheerleaders performed sideline routines, and swam, ran, jet-skiied, rowed rubber rafts, and roller-skated before an appreciative and ogling television audience. While ABC's Wide World of Sports remained a paragon of decorum (retaining its top-rated anthology show standing), CBS and Einhorn's cheerleaders easily outdrew NBC's SportsWorld. Einhorn defended his CBS Spectacular contributions with a euphemism that will long be remembered in the annals of TV sports: "I don't call them trash sports. I call them entertainment features within the anthology format."

One of the more intriguing and surprisingly successful made-for-television inventions was The Skins Game, created by Don Ohlmeyer, one of TV sports' top producers who had earned twelve Emmy Awards during his tenure at two networks. Ohlemeyer was a protégé of Roone Arledge while at ABC, producing everything from Monday Night Football and the Olympics to Battle of the Network Stars. He left ABC in 1977 to become executive producer of NBC sports, revitalizing a moribund and dispirited division in only three years. When NBC lost the 1980 Moscow Olympics they had negotiated to televise, at the hands of President Carter's boycott, Ohlmeyer himself became dispirited and restless for new challenges. He started his own production company in 1981, a joint venture with RJR Nabisco, which shows how interlocking and inbred corporate television can be. Nabisco is part owner of ESPN, which is also partly owned by Ohlmeyer's alma mater, ABC.

Ohlmeyer brought the idea of The Skins Game to NBC in 1983 to help the network counter-program NFL games on CBS and college football on ABC. He bought the time from the network and sold the commercials himself. When most TV sports ratings were beginning to decline, The Skins Game was profitable, more than holding its own in the ratings against older, more established network competition. By 1986, The Skins Game was rating higher than any other golf tournament on television except the Masters, with 30-second commercials selling for more than $50,000 each to advertisers interested in reaching an upscale, male audience.

The Skins Game involves wagering on each of the 18 holes, and is nothing more than a television version of a gambling game that golfers have played for many years. At country clubs, golfers bet their own money. On TV, they play for the sponsors' money, and the stakes are high. Ohlmeyer based the success of The Skins Game on his ability to attract some of the legendary golfers who were no longer on the pro tour. Ohlemeyer's sense of showmanship convinced him that Jack Nicklaus, Arnold Palmer, Lee Trevino, and Fuzzy Zoeller were still a formidable foursome who could attract a sizable TV audience in a match whose rules were simple—winners were paid for every hole they won. The first six holes were each worth $15,000, the next six $25,000, and the last six holes $35,000. In 1988 the first Senior Skins Game found Arnold Palmer, Gary Player, Chi Chi Rodriguez, and Sam Snead competing for $360,000 in prize money. For the golfers and TV audience, The Skins Game is like a combination of Happy Days and Strike It Rich, and, while it is a relative ratings success, it is nevertheless scorned by many critics and golf purists as just one more of TV's ventures into the world of make-believe sports and real trash.

ABC's Wide World of Sports, with its weekly need to satisfy a voracious appetite for programming, is generally credited with spawning The Superstars, the first and perhaps best-known of the challenge sports. If television is anything, it is imitative, and the progeny bred by The Superstars reads like a list of biblical begats: The Women Superstars,

The World Superstars, Superteams, Challenge of the Sexes, Celebrity Challenge of the Sexes, Battle of the Network Stars, Dynamic Duos, All*Star Anything Goes, and the First Annual Rock and Roll Sports Classic.

The Superstars began in 1973 when, in an act of retribution, Roone Arledge scheduled the new made-for-TV series on Sunday afternoons opposite NBA basketball on CBS. In 1965, Arledge had bought the rights to the NBA, a move which proved to be successful both for the league and for ABC for almost nine years. However, in 1973, the NBA was lured to CBS by a $27 million offer. Arledge felt betrayed, having invested a considerable amount of money and effort in NBA coverage which helped the pro league regain a measure of popularity. Using the growing success of Wide World of Sports on Saturday afternoons, he created a Sunday version of the series that he scheduled opposite CBS's NBA games. Within five weeks, Wide World was handily outrating pro basketball, but Arledge was far from satisfied. He administered the coup de grace by scheduling The Superstars, then an untried but potentially successful series, to accompany Wide World. In tandem, the two programs all but finished the NBA until the end of the decade.

In February 1973 a hand-picked group of well-known American athletes was assembled in Rotonda, Florida, to tape the first program in The Superstars. They competed against one another in a series of ten events designed to test their skill in sports other than their own specialty. The idea of finding "super athletes" was the brainchild of two-time Olympic gold medal winner and world champion figure skater Dick Button, who was fascinated by the self-realization that, even though he excelled in one sport, he was far from being an all-around athlete. In the mid-1960s, he presented the idea of a "mini-Olympics" to Barry Frank, then vice president of Sports Planning for ABC. The purpose of the show, which Button's company, Candid Productions, would produce, would be to identify and reward the best all-around performer from a gathering of some of America's top athletes.

While Frank was not immediately attracted to the idea, he reconsidered it when he joined Trans World International (TWI), the sports producing and distributing arm of International Management Group (IMG). With the Automotive Division of the Fram Corporation as its first sponsor, The Superstars was launched in 1973 as a three-way production between ABC, Dick Button's Candid Productions, and TWI. In later years, TWI and Candid took over full production responsibilities, furnishing the network fully recorded and edited programs. In 1984, ABC dropped The Superstars, the same year that the network began covering USFL football games in late winter and early spring. NBC bought the rights, scheduling The Superstars to fill the usual mid-winter lull in live sports coverage.

In its first year, Superstar athletes competed in ten events: tennis, swimming, gold, bowling, weightlifting, 100-yard dash, half-mile run, a one-mile bicycle race, baseball-hitting, and table tennis. The first year's competition, which gave out nearly $40,000 in prize money, was won by Olympic pole vault champion Bob Seagren. In 1974, when soccer star Kyle Rote, Jr., won more than $53,000, a challenging obstacle course race had replaced table tennis as an event. In subsequent years, rowing replaced golf, although the producers later reinstituted golf to replace baseball-hitting. Golf was dropped a second time in 1987, replaced by basketball-shooting.

Many of even the most sympathetic viewers of The Superstars doubt whether or not the series' competition actually proves who is the best all-around athlete, which perhaps misses the point of the series by taking it too seriously. While Dick Button's original concept may have been born out of the idealism of a world-class champion, the series is intended to do nothing more than attract a sizable TV audience to watch famous athletes compete in various events in which they have limited expertise.

One of the lures in attracting top-name athletes is the location where Superstars is produced. In its first five years the series was taped in mid-winter at Rotonda, Florida, before moving to the Bahamas for three years. Since 1981, the series has been produced in Miami. From the point of view of the participants, The Superstars is literally as much fun as a day at the beach.

Each show takes two days to produce. The athletes receive first-class air and hotel accommodations for two people, and a $1000 guarantee against their winnings. Money is clearly not the attraction. While some top-level athletes refuse to participate for fear of spoiling their macho image and appearing less than perfect by appearing in events outside their element, most look to the The Superstars as a time to relax, enjoy the camaraderie of other athletes, and test their endurance and all-around athletic prowess. Occasionally, what starts as "a day at the beach" turns into something fierce when arguments arise over which rowboat got to the finish line first, who won in the foot races, or whether or not a batted ball was fair or foul.

From the audience's point of view, the appeal of The Superstars or other challenge sports is simple(minded) entertainment, sometimes bordering on the voyeuristic. The sight of New York Jets defensive lineman Mark Gastineau, destroyer of mortals on a football field, rowing a small boat conjures up an image of what Captain Ahab's whaler would look like if Moby Dick took control. The sight of All-Pro running back Herschel

Walker wielding a tennis racquet more resembles an explorer in short pants hacking his way through a jungle thicket than a superb football player trapped on a tennis court attempting overhead slams.

If The Superstars and its ilk merely appeal to viewers, most critics begrudgingly bestow an uncommonly high level of respect for made-for-television anthology series like ABC's Wide World of Sports and the attempts of other networks to produce similar magazines. Even the most hard-hearted critics seem to appreciate the sheer level of skill, energy, and imagination that the networks spend on pursuing little known events around the world, and packaging them for television. Unlike their negative response to challenge sports, many critics claim that they are only mildly offended at having to watch "athletes" on sports anthology programs pulling tractors, demolishing automobiles, tagging sharks, wrist-wrestling, diving from Acapulcan cliffs, or engaging in one-man volleyball games.

ABC's Wide World of Sports, whose story has been well chronicled in a number of excellent accounts, is television's longest running sports magazine and stands alone in its genre. If measured by no other standard, its record-shattering longevity borders on the miraculous in a business where cancellation comes quickly for programs that falter. The series propelled ABC's sports division to the top of its class, and it was the breeding ground for some of the most influential and accomplished producers and directors in the history of television sports. While not the first series of its kind on the air, Wide World set a standard for TV sports anthologies almost from its beginning. In an industry known for imitation, CBS and NBC's Sports Spectaculars and Sports Saturday/Sundays, Grandstands and SportsWorlds have been generally unable to match ABC's record with Wide World of Sports.

From its first program in April 1961, the series strived to live up to its accurate, if somewhat pretentious, slogan which suggests that ABC "spanned the globe to bring the constant variety of sport" to its weekend audience. What happened in 1961 was the kind of romantic drama once reserved solely for MGM and its Judy Garland/Mickey Rooney "Let's do a show in my father's barn" musicals.

When viewed in the context of its background of a struggle for parental approval and an idea undernourished by the milk of advertising, the fact that Wide World of Sports ever survived its rocky beginnings is wondrous. Its creation and ultimate survival demonstrate the classic ingredients necessary for success—sheer persistence and fortuitous timing. At Wide World's birth, commercial television was a young industry in a seller's market. Producers could afford to experiment, rights to sports events were readily available, and the viewing audience was unjaded by a surfeit of televised sports.

In the early 1960s, ABC was the weakest of the three networks. It claimed many fewer affiliates than CBS and NBC and could not deliver as large an audience to its advertisers as its competitors. The president of ABC was Oliver "Ollie" Treyz, whose background was primarily in sales and research. Treyz, who had little appreciation for sports in general, saw little value for sports programs in light of the high production costs and small financial return. During Treyz's tenure, the network contracted out much of its sports productions, many of them to Edgar Scherick, a skilled and peripatetic independent producer.

In late 1960, Scherick sold the idea of a sports magazine that would rival CBS's documentary series, Sports Spectacular, to Tom Moore, ABC's vice president for Programming. CBS was airing its program on Thursday nights; Scherick had the weekend in mind. Moore and Scherick hired Roone Arledge, a young NBC alumnus, to design the series which was to be an amalgam of filmed and taped sporting events not usually seen on television.

Using the NBC library as his base of research—a perfect 10 on the "chutzpah" scale—Arledge and his small staff uncovered a variety of lesser sports which barely received any attention on the sports pages of daily newspapers. Not only were most of the promoters of these events receptive to TV coverage, some even agreed to pay for it. The ABC sports brain trust could hardly resist this price.

At about the same time ABC was considering Wide World, the network bought out Scherick's producing company, retaining his services and making him the company's second largest individual stockholder. This buyout was the beginning of ABC Sports as we know it today.

The Sports division now had the full support of Moore, who had replaced the recalcitrant Treyz as network president. Under the careful and creative eye of Roone Arledge, Wide World of Sports assumed a life of its own. Horse shows, hydroplane races, and surfing championships became as commonplace as track and field events, skiing and swimming meets, auto racing (which eventually became one of the series' most popular features, outrating NBC's baseball games) and boxing macthes (second only to auto racing in audience appeal).

Moore and Arledge withstood the criticism leveled by other networks that the series only showed taped—not live—events. While accurate, this fact was undoubtedly lost on most TV viewers who, even today, can barely distinguish between network and local programs, and to whom it is immaterial whether or not demolition derbies and rodeos are live or on tape or film.

In addition to its commercial success, Wide World of Sports has become a testing ground for other ABC series over the years. For example, its extensive bowling coverage led Arledge, who became president of

ABC's Sports and News divisions in 1977, to produce ABC's highly popular Pro Bowlers Tour. The American Sportsman series was first shown on an early Wide World program and later became a regularly scheduled ABC series. The Olympics, of course, is the most notable example of how Wide World prepared a network and its audience for the grandeur of international competition.

One of the keys to Arledge's success with Wide World was his ability to translate athletic contests into the personal stories of the participating athletes. Wide World's viewers came to know the participants as people and not as impersonal figures in a sports competition. This "up close and personal" treatment was an ABC Sports feature long before it became formalized as part of ABC's quadrennial Olympics coverage.

By the mid-1970s, the technical virtuosity, production excellence, and aggressive programming of ABC Sports under Roone Arledge's leadership were the envy of the other networks. As Wide World's popularity grew, largely on the basis of opportunistic and highly promotable (and exploitable) programming coups—track meets from Russia; the stunts of Evel Knievel; Howard Cosell's exclusive interviews with Muhammed Ali—so too did its appeal to advertisers.

Prior to going on the air in April 1961, Wide World had attracted little sponsor interest. Advertisers took a conservative "show me" attitude before they would commit to an untried series. Complicating matters for Moore, Scherick, and Arledge was ABC's policy which mandated that all programs had to have sponsors on line before being scheduled. In a dramatic last-minute play rivaling for suspense Bobby Thomson's playoff game home run against the Dodgers, Ed Scherick sold the required commercial time only hours before the ABC hierarchy's go/no go deadline went into effect. This was less than one month before Wide World's premiere telecast.

After a less-than-auspicious beginning caused by normal internal strains that accompany the development of any new series, Wide World's financial success was assured after achieving a 6 rating in its first year. Since then, the series has regularly outrated NBC and CBS's anthologies, and between 1980 and 1985, averaged almost a 9 rating. During this same period of time, Wide World was contributing annual revenues of approximately $200 million to ABC's profitable Sports division.

In structuring each week's program, Arledge scheduled the most popular segments towards the end of each broadcast. Usually, he would tease the audience by showing the start of an event—the early races of a ski meet—and delay showing the outcome until the end of the program. This ploy was possible since the events were all on tape and could be edited and scheduled at random. Events such as a major boxing match, for example, were heavily promoted during the course of each show with billboards before commercial breaks, suggesting to viewers that if they left the room, they would miss the big event.

After its first few years, sponsors were attracted both by the series' ratings and its mass appeal. They rushed to buy in, hoping to pick and choose their spots adjacent to the show's more noteworthy events. ABC, however, limited sponsor participation by requiring advertisers to buy time on a rotating basis. Some weeks a sponsor's commercials would appear at the less opportune beginning of the program (perhaps in the middle of a dart-throwing competition from an Irish pub). Subsequently, the commercials would be rotated so that eventually they would reach the end of a program when some of the more exciting and more highly promoted segments were aired.

If Wide World of Sports accomplished nothing else, it redefined the meaning of sports. In *Supertube,* Ron Powers's excellent history of television sports in America, the author describes the impact that ABC has had in the realm of made-for-TV sports: "With Wide World, they made a seminal discovery: that instead of telecasting events because people were interested in them, they could make people interested in events *because they were on television.* In the years following this breakthrough, television would become an active, agenda-setting force in America's relationship with athletics—and with the styles, economics, political dynamics, and moral values that devolved from the relationship as well.

"Wide World of Sports, extravagantly successful in its own right, formed a kind of elite division-within-a-division: it became a training and experimental laboratory for the most promising of ABC's young cameramen, producers, directors, logistical staff and on-air talent. Beginning in 1964, Roone Arledge was able to transfer this well-drilled cadre, along with the Wide World methodology itself, to ABC's coverage of the Olympics, an international event that the vast majority of Americans had previously shown little inclination to follow."

To complain that Wide World of Sports and the other networks' anthology series are nothing more than glorified trashsports, is to miss the point of how commercial broadcasting works. Sports programs, whether live or taped; whether covering traditional games like football, baseball, or basketball, or less common events like wrist-wrestling or demolition derbies, are nothing more than diversions manufactured for the purpose of filling time, selling commercials, and making profits—for the networks, their affiliates, promoters, and participants. In this regard, The Superstars, Wide World of Sports, and future generations of made-for-television programs are all alike. If the history and economics of televised sports have taught us anything, it is that aficionados of celebrity challenge sports, cliff-diving, roller derby, arena football, and tag-team wrestling will never be wanting for diversion as long as they keep watching.

8

GOING FOR THE GOLD

EVERY FOUR YEARS, network television pulls out all the stops and mounts the most extensive, expensive high-tech showcase production it can possibly handle. The Olympic Games represent not only an immensely popular programming format but the hopes and dreams (occasionally nightmares) of the networks themselves: they are regarded by insiders as the "signature" programs of the Sports divisions—and the standard against which all sports programming is judged. Behind each gloriously spectacular quadrennial production lies at least four years' planning, fierce (often cutthroat) competition for the broadcast rights, a trail of international intrigue worthy of a dime-store novel, agonizing doubts and reappraisals, and enough hard feelings and name-calling to shame the script-writers on "Dallas." In short, Olympic television resembles the old adage about sausages: "If you like eating them, never watch them being made."

The public perception of the televised Games has always reflected the intense barrage of publicity and promotion which surrounds them. The Games themselves appear only after many months of on-air promotion, a welter of fund-raising and marketing campaigns, the appearance of "Olympic type" anthology formats designed as practice runs for the real thing, and a steady drumbeat of programming announcements, all intended to increase ratings. When the Games themselves actually begin, selected images of bright young "student athletes" and idealized amateurs fill the screen, accompanied by pageantry, stirring Olympian music, sweeping philosophic pronouncements, and just the right touch of nationalistic fervor. To the average viewer, the Games offer competitive drama, a never-ending variety and availability of events (many seen for the first time), non-stop boosterism, and the comfortable delusion of the Olympic Ideal—athletic competition without the many problems attendant in professional sports. These attitudes, indeed the whole atmosphere surrounding Olympic television, are in many ways uniquely American, and as a result, the Games themselves have been adapted to the necessities of American television.

The size, scale, and monetary impact of American coverage dwarf that of the rest of the world, distorting not only the International Olympic Organizing Committee's priorities in planning the Games, but also the networks' ability to evaluate objectively their own potential for success. The acquisition of broadcast rights has become an end unto itself, a virtual test of management's manhood, rather than a carefully designed element in the overall business plan. As the networks have engaged in ever-more-urgent campaigns to acquire the rights, they have driven rights fees to stratospheric levels—often outstripping their ability to sell advertising. Getting the broadcast rights, in too many instances, has turned out to be a pyrrhic victory—what has amounted to a commitment to put an extremely pretty public face on a profoundly ugly financial picture. The Games have rarely returned a significant profit to the networks and have frequently lost money. Given current network management's near-religious veneration of the bottom line, their continued willingness to engage in such high-stakes poker in pursuit of intangible rewards marks the Olympics as a television phenomenon.

Despite current popular opinion, the Olympics have had a short fifteen-year history as successful television fare in this country, and even that assessment is colored by one's definition of success. At the networks, Olympic success is most often defined in uncharacteristic terms of "overall value" that stress the benefits of goodwill, publicity and attention-getting, status and stature, energy and enthusiasm, and the satisfaction of having beaten the other networks to a property dearly coveted by all three. The networks are far less willing to talk about the financial details, preferring to cast the Games as grand patriotic adventures; this atypical benevolence, and the apparent willingness to suspend the executioner's axe for such financially marginal programming, reveals much about the special status the Games have attained. In a cyclical pattern of action and reaction most reminiscent of the superpower arms race, the networks have fought each other for each opportunity to air the Games, disbursing ever-increasing amounts from their war-chests, and in the process committing themselves to bigger, better, shinier productions each time. The inflation of both expenses and expectations can be traced directly to the competitive instincts of the networks themselves, which now find themselves hard-pressed to satisfy either.

For most of the early years, the Games (particularly the Winter Games) received little notice from U.S. broadcasters and were covered as news, not sports, receiving rather brusque, cursory coverage at that. For example, when CBS paid the petty cash sum of $50,000 to cover the 1960 Winter Games in Squaw Valley, California, it refused to send a sports anchorman; instead, CBS news anchor Walter Cronkite covered it in the style of a modified "See it Now" or "You Are There." Although the events were available "live" and were staged in the United States, most were recorded on black and white film and shown after completion, or as excerpted highlights. The public showed only elightly less interest than CBS, in spite of the U.S. hockey team's unexpected success (a triumph which presaged the same result at Lake Placid, but which was treated as a good story for the print media, notably *Life* magazine). The same year, CBS paid $394,000 for the Summer Games in Rome, and relegated to them the same sort of coverage, further diluted by the difference in time zones, and the difficulties of getting footage back to New York for transmission to the affiliates. CBS, discouraged by the results, became somewhat passive in pursuit of further Olympic coverage and chose for a time to concentrate its Sports resources on the very successful National Football League and other packages. It was a strategic withdrawal from an event which seemed at the time to hardly merit serious attention or money; little could the executives at CBS imagine that within a decade an unbridled bidding war would develop, and their early disinterest would place them in a chronically weak competitive position compared with the passionate, free-spending Olympian suitors at ABC and NBC.

The 1964 Tokyo Games went to NBC for $1.5 million, a figure of no special importance to the network, then basking in the glow of strong profits and buffered by the immense financial clout of RCA, its parent company. However, the amount paid for rights was still nearly quadruple what CBS paid four years earlier, and it signified two trends that would continue for many years: the steady increase in rights fees (later compounded by increases in the rate of the inflation), and the fact that Summer rights were, on average, more than two and one half times more expensive than Winter rights from 1960 until 1984. Not until ABC's stupendous bid of $309 million for the 1988 Calgary Games, did anyone think to pay more for the Winter Games than the Summer. The Tokyo Games proved a modest success for NBC, which was able to provide somewhat better coverage than CBS had, despite the continuing technical, logistic, and time-zone problems. The Winter Games went to ABC, the weakling network, whose upstart Sports division was aggressively seeking inexpensive opportunities to carry recognizable events. The games in Innsbruck, Austria, cost ABC only $597,000 in rights fees, and, more importantly, provided the network a working laboratory to experiment with personnel and production techniques developed especially for the Games. Many of these were to become fixtures in the ABC approach to future Olympiads. Most significant of all, however, was the fact that Innsbruck infected the key executives at ABC Sports—and none more so than Roone Arledge—with the almost religious belief that the Olympics and ABC were made for each other.

In 1968 ABC made a clean sweep of the Games, getting Mexico City for $4.5 million in Summer and Grenoble, France, for $2.5 million in Winter. Arledge's commitment to the Games, and to developing a unique, "signature" look to ABC Sports' Olympic productions was most starkly revealed when he committed $3 million to facilities and production costs at Grenoble, 20 percent more than the rights fee. This was the first but certainly not the last time he would overwhelm an event—and his competitors—with the sheer tonnage of men, money, and material ABC was willing to dedicate to special events. His seemingly limitless resources (in fact, ABC as a whole was the most short-handed and underfunded network by far) also paid grand dividends whenever he negotiated with the International Olympic Committee or a host organizing committee for the rights to future Games; he could always claim, with considerable justification, that no one could match ABC's commitment to absolutely first-class coverage, in which money seemed no object. The other networks, secure in their long list of professional and amateur sports packages, would not awaken to the importance of ABC's head start with the international Olympic movement until its warm embrace had become a stranglehold.

As recently as 1972 there was only moderate competition for the broadcast rights. ABC locked up the Munich Summer Games for $7.5 million, and NBC returned to Japan by securing the Sapporo Winter Games at a cost of $6.4 million; both figures represented significant increases over the previous level but were small in comparison with the rights being paid professional sports. The telecasts still garnered relatively small audiences, and the advertising community could barely stifle a yawn. Who, after all, would want to watch endless hours of obscure events, foreign athletes, and a parade of third-world flags no one save a geography teacher could identify? Indeed, when advertisers had so many established, successful All-American sports to choose from, and with their target adult male audience already happily parked in front of the set, watching football, baseball, bowling, boxing, and all manner of events, why invest in the modern pentathlon, or field hockey, or luge? It took a combination of factors, most unanticipated, to change the status of the Games in this country, and to elevate them to the level of mega-programming worthy of the money, attention, and effort television now lavishes on them.

The 1972 Munich kidnapping and massacre of Israeli athletes turned an otherwise sleepy American awareness of the Games into riveted, near-obsessive viewing. The intensity of the public's attention could not be matched by any other programming, nor could the networks fail to realize that the Games would henceforth be considered major news events, dramas acted out on the stage of international politics. Even commercial advertisers realized a grisly profit: they had paid low rates in anticipation of the usual low Olympic ratings and were the unintended beneficiaries of the skyrocketing audience as the crisis wore on. One advertiser, Lincoln National Life, saw its name-recognition soar some forty places in the insurance industry rankings as a result of having bought an extensive schedule of inexpensive ABC commercial slots. ABC itself basked in the attention and accolades afforded its broadcasts, due in no small part to its receipt of multiple Emmy Awards for news coverage, as well as sports. The other networks realized, albeit tardily, that the grandeur and import of the Games transcended sports, and they prepared to get serious about wresting them from ABC.

The next Games took place in 1976, and, as luck would have it, the Summer Games were staged in North America during the hoopla and patriotism of the United States Bicentennial Year celebration. Montreal and (four years later) Lake Placid would afford the winning network and American viewers the full panoply of events in prime time, made easier and more accessible by friendly governments, nearby locations, and a full appreciation of the needs of television. NBC and CBS began preparing their bids in earnest, waiting for the time to submit them to the Olympic Committee. To their astonishment and outrage, that chance never came. The Montreal Committee joined the IOOC in announcing that the Games had been awarded to ABC for the sum of $25 million. Upon further investigation, it was learned that Arledge had made the offer, on a 24-hour, take-it-or-leave-it basis, while in the midst of directing the Munich coverage on the scene. This brazen, almost arrogant technique of offering a quantum increase coupled with strict deadline pressure, known as "the ABC closer," became a fixture in Arledge's negotiating technique, sometimes to the grave apprenhension of ABC accountants and salesmen. ABC also carried off the 1976 Innsbruck Winter Games (which had been scheduled for Denver, but were returned to the Innsbruck facilities when Colorado voters refused to back certain necessary bond issues) for $8 million in rights fees. The prominence and nightly availability of the Games coincided with the emergence of gymnastics and ice skating as sports attracting a new, more heavily female audience. When the U.S. teams did exceptionally well, especially in track and field (Bruce Jenner and friends), boxing, and ice skating, audiences rose further—and watched more. It was a good year for the Olympics, and a very good one for ABC Sports, which tried its hardest to make sure the two entities were re-garded as inseparable. It promoted itself as "The Network of the Olym-pics" and painted the five-ringed logo on production trucks and equip-ment; there was a painful sense, especially at CBS and NBC, that ABC regarded the Olympics as proprietary property, essential to the health of the network.

It had become clear that, whatever the bottom line on the broadcast of the Games themselves might be, the real importance of the Olympics was as an unmatched promotional soapbox for the rest of the network's enter-tainment programming. Millions of additional viewers were sampling ABC during two crucial times in the broadcast year: just before the introduc-tion of the new fall programs, and between the winter holidays and the spring ratings book. Some percentage of those viewers would be retained by the other ABC programs, whose ratings would improve, thus driving up advertising rates across the board. Given the unique circumstances of 1976, the Olympics seemed to be a "win-win" proposition; events over the next ten years would prove the high cost of this illusion, and how the net-works' competitive instincts led them to throw good money after bad in competing with each other to underwrite the Games.

The Montreal Games gave powerful impetus to the ABC Television Network's surge from the obscure bottom of the ratings ladder (ABC stood for the Almost Broadcasting Company, cynics had sneered) to a position of dominance that was to last throughout the late 1970s. Launched by a drumbeat of promotion inserted into Olympic programming, aimed at the same young, upscale audience as the Games, and buoyed by spill-over ratings, a brace of fledgling prime-time entertainment programs be-came successful—in large measure thanks to "The Network of the Olym-pics." Arledge had not only scored a coup for ABC Sports, but had managed in the process to elevate the stature of the entire network, now basking in the glow of his success. Confident that his combination of boldness and almost mythical "gut instinct" for programming, events, and personnel could bring equally impressive results under different circum-stances, ABC in 1977 handed the News division to Arledge, as well; de-spite some early mis-steps, he soon made ABC News a force to be reckoned with.

The idea that the Olympics might be beneficial to year-round prime-time programming was soon established as gospel in network executive suites. After 1976, it became common to hear this rationale offered as justification for paying sky-high rights fees: in some circles, the "rub-off" effect on other programming became *the* reason for carrying the Games, with only secondary importance assigned to the evaluation of the Games themselves and the intrinsic worth of acquiring, producing, and selling them. In reality, the 1976 discovery of the "rub-off" should have been viewed as a happy accident, not the precursor of a predictably effective network strategy that could be depended upon to float otherwise leaden programming. Eight years later, however, ABC tried the same strategy again, paying a record-breaking amount for Los Angeles, and using the Games and the recent release of Tom Wolfe's stylishly successful *The Right Stuff* to incessantly—albeit vainly—promote an expensive flyboy drama, *Call to Glory*.

Whether Calgary will be the death-knell for the concept of Olympics-as-loss-leader remains an open question, particularly given the strict financial controls which new management and shrinking market share have imposed on network television. There is no doubt that the televized Games provide an unmatched podium from which to promote other programming. However, the losses incurred in the process may prove greater than the cost of a simple alternative: spending money on non-Olympic promotion, and eschewing the temptation to own the Games. A $65 million income/expenditure gap may be more expensive, relative to the promotional impact on prime-time programming, than a direct investment of only $15 million in non-Olympic promotion for the same programs. Buying the Olympics may be a very inefficient, perhaps foolhardy, means to any end, save that of great sports programming.

Star-crossed NBC Sports had carried 18 hours of the 1972 Sapporo Winter Games live, to emphasize its claim as the network leader in "live" sports, but production problems, the vast difference in time zones, the relative indifference of U.S. audiences to the winter events, and the lack (fortunately, for the rest of the planet) of any transcendant news angle like Munich's, had earned the network only average ratings—acceptable, given the time zone problems, but nothing special. However, NBC styled itself "the leader in live TV sports"—a not-so-subtle dig at ABC and "Wide World of Sports"—and was aching to bring ABC down a peg or two by breaking its recent hold on the Games. After a titanic three-way struggle (CBS, as usual, dropped out first), NBC acquired the rights to the 1980 Moscow Games for $85 million, plus numerous "considerations." However, when the Soviet Union invaded Afghanistan, President Jimmy Carter led a boycott of the Games, and NBC was left high and dry: no Olympics (despite huge expenses, the loss of equipment installed in Moscow, and the virtual renovation of the NBC Sports staff and facilities, all of which cost some $36 million) at precisely the time when its promotional and programming strategy had been predicated on the Olympics keynoting bold new network programming throughout the schedule. The network had even created "NBC Sportsworld" to do for NBC what "Wide World of Sports" had done for ABC—systematically cover pre-Olympic events and athletes, and build audiences for the eventual Games themselves. NBC's embarrassment and anger were public, but ultimately futile, and the Moscow debacle would usher in a disastrous era for the network.

Any misapprehension that the Soviets were not sophisticated in the ways of capitalist negotiations or did not understand the complexities of American commercial television were quickly swept away. Faced with a savvy, polished team of Soviet "negotiators," the U.S. networks soon found themselves being dictated to in a manner unlike anything they had experienced with other host countries, and it was clear to all parties who held the upper hand. The Soviets, in addition to outright demands for certain concessions, also hinted broadly that there were ways in which the networks could show their special interest in doing business. The networks' response to these unexpected circumstances was not one of which they are terribly proud.

All three networks were very anxious to get the Moscow rights, and the Soviets knew this. The fact that the Games would be taking place in the heart of the Soviet Empire was of great interest to network News as well as Sports, as it represented perhaps an unparalleled opportunity to pierce, even in a limited way, the Iron Curtain with the all-seeing television lens. From the standpoint of athletic competition, the U.S. vs. Soviet rivalry would be a constant highlight of the Games; the corporate competition among the networks would be no less fierce. ABC was, as usual, determined to hang on to the advantage it had gained by carrying six of the last eight Games, and prepared an aggressive strategy that included a pre-emptive bid like the one which had snookered the others out of Montreal. NBC was still smarting over its eclipse by ABC, and resentful of the latter's tactics and attitude. CBS, which had never supported its Sports division the way the other two had, had finally yielded to Sports' blandishments to get serious, and to compete vigorously for the Games. In short, Moscow not only was a great opportunity, but its rights became a matter of intense corporate pride in all three executive suites.

Although formal bidding would not start until the Montreal Games, the networks began to ingratiate themselves to the Soviets as early as 1974, purchasing the rights to various films and videotapes produced in the Soviet Union. Many of the titles were of dubious interest, at best, in this country, celebrating as they did the heroic efforts of farm labor, new production quotas at lumber mills, and the glories of life on the collective farm. The official Russian propaganda film is nothing if not boring, and almost none of these collectivist epics were ever televised in this country, and that included a particularly mind-numbing authorized film biography of Leonid Brezhnev, and "the Russian Festival of Music and Dance," which cost $1.2 million. Other fare, most notably a prime-time special from the Bolshoi Ballet, was aired. Whether these lamentable efforts at ingratiating themselves had any effect on the negotiations is doubtful. All three succumbed to the temptation, so they effectively cancelled each other out. Besides, the Soviets, who seemed never to have put much credence in the exercise, were said to have regarded the whole episode as a chance to tweak the Americans a bit, watch them squirm, and dump on them a bunch of worthless productions gathering dust in some Ministry of Culture film library.

CBS decided to break the spiral of unseemly Soviet demands by hauling up its biggest gun: Chairman William Paley personally flew to Moscow in his private jet—thought to be the first private plane ever allowed to do so—in hopes of sealing a deal. He also hired Lothar Bock, a secretive West German impresario reputed to have the inside track with the Soviets (a man of much mystery, he was rumored to have all sorts of political connections to various governments, political figures, and intelligence agencies in the Eastern bloc, and was regarded as a designated intermediary for them), to act as intermediary for CBS. Several times CBS thought it had reached a final agreement, only to have the Soviets, through Bock, reopen negotiations, always at a higher price. This sort of game was apparently being played with NBC and ABC at the same time. Eventually, the Soviets made it clear to all three networks that they wanted a rights fee of $210 million, plus another $50 million in equipment and facilities which were to be installed at network expense and left in the Soviet Union after the Games. After some consultation among themselves, the networks agreed they were being played for fools and decided to make a stand.

The three networks decided either to boycott the bidding or to approach Congress for the purposes of obtaining an anti-trust exemption allowing them to pool their coverage of the Games. While they were waiting word from Washington and their attorneys, Bock—apparently chastened by the potential loss of his million-dollar commission—managed to secure the deal for CBS, or so he said. However, on Paley's orders, CBS now declined, dropped out of the bidding, and stayed home in New York. Bock, suddenly lacking a buyer for the deal he had apparently brokered, turned around and sold it to NBC, which was desperately seeking so prestigious an event. The Games, NBC hoped, would restore it to the pinnacle of live sports production. NBC paid $85 million, plus the cost of facilities and equipment. The network also agreed to terms which included an additional package of films and a multi-year $7 million "consultancy" for Bock. To the very end, ABC attempted to beat NBC's offer, but, according to ABC executives, they were never given a fair chance to compete, nor even told what the final bid had been, because the mysterious Mr. Bock was in cahoots with the Russians and his new-found clients. An ABC delegation headed by Arledge flew off to Moscow prepared to forestall the NBC victory at nearly any cost, but they arrived just after the contract was signed. The NBC triumph, achieved at the troubling sacrifice of money and ethics, was to be snatched away by the U.S. boycott, leaving NBC Sports dispirited and embarrassed. It was a blow not only to the network itself but to affiliates throughout the country, which were counting on the Olympics to provide a needed ratings boost, as well as the opportunity to sell lucrative local commercial inserts.

If Moscow was the low point for NBC, the opposite could be said for ABC and Lake Placid. It seemed that ABC was not only good, but lucky, too. For approximately $15 million it had bought the United States and Canadian rights, figuring the Games offered the advantages of proximate location but expecting them to be subordinate, as usual to the Big Show in Moscow, which it had so badly wanted. Instead, what ABC got was, in effect, the only show in town, and a marvelous, stirring show it was. The dominant mastery of speed skater Eric Heiden was exceeded only by the unexpected surging triumph of the U.S. ice hockey team, whose stunning march through the medal round seemed to encapsulate everything noble about the Olympics, American youth, and, indeed, the thrill of victory. Audiences swelled throughout the 53 hours of television, and ABC, surprised and happy, rode the wave of enthusiasm and interest all the way to the bank. Announcer Al Michaels might well have spoken for the entire network management when he cried, "Do you believe in miracles? YESSSSS!"

The lack of any substantial coverage of the 1980 Moscow Games (NBC was forced to settle for late-night and early-morning highlights bought from European and Soviet television) only whetted the public's appetite for the next opportunity, scheduled for Los Angeles in 1984, and the competition for television rights was again fierce. Los Angeles seemed to present all the same advantages of Montreal and Lake Placid, including location, time zone, friendly government, patriotism (or, at least, nationalism), and willingness to cooperate in every way with television. In addition, the audience had grown increasingly heterogeneous over the years—more female, younger, better-educated, more "yuppie." These changes had by now become an accepted part of Olympic bidding, and the more diverse demographics had attracted the attention of a much wider range of potential advertisers, which emboldened the networks to increase their predicted ad revenues. Most significant, however was the "pride" factor among the networks: all three now attached an almost mystical importance to the acquisition of the rights, and there was much talk about their prestige being on the line in the bidding. CBS felt it had to become a major player in the negotiations, since it hadn't carried anything since 1960, and had dropped out of the bidding in other years when the price had gone too high; NBC was still smarting from the humiliation of 1980 and the disappointment of 1972, and was chafing under ABC's public identification as "THE network for sports" and "The network of the Olympics"; ABC was determined never to let its two competitors recover from its stranglehold, especially for Games staged in the United States. Committed to (and perhaps a prisoner of) its own image, ABC paid enormous sums for Los Angeles ($225 million) and the Winter Games in Sarajevo, Yugoslavia ($91 million). Los Angeles succeeded, but Sarajevo failed (commercial rebates and compensatory low rates were later demanded by dissatisfied advertisers). Voices were heard in the advertising community about how the market had topped out, that ad rates could not go much higher and still remain an efficient buy, and that only network hubris kept driving negotiators onward and prices upward. The acquisition of the Olympics was now a matter of pride and emotion, unhitched from the dictates of financial realities and shrewd business calculation so unsparingly applied to other programming.

The next round in this heavyweight fight produced more of the same: ABC bid an astounding $309 million in rights fees alone (production costs would add much more) for the 1988 Calgary Winter Games, apparently based on the now-familiar lure of Games on the North American continent. The startling precedent of paying more for the Winter Games than NBC paid for the Summer Games in Seoul, Korea, was exceeded only by ABC's sheer effrontery in paying more than triple the $91 million price it had paid for the Sarajevo games, on which it had lost money. The colossal expenses for Calgary could not be made up through advertising, despite the sale of all available commercial inventory, for $460 million, and ABC itself predicted a loss of between $35 and 40 million.* Perhaps understandably, the new Cap Cities management was said to be unamused, and was unlikely to support a repeat performance at the negotiating table or on the balance sheet.

Just down the avenue at Rockefeller Center, NBC Sports was fretting

* See endnote.

over its latest opportunity for redemption: they got the Seoul Summer Games at a reasonable cost ($300 million, plus revenue sharing), but political instability in South Korea was spreading. The turmoil in Korea, and suggestions that the Games be moved to another city (Los Angeles volunteered itself), finally led IOC President Juan Antonio Samaranch to issue a blanket denial that the Games might be moved or canceled, saying, "The Games will be in Korea, or will not be played at all." Nevertheless, NBC was not about to risk the kind of financial exposure it had incurred in 1980. According to escape clauses it had insisted be written into its 1988 contract with a group of Korean banks, NBC would get its money back if the Games were cancelled; if all or most events were postponed for seven days; the Games and ceremonies were not held predominantly around Seoul; the U.S. team (or a large part of it) did not attend, or if NBC couldn't have access to all events. The management of General Electric, which had bought out RCA, was known to be concerned about the 1988 Games, and wary of rolling the dice yet again in 1992, when Barcelona, Spain, and Albertville, France, will be the host cities for the Summer and Winter Games.

The phenomenal and almost hypnotising lure of Olympic television is nowhere so strong as in this country. Throughout the rest of the world, television systems pay much less money—and attention—to the Games. Quite frequently they will carry only the worldwide feed made available by the host country, and will forgo any additional, unilateral coverage. Some countries will only carry limited highlights, or the coverage of specific events of great interest at home: field hockey in India and Pakistan, wrestling and weight-lifting in Iran and Turkey, for example. Rights fees from non-American television are minuscule: the European Broadcast Union, which represents thirty-two countries and a population of several hundred million, paid a total of $28 million for Seoul (compared with NBC's guarantee of $200 million, plus possible revenue-sharing); EBU paid $5.7 million for Calgary (compared with ABC's $309 million). The Soviet Union, its Eastern European allies, North Korea, and Cuba combined paid the grand total of $1.2 million. The astonishing difference in price is explained by the fact that only United States coverage is built entirely around advertiser-supported commercial television; most other nations will carry the Games on government-owned, non-commercial systems, which face no real competition for the rights and are not expected to realize a profit.

It should come as no surprise, therefore, that the influence of American television over the IOOC and the Games is immense. In return for providing the overwhelming percentage of total television revenues (nearly 95%), as well as the most extensive supplementary coverage of the events themselves, the chosen network is in a strong position to influence decisions regarding the schedule, location, venue, and organization of the events and ceremonies. The Calgary Olympic Organizing Committee (COOC) did everything in its power to lessen the pain and potential loss to ABC—after all, $309 million plus production costs ought to buy a lot of cooperation and support. The COOC lengthened the Games from 12 days to 16 days, thus providing an extra weekend of coverage: 50 percent of the events were scheduled for weekends or prime time in the United States. The number of events was increased from some ninety in Sarajevo to 128 in Calgary, including a number of "demonstration" sports with television appeal, such as freestyle skiing, short-circuit speed skating, and Olympic rodeo.

The ice hockey format was changed so that the games would be played every day, rather than on alternate days, and the number of teams qualifying for the medal round rose from four to six, greatly increasing the U.S. team's chances for a medal. COOC also agreed (allegedly after ABC paid $1.2 million to the International Ice Hockey Federation) to a pre-arranged schedule, which had the U.S. and Canada playing most of their games in prime time. In addition, the U.S. team was granted a special waiver from Group A, which would have meant first-round games against the powerhouse Soviet and Czech squads, and was placed in Group B, which meant first-round games against Austria and other second-level teams. This was good for the U.S. team, which in turn was good for ABC—which apparently came up with the idea in the first place.

There is nothing new about the networks' desire to organize the Games for their own maximum benefit. The significant change has come in the boldness of the concessions they seek to offset the skyrocketing rights fees and production costs to which they have committed themselves. Their intense self-interest sometimes takes a form that borders on the megalomaniacal: during the early bidding for the rights to the Seoul Games, ABC was said to have proposed that the entire nation of South Korea move its clocks ahead by one hour for the duration of the Games, to try to ameliorate the 13-hour time zone problems of viewers back home in the States. The astonished South Korean government declined to participate, citing the havoc it would wreak in military, industrial, and financial arrangements worldwide. The mind-set and attitudes of the American television executives were very different than those of the host country, and this "culture gap" (a chasm, really) is one of the peculiar features of Olympic television that crops up with great regularity. Foreign host committees are often mystified, and more than a little offended, by the American preoccupation with money; the size and scale of the U.S. coverage, the "up close and personal" emphasis on the personalities of certain star athletes; and the negotiating style of the network executives.

On occasion, the clash of cultures can be amusing. During the bidding for the 1968 Grenoble Games, the NBC negotiating team mounted a jazzy presentation based on their experience at handling large, live events such as college bowl games. When they were finished, the head of the host committee is said to have shaken his head, saying, "I can't understand why you keep talking about bowel games—it's in very bad taste." Another time, Roone Arledge spent all day talking to the head of the Innsbruck Organizing Committee, reviewing details of ABC's production, programming, and financial plans. When Arledge finally rose to leave, he embraced the man, and promised to provide even more detailed materials concerning the proposed telecasts. The Austrian gentleman said, haltingly in English, "Hello."

In other instances, however, there has been nothing amusing about the progress of negotiations and bidding. In any language, money still talks, and the escalation of rights fees has been a direct result of the host committee's shrewdly playing one network off against the others, all the while extracting more and more treasure. Sometimes the networks, in an attempt to short-circuit the hosts' divide-and-conquer strategy have made a pre-emptive high bid: the most frequent proponent of this technique has been ABC utilizing the "ABC Closer." ABC's bulging Sports budget (by the early '80s ABC Sports was contributing between $180 and 200 million to the company coffers annually), its long and successful track record of Olympic coverage, and its unbridled self-confidence, bordering on arrogance, gave it the clout to make these deals. By 1987, with Cap Cities firmly astride the Sports budget, and with Arledge and his key deputies removed from operational control, the "ABC Closer" may be a thing of the past.

ABC had predicated its pre-emptive bids on the expectation that advertising rates would rise sufficiently in the years between the rights fee negotiations and the date of the Games to pay the outlandish expenses. Inflation is an important element in the pricing of any long-term contract, and ABC guessed right several times using interim inflation to cover costs at Munich, Montreal, Innsbruck, and Lake Placid. However, this practice eventually caught up with them, as the network overbid—in terms of total dollars and the competition—for Los Angeles and Sarajevo in 1984. Arledge's Los Angeles bid of $225 million was an amazing $75 million more then runner-up CBS, and the $91 million paid for Sarajevo turned out to be more than the advertising market could bear. Apparently undaunted by the experience, and given free rein by ABC management, Arledge was still willing to commit the staggering $309 million (some $5 million higher than NBC), plus enormous production costs, to the Calgary Winter Games. Those costs beyond the capacity of the advertising community to subsidize, may ironically represent Arledge's last hurrah, and may mark the end of an era.

In fact ABC and NBC will have to generate about $1 billion in advertising revenues just to cover their costs for rights fees and production in the 1988 Games. Since it is estimated that in 1988 there will be a total of $8.5 billion available to all U.S. television and of that approximately $1.2 billion will be spread among all sports programming, the Olympics draining off $1 billion will leave only $250 million for all other sports combined: NFL, MLB, World Series, NBA, College Sports, anthology programs, etc. The Olympic telecasts have become so expensive as to threaten the willingness and capacity of the advertisers to support television sports. In partial recognition of this fact, the IOOC voted in 1986 that, following the 1992 Games, the Winter Games would thereafter be held two years after the Summer Games, to avoid head-to-head competition for the advertiser support and marketing tie-ins so crucial to American television. The hope is that the advertisers will have two years' respite to rebuild their war chests between Olympic negotiations. Another potential effect of shifting the Winter Games is the tantalizing possibility that they could be held in the Southern Hemisphere, when it is summer in the Northern Hemisphere, thus creating what amounts to two different "summer" Games for viewers in the U.S. and most of the developed world. At present, when the two Games take place the same year, it is not possible for one to be scheduled in the Southern Hemisphere, as it would conflict with the telecast of the other. However, the time-shift makes intriguing the possibility that after 1992 just such a proposal will be brought forward, in all probability by American television.

Affiliates have traditionally egged their networks onward and upward in the checkbook battle for the Olympics. Their interest had always been in the ready supply of immensely popular network programming at key points in the year. The Olympics provided this, as well as an energizing injection of enthusiasm, which seemed to galvanize local salesmen and advertisers alike. They stood to profit immensely from a successful network bid but really didn't share much downside risk, should the network lose money on the deal. However, as the most recent rights fees have demonstrated, profits at the network level may be greatly diminished or non-existent. Calgary was a large hole into which ABC threw money. To minimize that loss, ABC was less generous in giving affiliates commercial availabilities to sell on a local basis; the network retained every possible commercial slot to sell itself, and kept the money to reduce its loss.

An examination of how one ABC affiliate in a small city planned to sell its commercial time during Calgary reveals much about Olympic ratings and demographics. KCRG-TV in Cedar Rapids, Iowa, planned to clear 96 hours of Olympic programming over 16 days (February 13–28), estimating the following audience delivery:

	Weekends	Prime Time	Late Night
	(rating/share)	(rating/share)	(rating/share)
Total Market	26/61	25/41	14/32
All Women	15/56	20/74	10/38
Women 18–49	14/32	17/38	8/19
Women 25–54	17/32	21/39	11/21
All Men	19/65	15/52	10/34
Men 18–49	19/65	10/24	7/17
Men 25–54	18/33	11/21	9/17

The enormous ratings and splendid demographics predicted by KCRG-TV reveal not only the salesman's natural optimism about his product but also the same kind of wishful thinking that impels the networks to pay ever increasing fees in the face of mounting losses. A comparison of the predicted Calgary audience delivery with the ratings actually achieved by recent Winter Games is instructive:

Average Network Ratings and Share

1968	Grenoble	12/25
1972	Sapporo	15/30
1976	Innsbruck	19/35
1980	Lake Placid	21/39
1984	Sarajevo	15/27

The Calgary Games would have to have averaged ratings performance significantly higher than any previous Winter Games to meet the expectations of the Cedar Rapids affiliate, its salesmen, and the advertisers buying time in whatever local commercial slots made available to the station by ABC. The network's most recent experience, at Sarajevo, was a ratings disappointment, although the total cumulative reach of its coverage was still impressive: Some 87 percent of all television households watched at least some of the Sarajevo telecasts; 93 percent of those having at least four years of college education tuned in, as did 91 percent of those earning at least $30,000 per year in professional or managerial careers; 91 percent of families of four persons or more watched, and in at least 89 percent of the households, the "lady of the house" aged 18–54 viewed at least part of the telecasts. These are attractive demographic categories, and the numbers reveal that ABC did very well in getting most people to sample the product.

Promotion and publicity can be effective in stimulating viewers to sample a sports program, but it is production which must retain them. Nowhere are the challenges of remote production more daunting and complex than in the Olympics. In part this is due to the immense scale and scope of the events; to the technological considerations of getting signals from remote locations and transmitting them around the world; and to the constant exhaustion of both crew and equipment. Additionally, the special nature of the Olympics—its international committees and jurisdictions; the ancient, philosophic "Olympic Creed" of non-commercial amateur idealism and international harmony—affects the production and its portrayal of the Games. Planning for the production of the Olympics is itself worthy of inclusion as an event, since it requires as many years of dedication and thankless hard work and offers as many obstacles as the decathlon.

The first major Olympic production was in 1968 at Grenoble, to which Roone Arledge and ABC committed 27 hours of programming, including one whole prime-time week night, and some 250 people. The coverage was fed to New York by the Early Bird satellite, and plugged into the network. Live coverage had been possible since the 1962 launch of Telstar, but it was of little use to sports programmers, since it rotated around the Earth in such a way that it passed over the downlink in Maine (and thus was usable) only a few hours per day. In 1964, the geosynchronous Syncom satellite, parked in a "stationary" orbit, transmitted live from Tokyo, but virtually no one watched the 14 hours of NBC coverage because of the immense difference in time zones (ABC covered the 1964 Innsbruck Winter Games on film, which was flown to New York and aired the next night as a highlights package). The 1968 Mexico City Summer Games were covered with land lines, and their location in a North American time zone encouraged ABC to originate 44 hours of programming. However, ABC executives, made nervous by the street rioting in Mexico City and the "Black Power" protest of some U.S. athletes (and the effect on the rate card), decreed that most of the Games be shown on delayed videotape. In 1972 the U.S. Olympic team sent 470 athletes to Munich; Arledge sent 330 ABC people, a decision fully vindicated by the extraordinary demands of covering for 63 hours the crisis which overtook the Games (some of the key ABC production people nevertheless spent days without sleep in production trucks and studios during the worst of it— their commitment to the unfolding drama was fully the equal of any seasoned News team).

To appreciate the magnificent job the networks usually do in covering the Games, one should not only watch the superb technical artistry displayed on the television screen, but also consider the behind-the-scenes logistics which make it all possible. At Los Angeles, for example, while ABC viewers were watching the exploits of Carl Lewis, Greg Louganis,

Joan Benoit, and dozens of others, some 1400 engineers, 1800 support personnel, and 300 network production and management people were working to capture the imagery and transmit it. They produced 188 hours of programming, more than twice the amount at Montreal in 1976, and were responsible for worldwide coverage of 1300 hours of competition. 205 cameras, and 660 miles of camera cables, plus a complex web of microwave relays, were necessary to cover thirty Olympic venues, some of which were nearly two hundred miles apart. In addition a fleet of specially-designed vehicles included four helicopters, three houseboats for camera platforms, twenty-six mobile units, two custom-designed boats, six motorcycles (2 electric), and thirty-five office trailers. ABC announcers could describe the action from 404 "hard wired" commentary positions.

ABC viewers were treated to—and have come to expect—the most imaginative use of cameras and microphones in bringing home the full panoply of the Games in revealing detail. Underwater cameras and waterproof microphones captured the techniques of swimming and diving; the marathons were covered by relays of stationary and motorized cameras; there were microphones in boxing ringposts, equestrian saddles, and basketball backboards. That winter in Sarajevo, ABC's miniature wireless cameras and mikes were mounted on skiers' helmets and boots, and in the nose of a speeding luge, giving viewers a stomach-churning opportunity to put themselves in the athletes' place. In Calgary, a camera was attached to a hockey puck. The technical brilliance of Olympic coverage is perhaps matched only by the creative energy of the production personnel. For them, it is a time to pull out all the stops: to push themselves and their equipment to the limit in pursuit of ever more imaginative and revealing coverage. Their zeal is expensive (ABC budgeted $100 million in production costs at Los Angeles), but most viewers would agree that the results justify the expenditure.

Whether it takes the form of a boycott, international wrangling, the exclusion of one country or another, or something as heinous as murder in the name of a political cause, international politics has been associated with the Olympics since at least the 1936 Berlin Games, Adolph Hitler's planned showcase for the glories of Aryan youth. In 1952 the announcement that the Soviet Union would send a team to Helsinki spurred a furious American fund-raising campaign to "defeat the Reds." This constant, nearly universal inclination to politicize the Games runs directly counter to the IOOC's stated philosophies and the Olympian ideal. It also runs counter to the interests of the networks, for although a little nationalist pride is a good thing when building audiences (clearly, American viewers want to see our athletes competing with—and hopefully defeating— those from the Soviet Union, Cuba, East Germany and Japan, rather than those from Brazil, Finland, or Belgium), it too easily gets out of hand, and threatens the attractiveness of the event, as well as the smooth organization of the Games. The networks do not like surprises, particularly the kind that threaten half-billion dollar investments.

When things are going smoothly, the Games provide an arresting glimpse at athletes and customs in many countries not usually examined by U.S. television. In a sense, the telecasts provide a travelogue of sorts, exploring the various societies which have produced the great athletes of the day, often visiting them at home while they train and prepare for the competition; the "up close and personal" style adopted by all three networks has enabled American viewers to know something about the otherwise faceless foreigners, and in many cases, to become fans and admirers. To a great extent, the phenomenal popularity achieved by Olga Korbut, Nadia Comaneci, and many other foreign athletes is a tribute to the supportive, sensitive portrayals they received on American television. Many television production executives with Olympic experience mention this element of their telecasts as among the most satsfying contribution they can make to the total coverage.

Preparing to cover so large a number of athletes and events is a formidable task, which begins in earnest several years in advance. Large research units are established at the network, staffed by specialists who assemble statistical information about thousands of athletes, as well as personal profiles, and competitive histories. Some of the athletes judged most likely to succeed (or at least, to make interesting copy) at the Games, will be the subject of videotaped mini-documentaries which are shot on location, and can be inserted into the telecast at the appropriate moment. The network will shoot some of these itself, and turn over the remainder to experienced Olympic production specialists, such as Bud Greenspan's Cappy Productions. As NBC began preparation for Seoul, Peter Diamond (the acknowledged wizard of Olympic research) and a team of five researchers had been hard at work since mid 1986, compiling a customized encyclopedia of international athletic competition that would eventually contain information on thousands of individual athletes, and the results of every significant event.

Research and preparation are also important in preparing the on-air talent and audience alike for the fine points of many sports not commonly followed or understood in the U.S. Audience research has shown that one of the most pleasing elements of past telecasts has been the audience's exposure to events from around the world. Thus the educational function of the telecasts is much greater than that for a football or basketball game, where the operating assumption is that only knowledgeable fans are watching. During the Olympics, viewers need (and apparently want) to be educated about techniques, training methods, competitive histories, and "star" athletes. For the program producers, this means having a surplus of informative and illustrative material on hand at all times, and that material must be gathered and packaged well in advance. It also means that a delicate balance must be struck between focusing entirely on a few prominent American athletes and boring the audience with more information than they ever wanted to know about Bulgarian shot-putters; between losing the attention of the casual fan and offending the sensibilities of the knowledgeable one. The Games are a rarity, in that they attract casual fans (non-fans as well) in addition to the usual sports viewers, and this diverse audience must be served in a unique and sophisticated manner.

Much of the burden for striking that delicate balance falls on the shoulders of the on-air personnel, even though they do not make many policy decisions regarding program content. Nevertheless, it is their faces and voices the audience identifies with, and they confront the unenviable challenge of remaining fresh, innovative, and informative over the whole exhausting grind. Selecting on-air personnel is therefore very tricky. Olympic announcers are expected to be particularly insightful and expert on the sport(s) they are covering. The sheer size and variety of the Games often means that the networks have to use people who are either experts or great communicators, but not necessarily both at the same time. The employment of so many ex-athletes as commentators increases the likelihood that an experienced anchorman (ABC's Jim McKay being the prototype) will have to be alert to smooth over their glitches, to soften their partisan rooting interest, place their unsophisticated views of international politics in a larger context, and simply help them with the complexities of the television technology arrayed around the venues. A skilled anchorman (in reality, a team of experienced, qualified people is required to cover all the on-air shifts) can be, as McKay proved in Munich, the critical link in establishing credibility, as well as actng as the all-important switching point among the myriad locations and events. Not surprisingly, competition for that treasured assignment is heated.

The undeniably political nature of the Games mandates that on-air talent be prepared to function as journalists, even including contingency planning for the coverage of a serious disruption; the Munich experience convinced the networks never to be caught unprepared again. The broadcasters must be attuned to the sensitivities of nationalism, regional, racial, and ethnic disruption; the Munich experience convinced the networks never to be caught unprepared again. The broadcasters must be attuned to the sensitivities of nationalism, regional, racial and ethnic pride, and a host of other factors which might legitimately be part of the overall Olympic story. Unfortunately, these realities run directly counter to the official IOC position regarding the role, purpose, and philosophy of the Games. The IOC insists there be reduced attention paid to these political differences, and also frowns on too much overt emphasis on money, individual "star" athletes, and on keeping score of medal counts, national totals, etc. This deliberately antiquated attitude runs directly counter to every habit and preference of American sports television, and it leads to some awkward relations between the U.S. network, the IOOC, and other television systems which may be carrying the international feed.

Perhaps the most wrenching disputes between U.S. networks and the Olympics came during the long tenure of Avery Brundage as head of the IOC. Although his American citizenship might have predisposed him to a greater understanding of network television, Brundage remained an obdurate conservative when it came to upholding the image of "The Olympic Ideal": in his eyes, neither commercialism nor nationalism should mar the competition on the field, and no political disruption— no matter how heinous—should be permitted to alter the Games or the coverage thereof. After the Munich massacre, the Montreal anti-apartheid boycott, the U.S. and Soviet boycotts of Moscow and Los Angeles, and a host of lesser conflicts, Brundage remained unmoved, saying, "The Games Must Go On."

Brundage and his successors in the international Olympic movement came to regard the Games as a privileged sanctuary, while journalists saw them as a treasure trove of stories. Officials from many nations are suspicious of the U.S. mass media, and of their penchant for discovering and covering troubling issues. At the 1987 Pan American Games, in Indianapolis, there were violent confrontations between members of the Cuban team and expatriot Cubans urging them to defect. The Cubans laid some of the blame on U.S. media, claiming the exposure given these "hooligans" incited them to further acts and ran counter to the spirit of the Games. Tighter restrictions on the media were urged, to bring them "up" to the exclusionary standards of the Olympics. As Pete Axthelm noted in the *Gannett Center Journal*," published at Columbia University, the Olympics control the press even more effectively than the Super Bowl: at the latter, reporters are allowed, even offered, as much access as the players' practice time and the media's own numbers permit. At the Games, on the other hand, "access is as limited as bureaucrats can make it."

In both Los Angeles and Sarajevo, ABC was sharply criticized for providing an international feed which over-emphasized the exploits of American athletes. Soothing the hurt feelings of so many different nations, while simultaneously appealing to the cricial domestic audience, was a thankless task. Viewers in this country—accustomed to watching extensive nightly sportscasts on the evening news, and to reading detailed sports summaries and statistics every day in the paper—demand to know the details of medal standings, national totals, the performances of big-name athletes, and the personal struggles of many others, and ABC was expected to oblige. American viewers and advertisers are more important to the financial success of the Games than the rest of the world combined, so ABC's single-minded concentration on U.S. athletes can readily be understood.

The news value of the Games is tremendous even without any disruption or unexpected events. The U.S. network will have gone out of its way to promote the highest possible interest in viewing the Games, and many other corporations with marketing tie-ins (Coca Cola spent $1.3 million just on free drinks for the athletes in Montreal) will have launched their own promotion and publicity campaigns. After deliberately focusing so much attention on the Games, the U.S. network rights-holder jealously guards its "exclusive" rights. But as we saw in Chapter 3, upholding those rights when a sports event becomes a news event can be tricky. Olympic broadcasters are tempted to declare anything and everything which takes place on the grounds to be exclusive material. When, in 1980, NBC showed no more than ten seconds of a Sarajevo flag-raising ceremony as part of a short news clip, ABC took them to court to enjoin them from poaching on what ABC considered its territory. Ten seconds of video unrelated to any competition may seem a tempest in a teapot, but ABC was dead serious about asserting its complete exclusivity over anything taking place within the confines of the Olympic Village. With the possibility of many news stories emanating from Seoul, and the threat of political demonstration or upheaval high, NBC's policies and its competitors' plans will be the subject of much debate and scrutiny, as will those of both North and South Korean governments, each of which will control some aspects of the Games.

The role of corporate sponsors has grown dramatically in recent years, with corporations vying with each other to be the "official" something-or-other of the Olympics, or an underwriter of specific facilities, or even as employer of American athletes-in-training. Not only must the broadcaster be solicitous of the IOOC's sensibilities regarding amateurism and commercialism, when mentioning these entanglements, but he sometimes finds himself in an awkward conflict, as when the corporate sponsor of an event or venue is a competitor of the paid advertiser on the broadcast itself. In Los Angeles, for example, some 146 corporations were "official sponsors" of various elements; this does not include hundreds of foreign corporations similarly affiliated with other teams. Logos and announcements were ever more prominently displayed, often to the chagrin of ABC and its advertisers.

ABC sold some $460 million in advertising during the 1988 Calgary Winter Olympics, with the biggest buyers, including Chrysler, Ford, and Anheuser-Busch paying $25 million each (NBC predicted advertising sales in excess of $600 million for the Seoul Summer Olympics.) In addition, nearly one hundred other corporations paid fees, or contributed goods and services, totaling $87 million, for the right to associate their American marketing campaigns with the Calgary Games. A complex pricing structure distinguished twenty-one "official sponsors" from thirty-six "official suppliers," and both groups from a third category of companies permitted only to reproduce the Olympic logo on their merchandise. For nine really big spenders, a special marketing category dubbed The Olympic Program (TOP) was devised, which allowed them to print their names in all official programs for both the Calgary and Seoul Games. Moreover, since aggressive corporate sponsorship is hardly an American preserve, corporations based in the economic powers of West ern Europe, East Asia, and Australia dramatically swelled Calgary's sponsorship revenues.

The physical size, scope, complexity, and grandeur of the Games make them a daunting organizational challenge to the broadcaster. There is so much to cover, much of it happening simultaneously at several different venues, so many athletes, so much athletic excellence (all the competitors are, after all, champions on some level), so much inherent drama, that one is hard pressed to keep up the pace day after day. Language barriers, unfamiliar personalities, and differing team policies regarding media access and cooperation only add to the difficulty of the task at hand. Technical facilities provided by the host country may be incompatible with the American network, or staffed by less skilled technicians, or dedicated to events of little interest to the U.S. Interfacing with the host country feed or the world feed may be fraught with danger. In 1986, for example the World Cup soccer championship in Mexico was televised almost unilaterally by Mexican television, and the feed accepted throughout the world. In a comedy of errors, the understaffed and inexperienced Mexican crews frequently scrambled pictures and audio, mismatched feeds to the wrong countries, lost cameras and sound during several matches, and otherwise botched the job in humiliating fashion. NBC, which took the feed, and attempted to augment it with voice-over narration from studios in the United States, was equally embarrassed, but it learned an important lesson in preparing for Seoul: if you want it done right (by American broadcast sports standards) you had better do it yourself, even if that means considerable extra expense, building your own facilities from scratch, and "donating" some of it to the host country at the conclusion of the event. It may also mean providing the international feed, even though that requires additional, 'round the clock production to accommodate the various interests of nations around the globe, and in every time zone; it's always prime viewing time somewhere, and they've all got a favorite sport or event which they want covered.

Time zones and the location of the Games have traditionally represented the greatest challenge to the networks, and have come to represent the most important consideration in bidding for Olympic rights. Even with the advent of synchronous satellites capable of sending crisp, high-quality pictures from anywhere on the globe to American living rooms, the complications posed by the difference in time zone between the site of the Games and the East Coast are profound. The network's interest is in getting the organizing committee to schedule as many events as possible—particularly those involving the U.S. teams—so they will occur when it is prime time in the U.S., regardless of the time of day at the Games. Thus in Korea, a number of events were scheduled at 8 a.m. to accommodate this desire, even though the other nations' teams were unhappy about it. The early hour may actually serve to handicap U.S. teams, who must be able to perform at a time when they are usually asleep. Conversely, some events which would were scheduled for late afternoon or early evening had to be shifted, as it would be in the middle of the night on the East Coast, when the available audience is small, indeed.

The network attempted to include as many weekend days as possible in the athletic competition, thus increasing the number of hours of broadcasting (and thereby, commercial inventory) in time periods when most of the population is at home, they are accustomed to watching sports, and the programs being pre-empted are of little commercial value to the network or its affiliates. The broadcaster will also attempt to get the organizing committee to spread out those events considered prestigious in this country, so that none overlaps or conflicts with another, and to guarantee a steady supply of same, building towards dramatic climaxes in the last days of competition. The network must also take care to protect the affiliates' local evening newscasts, which are major revenue sources for the stations. Both early and late evening news must be bracketed by Olympic programming, but not overwhelmed by it, or pre-empted; this is further complicated by the fact that in different time zones within the U.S., local newscasts are scheduled to air at different times in relation to the Games. More worrisome still, if the network records and saves for tape delay certain events and results, can it prevent its own affiliates (or those of its competitors) from trumpeting those results on the local news, before the network has had the opportunity to run the tape?

Another problem facing network programmers is how to deal with the counterprogramming efforts of competing broadcasters. In some cases, this means placing a strict embargo on news and pictures from the Games until they have aired on the "official" network, so that competitors cannot steal their thunder. In other cases, this means convincing the audience that the Olympic-style programming they are watching on a competing network is not the real thing. It is not uncommon for unsuccessful Olympic bidders deliberately to acquire the rights to the Pan American Games, Goodwill Games, World Track and Field Championships, National Sports Festival, Spartikiad or Commonwealth Games, and then cover them extensively, as though they were pre-Olympic (or related) events. The clear intention is to soft-pedal the exclusivity of the designated Olympic network, without actually violating any of its contracts or copyright protections, and to dilute its audience. In 1988, ABC deliberately pursued and won the rights to the U.S. Summer Olympic Trials, despite (or, perhaps, because of) NBC's possession of the Seoul Games rights.

The list of possible problems facing the successful network bidder is long, indeed, and it includes more headaches and risks than can be easily enumerated: the staggering costs, with little hope of significant profits; the immense production difficulties; the specter of international politics, disruption, or cancellation; the constant negotiating with a bevy of foreign governments, agencies, boards, and commissions; the technical puzzles of interfacing dissimilar production facilities and personnel; the scheduling problems; the resistance of advertisers and selfishness of affiliates; the counterprogramming of competitors, and a host of other factors beyond control or prediction. It is no small wonder, then, that the American networks have over the years become more and more insistent in their demands for cooperation in staging the Games as they would like. Given the percentage of financial support coming from these networks, and from corporations interested in being associated with the telecasts, it seems to them only business prudence that the IOOC and local organizing committees acknowledge (implicitly, through cooperation and flexibility) the fact that without U.S. television, the Games simply could not continue to exist as we know them today.

Whether this system can survive much longer is open to question. Many observers believe that the upward spiral in rights fees and production costs has reached the point at which no single, advertiser-supported network can prudently afford to buy the exclusive rights. The growth of cable and other communication technologies has brought a new group of companies, hungry for prestige programming, into the picture. Some discussions have already been held between representatives of broadcast and cable television, with an eye towards eventual splitting, pooling, or tiering of the coverage. Under this scenario, each company's financial contribution would be limited, as would its risk. The IOOC could still receive a significant total rights fee, and perhaps even a greater number of hours of coverage. However, it might lose much of its negotiating leverage when dealing with U.S. network bidders, as the old ploy of playing one off against the other would be less effective in a cooperative market. For many years the prospect of subscriber-based pay cable acquiring Olympic rights has been a tantalizing one. Simple arithmetic easily demonstrates the theoretically huge amount of money available to such a bidder: if only 40 million households were willing to pay twenty dollars to watch the exclusive coverage of the Games, then $800 million would be on hand to make it happen. It hasn't happened yet—and may never—but then many equally implausible ideas have already become reality since television got serious about the Games.

Perhaps the greatest single obstacle to achieving any new system of televising the Games would be the very element which has done so much to create so many of the problems in the first place: the networks have allowed the Olympics to become so emotional an issue, so much a matter of pride and self-importance, that they no longer measure it by any reasonable business standard normally applied to programming decisions. The televised Games have, like Frankenstein's monster, taken on a life of their own, and their importance is magnified by the pride of authorship and ownership vested in them by the networks. The possible entry of cable may only add another group of competitors to the relentless pursuit of the rights, further raising the stakes and the intensity of the competition: the Games would certainly loom even more important for any cable system willing to put up such enormous sums (the broadcast networks, by comparison, have many other popular programs, and therefore "need" the Olympics less) in hopes of establishing a "signature" with the audience. It remains to be seen whether the hard-headed, unsentimental management now at the networks' helms will continue to find them so irresistible.

NOTE: Capital Cities/ABC executives later admitted the network had lost $65 million at Calgary. Within a few weeks, CBS secured the 1992 Albertville Winter Games for $243 million, $68 million higher than runner-up NBC.

9

SPORTS FOR SALE; APPETIZING SPORTS FOR SALE

CARL ERSKINE looked in to get the signal from his catcher. He shook off one sign before starting his windup. Crouched down behind the plate flashing the signs to Brooklyn's beloved "Oisk" was another former Dodger, all-star catcher Mickey Owen.

A scene from a 1940s World Series game? More like a miracle of modern-day geriatrics. The scene was not Brooklyn's Ebbetts Field but Shea Stadium, home of the New York Mets. And Carl Erskine was far from the prime of his career. The event was an old-timers game which has become a traditional part of the baseball season for all twenty-six major league teams. In this 1987 game Erskine was a sixty-year old gray-haired bank president and Mickey Owen a seventy-one-year-old retiree.

Sports on network television is on the verge of becoming a depressed industry partly because companies like Equitable Finance Company, which is responsible for making old-timers games possible, have turned to sponsoring live events instead of putting all of their advertising dollars into buying commercials in an expensive and fragmented TV market. Like countless other companies, Equitable has found that on-site event sponsorship is more efficient than spots on television, considering TV's inherent problems of high costs and waste circulation. Most of these events are not shown on TV or cable, but the sponsoring companies benefit sufficiently from the impressions made on live spectators and often from substantial news coverage.

Tennis is a prime example of a once-popular TV sport that advertisers used to reach upscale viewers. When tennis TV ratings declined as a result of over-exposure, commercial sponsors left television to pursue the safer and less expensive route of "buying" an entire tournament (the Volvo International, for example.) Other companies just bought on-site space at tournaments to display corporate banners and entertain clients at gala parties.

Capital Sports, Inc., is a New York-based marketing firm, one of a growing list of sports marketing specialists which tie sports events together with the interests and objectives of corporate sponsors. For example, Capital is totally responsible for running all of the Equitable old-timers games, a logistical exercise which involves bringing together approximately thirty-five former major league players—some who played in the city where the game takes place, some Hall-of-Fame members, and others who are ex-major leaguers willing to attend and who are still able to swing a bat and carry a glove.

In addition to paying Capital a fee to promote and market the games, Equitable pays expenses for each player and his wife, and a $1,000 honorarium. In addition, the company donates $10,000 for each game (amounting to $260,000 a year) to a charitable foundation which assists former major leaguers in financial need. Equitable's precise financial return is hard to calculate, but its management feels that gathering former sports heroes at a well-promoted event that carries the Equitable name is sound business for a company that endorses health and longevity.

The Olympics, the profound celebration of amateur athletics, is probably the best-known event for attracting marketing-conscious companies. Ironically, the 1984 games in Los Angeles reached what was perhaps the apotheosis of commercialism, virtually rewriting the rules of sports marketing. Nearly every turn of Olympian endeavor was accompanied by a sponsor willing to pay dearly to have its name associated with some part of the world's foremost athletic festival: Canon was the official 35-mm. camera, Kodak was the official non-35-mm. camera, and Fuji the official film. Kellogg was the official cereal, and A. H. Robins and Z-BEC brands were the official vitamin pills. The 7–11 convenience stores donated a velodrome, and McDonald's contributed a multi-million dollar swimming pool. While these companies, and hundreds like them, were "official" suppliers of goods and services, none were "sponsors" of the L.A. Oympics. This designation was reserved for companies willing to pay nearly $14 million each to the Los Angeles Organizing Committee, in return for which they received permission to use the official five-ring

Olympic logo in their advertising campaigns. Non-sponsors, who could still lay claim to being the official this-or-that, paid much less.

The commercialization of the Olympics does not stop with local organizing committees, as international marketers take increasing advantage of the Olympics' unique global appeal. In 1983 the International Olympic Committee (IOC) appointed ISL Marketing, a Swiss-based firm, as the sole organization responsible for securing and selling international sponsorship rights to the 1988 Olympics in Seoul and Calgary. ISL guaranteed exclusive rights within product categories to companies involved in multi-national marketing and which needed international exposure. Each of these firms was guaranteed worldwide use of the Olympic symbols in its marketing campaigns.

Through ISL, the IOC received a total of $120 million from nine companies (Eastman Kodak, Visa International, Federal Express, Brother, Panasonic, Phillips, Coca-Cola, 3M, and Time), granting them worldwide rights which allowed these companies to attach their corporate logos to the 1988 Calgary and Seoul games. In addition to paying sponsorship fees, each company spent approximately $30–40 million more on advertising campaigns and promotional activities.

While the Olympics are clearly one of the most obvious—and expensive—marketing outlets, no sports event is safe from corporate involvement. The International Ski Federation allows national teams to sell advertising on racers' uniforms, permitting up to 30 square centimeters of ads per outfit, with lettering limited to a height of 15 millimeters. While the Federation allows beer ads, it prohibits cigarettes and whiskey. Individual ad-clad racers on the U.S. Ski Team share proceeds from the sale. Each member receives 15 percent of the ad fee, and the remainder goes to the team organization. Skiiers are also allowed to sell space on their crash helmets and ski caps. For this prime location, they pocket as much as 90 percent of the fee.

The concept of sports marketing originally focused on advertisements in which athletes endorsed product lines associated with the sport in which they participated. According to industry estimates, corporations currently spend $50 million on endorsements by sports figures, twice the amount they spent collectively as recently as 1983. From the athlete's point of view, a lost race or game wasn't always disastrous, but to the victors generally went the endorsements. For example, after Boris Becker won the tennis title at Wimbledon in 1986, Puma, the West German company, whose tennis shoes and racquets bore the champion's name, rejoiced at the prospect of increasing its U.S. market share. In the mid-1980s, Puma lagged well behind Reebok, Nike, and Adidas, its German-based competitor. When Becker signed a six-year, multi-million dollar endorsement contract in 1985, Puma's worldwide sales of tennis shoes increased by 25 percent. After Becker's Wimbledon victory, Puma's tennis racquet sales also increased, but not as dramatically as its shoes.

Today, sports marketers also try to sell the intrinsic value of their athlete/clients, arguing that the image of excellence in sports is transferable to excellence in any field. Thus, an Arnold Palmer sells tractors, Jimmie Connors sells investments, and O. J. Simpson sells car rentals. (In December 1987 the *Wall Street Journal* reported that Palmer earned an estimated $8 million per year through endorsements, making him the top product endorser in the sports world.)

While it is hard to quantify the effectiveness of athlete endorsements, success stories abound. For example, John McEnroe's association with Bic disposable razors was credited with increasing that company's market share from 12 percent to 23 percent in the mid-1980's. Similarly, Dunlop Sports Company increased sales of tennis racquets by 170 percent, doubling its U.S. market share in one year after McEnroe began to endorse them.

Marketing companies which were once solely in the business of providing client services—everything from securing endorsements, negotiating contracts, and handling public relations to managing their clients' legal and financial affairs—have branched out considerably. Today, sports marketing companies package and manage sports tournaments and events, and attract corporate sponsors willing to lend their name and promotion budgets. Needless to say, if the event is televised, the company's exposure is greater. Thus many of these firms also produce TV sports programs, and in this regard are today positioned in an enviable "catbird's seat." Rights-holders look to the marketing companies to package their event, including event sponsors. And because of the soft advertising market, the networks have become increasingly dependent on sports marketing firms to bring pre-sponsored programs to them.

While literally hundreds of sports marketing firms have entered the business, the field is today dominated by three companies: International Management Group (IMG), ProServ, and Advantage International. Each began by representing athletes, but as their client lists grew, and as events like the 1984 Los Angeles Olympics drove home the enormous benefits of associating corporations with sports, these marketing companies capitalized on the new climate of sports involvement. They sought out events and "sold" them to corporations, which saw a link between their business and the sports culture. IMG is a good example.

The Cleveland-based company was started in the early 1960s by Mark McCormack, recognized as the *Wunderkind* of sports marketing. Most of McCormack's early clients were golfers, including Arnold Palmer,

Jack Nicklaus, and Gary Player, all of whom dominated the circuit in the 1960s and each of whom was an attractive off-the-links spokesman for commercial products. (In 1961, Arnold Palmer became one of the first athletes used in a TV commercial, performing in a television ad for L&M cigarettes.)

Nearly three decades later, IMG has become a virtual sports and entertainment empire, with more than four hundred employees in thirteen divisions and offices in fifteen countries. The company serves more than five hundred clients in sports and entertainment, earning annual revenues of approximately $300 million.

Most sports marketing firms freely admit that measuring the value of event sponsorship is more difficult for companies than assessing the value of athlete endorsements. Subsequently, those that approach these activities often rely more on instinct than hard data to justify their corporate involvement. Some companies which sponsor events echo Coors Beer, which flatly recognizes that "Coors likes sports because sports sells beer." Myer's Rum pursues the affluent post-teenage market by sponsoring wind-surfing competitions. Others, like Manufacturers Hanover Corporation, which sells financial services to young corporate executives, sponsor road races for corporate running teams. The management of Manufacturers Hanover says confidently that, "while other banks are spending huge amounts on TV ads, we can attract thousands of business people at about $60,000 per race, which is a lot of bang for the bucks." The John Hancock Company sees its corporate identification with the Boston and New York Marathons as a way to instill a sense of pride among its employees.

Whether company pride or increased sales (probably a combination of both) is behind corporate decision-making, one thing is clear. As event promoters look for ways to meet rising operational costs involved in running sports events, they are finding more companies willing to use sports events as a way to meet marketing objectives. In 1986 some 2100 corporations collectively spent more than $1 billion on event sponsorship and participation. The networks and TV sports advertising are the likely casualties of this dramatic shift from an advertiser-dominated industry to one which is sponsor-driven.

These marketing-conscious companies recognize that, while sports is entertainment, sports has valuable characteristics other than pure entertainment. Sports events generate considerable publicity on the sports pages and on television, are usually filled with drama, and often have a surprise ending. Sports is a universal language, and almost everyone wants to identify with people who excel.

In sports marketing and television, a picture may be worth a thousand words, but it is also worth millions in free publicity for companies seeking the attention of sports audiences. It is no accident that ubiquitous jugs of Gatorade or cups bearing Pepsi or Coca-Cola logos show up on the sidelines of tennis matches where players towel off. The players may be thirsty, but sponsors are even hungrier for the television exposure. That is why many corporations spend so heavily to place their banners strategically around stadiums and arenas where they will be picked up by TV cameras. When Boris Becker beat John McEnroe in a 1987 Davis Cup match, nearly one million TV households watching the dramatic six-hour event on ESPN saw two mammoth banners behind one of the end lines bearing the NEC logo. They were perfectly positioned to be included in every shot in the match, and they were not there, obviously, by a quirk of fate. (There is a New York-based service which logs and evaluates the amount of exposure that companies get when their signs appear in the background of televised events. While the networks do not receive any direct compensation for having provided this gratuitous publicity, they do take the value of the signage into account when they negotiate rights fees with the owner of the event.)

For approximately $750,000, Budweiser bought the rights to have its logo appear on the ring mat and ring posts during the heavily-promoted world middleweight fight in 1987 between Marvin Hagler and Sugar Ray Leonard. The logo was seen by countless viewers watching the fight on closed circuit television, on HBO's rebroadcast, and on news clips of the bout.

One of the earliest and most successful TV marketing promotions was a well-conceived event engineered in behalf of Ford Motors. Ford's Punt, Pass and Kick competition was a national contest in which youngsters in several age brackets competed against one another in three categories: passing, punting, and kicking a football for distance. Local competitions were held at the stadiums of NFL teams during the season, with winners representing their home town professional team in a series of regional competitions. The finals of each event were televised at half-time of a late-season NFL game. Ford had two audiences in mind. One was young people and future car-owners. But the more important audience was the parents of contest entrants, who had to obtain entry forms from their local Ford dealer. Rush-hour traffic jams in NFL cities were nothing compared with the traffic in Ford dealerships, where young passers, punters, and kickers filled out the forms while their parents eyed—and sometimes test-drove—Ford vehicles.

Other companies have used TV sports marketing as successfully. In 1986, McDonald's created a nationwide contest designed to stimulate local franchise business and widen the company's already significant sales advantage in the competitive fast-food industry. McDonald's "Win with the NFL" promotion, in conjunction with an extensive advertising campaign during football season, involved trading cards featuring photos of home team and All-Pro stars. By scratching off a panel on each card and matching it up with the next weekend's winning teams, entrants could qualify in a buy-one-and-get-one-for-free giveaway. McDonald's also bought exclusive food industry rights from the NFL and NFL Players Association to use team logos and photographs of players in uniform, which demonstrates just how competitive the sports marketing arena is and how much value there is in exclusive sponsorship.

Local TV stations have been successful in tying a company's marketing strategy into its commercial ad buys. Ballantine Blasts, Pepsi Grand Slams, Nissan Seventh Player Awards (for hockey; Tenth Player Awards for baseball), or Stop and Shop Player of the Game gifts are some of the countless promotions that sell goods and build in-store traffic for local companies. T-shirts and other giveaways, ticket discounts for customers, and parties, receptions, and meet-the-players nights for dealers and distributors are now stock-in-trade for the sports marketer.

Despite the benefits, however, sports marketing has also had its share of controversy, mostly in cases where the stakes were high. Marketing wars reached a new level of intensity in a struggle between two of the country's largest competing breweries, both deeply involved in sports advertising.

Anheuser-Busch, Inc., worked hard and spent lavishly to remain "king of the beers." With an annual advertising budget of $500 million, the St. Louis-based brewery was known for its aggressive and imaginative marketing, which brought it control of nearly 50 percent of the domestic beer market. In 1984, A-B was rocked with scandals involving corporate executives who allegedly offered illegal inducements to stadium owners and vendors to ensure that Budweiser retained its market monopoly. The U.S. Treasury Department's Bureau of Alcohol, Tobacco and Firearms charged that A-B used its leverage from buying advertising time on Chicago White Sox broadcasts to force vendors at Comiskey Park to sell only Budweiser products. A-B settled out of court without admitting to any wrong-doing, but its beer was removed from the ball park. Budweiser's arch rival, Miller Brewing Company, won the rights to the in-park beer concession, and took over the TV sponsorship of White Sox games.

Another sports marketing controversy focused on the tobacco industry, once a major TV sports advertiser and now an industry under siege. When tobacco advertising was banned from radio and TV broadcasts in 1970, cigarette companies were excluded from the ripe TV markets. They sought alternatives to retain their visibility with the sports audience and found them in event sponsorship, much to the anguish and protests of a vocal anti-tobacco, no-smoking lobby which often drew picket lines around stadiums and arenas. The Philip Morris Company was one of the first companies to step into the breach. It timed its leap with the movement started by touring female tennis players, who were smoking in anger about the lack of equal pay and equal treatment at tournaments. "You've come a long way, baby" was more than Gloria Steinem and Betty Friedan's anthem. It was the campaign slogan for Philip Morris's Virginia Slims cigarettes, and the picture of a slender 1920s' flapper holding a tennis racquet in one hand and a cigarette holder in the other became the logo for a national tournament featuring the world's foremost women players. Prize money and promotional campaigns were commensurate with the growing stature of the world's leading women players.

The R. J. Reynolds Company went in a different direction, sponsoring male-oriented events that were in keeping with the product profile it sought to create. Beneficiaries of the Reynolds promotion dollars were the Winston 30-event NASCAR stock car races and the Vantage golf tournament.

Sometimes the best-laid marketing plans embroil innocent companies in controversy. The Beatrice Food Company was the unhappy recipient of such an ill-fated public relations disaster. Two computer wizards broke the code of a simple contest Beatrice had created which involved guessing the scores of eight Monday Night Football games. The food company promoted the contest heavily during each of the games. Learning of the breakthrough and faced with the potential loss of approximately $21 million in prize money to these two contestants, Beatrice blew the whistle and stopped play. The code-breakers sued the food company, resulting in costly litigation that is typical of sales promotion contests gone awry.

As sports marketing moves away from being advertiser-driven to sponsor-dominated, the networks are increasingly threatened by the loss of ad revenues. They have adopted aggressive policies to match the aggressive marketing techniques of companies that sponsor events and include the corporate name in the title. CBS, for example, demands that a company whose name is part of the event title—e.g., The John Hancock Sun Bowl, or the Federal Expresss St. Jude PGA Golf Classic—must purchase at least 25 percent of the available air time in the game before the network will give on-air credit in its promotion or telecast of the event.

Many in the sports marketing industry disagree about whether corporate money used to sponsor events comes at the expense of advertising budgets. What is clear, however, is that the trend towards smaller network and cable shares is very real, and many companies are more than willing to sacrifice reaching television's mass audience in favor of a more efficiently targeted in-stadium audience. As TV ratings decline, advertisers pay lower rates, leaving the networks no option but to pay less for rights fees to events. With this cycle at work, event sponsorship is the new way for companies to reach TV viewers, and the trend is clear. It should come as no surprise to anyone that one day we will find ourselves enjoying events on television that carry titles like the FTD Rose Bowl, the Atlas World Series, and the Q-Tip Cotton Bowl.

Aggressive sports marketing may be the most effective way to induce additional corporate investments in event sponsorship and new television concepts. The experience of three companies may best illustrate the changing dynamics of sports marketing and its growing importance to entrepreneurs, rights-holders, and television.

Visitors cannot help but feel healthy waiting in the reception area of Reebok Shoes' contemporary offices, located in an industrial park carved out of an innocent sylvan setting fifteen miles from the congestion of downtown Boston. With sunlight streaming through skylights onto a nest of comfortable modular furniture, a reassuring sense of fitness is everywhere, personified by the presence of five life-sized mannequins. Each wears Reebok footwear and a rainbow of colorful lycra body suits bearing the company's insignia. Strategically placed within the mannequin community are photo enlargements, some in color and others in black and white. Each depicts a dramatic scene from actual foot races and tennis matches in which the bodies of some of the lean, muscular contestants are also decked out in Reebok shoes, apparel, and logos. You know immediately that you are not in the reception room of a law firm or an insurance company.

If this upbeat environment celebrates America's modern-day infatuation with sweating in high fashion, it also conveys the competitiveness of the billion-dollar health and fitness industry that has burgeoned internationally in the past twenty years. While Reebok's roots begin at the turn of the century, the company made its real fortunes in the early 1980s when it grew almost overnight from a small manufacturer of aerobic shoes to an industry leader with three divisions, eight footwear product lines, and revenues that rose from $3.5 million in 1982 to $919 million in 1986. The successful rise of Reebok to the top ranks of the country's athletic shoe and apparel firms was marked by its acquisition of two competitors: Rockport Shoes and AVIA. Along the way, Reebok also added the John Frye Shoe Company, a 150-year-old manufacturer of popular sturdy boots.

Reebok started in Bolton, England, in the early 1900s, when Joseph Foster, a passionate but mediocre runner, developed spiked shoes to help his performance on the track. Foster marketed his innovative product to British runners under his own name until after World War II, when the company's growth and success led to plans for worldwide expansion. But management felt, however, that more needed to be done if the company were to retain its preeminence in the field. A name change was a priority matter.

"Foster's was a family name, connected with British running," said one of Foster's heirs. "In the 1950's we were looking toward new directions and sought a new name. I wanted an animal and just had a feeling about the letter "r." So I went to the dictionary and found reebok—a swift and agile gazelle."

Reebok entered the competitive American marketplace under new ownership in 1979 by attempting to gain a share of the running shoe market, which was becoming one of the decade's fastest growing industries. The company's major breakthrough, however, occurred not in the running field. Rather, it was in aerobics, an activity befitting the lifestyle of the affluent who supported the new exercise form as healthier—and more chic—than running. Participants in search of "fitness" swore to the freer and more comprehensive benefits of aerobic exercises.

If Reebok's design of aerobic footwear was pioneering, its marketing of the shoe was inspired, and by the mid-1980s the company dominated the men's and women's market. To many new aerobics practitioners, it was gauche to wear running shoes or tennis sneakers to a "jazzercise" class, and Reebok made the point even clearer in its advertising. The marketing of Rockport Shoes followed similar lines. Rockport "invented" walking as an exercise form, a craze later fueled by the creation of walking clubs, magazines, and other marketing gimmicks that propelled Rockport into market leadership in the walking shoe category. While specific footwear for aerobics and walking were successful beyond management's dreams, Reebok's tennis, basketball, and running shoes more than held their own in the competitive marketplace; the company's apparel division—not as successful as its footwear division—brought high fashion to family recreation.

Athletic sportswear and sports equipment industries resemble an oligopoly, where four or five major manufacturers dominate. The stakes involved in increasing market share are high, and competition is keen and costly. Entry by newcomers is difficult. Each participant differentiates its product through aggressive advertising and marketing which gains product recognition by associating the company with top calibre athletes and events. Reebok is as aggressive as any of the other companies in its industry, as a comment by its CEO attests. "We're not a footwear company," said Paul Fireman.* "We're a marketing company."

Reebok's leadership in creating market demand for its products is based on coordinated advertising and marketing activities that follow traditional lines. Product endorsements and event sponsorship play a major role in supporting Reebok's print and TV advertising activities. In tennis, for example, the company has signed such leading international players as Hana Mandlikova and Miroslav Mecir to long-term contracts. The terms of these and other endorsement agreements depend on such factors as the players' ranking and age. Most contracts run anywhere from two to five years, and often include bonuses for winning grand slam events and televised tournaments and for improvement in the player's ranking during the year.

In addition to tournaments, most players are expected to make personal appearances at tennis clinics and at Reebok retail outlets. Like the rules governing skiers, the use of company logos on participating tennis players is tightly controlled by the United States Tennis Association (USTA) and other international governing boards. Each approves the size and location of logos and company names on players' garments, so companies like Reebok carefully design these instruments of corporate identification for maximum visibility.

Reebok considers several factors to gauge its return on investment when paying athletes for their endorsements. The first is the authenticity that the company gets from having a tennis player of the calibre of Hana Mandlikova or basketball players like Dennis Johnson or Danny Ainge endorse a Reebok product. A second benefit is the credibility that Reebok gets when it presents itself to retailers and distributors in the sportswear and equipment industry. A third benefit is product development. Companies like Reebok value the input they receive from athletes whose livelihoods depend on wearing quality apparel. They take their comments seriously regarding the comfort and durability of the shoes and equipment.

Reebok has based its strategy for sponsoring events upon careful selection and exclusivity. In the mid-1980s the company created the Reebok Teaching Pro Classic, an event designed to reach a market segment that is influential in promoting Reebok's tennis line. Although the event is not televised, it involves a year-long series of local and regional tournaments in which tennis instructors and professionals at clubs across the country compete. Elimination rounds led to the finals played at the Tennis Hall of Fame at Newport, Rhode Island. There, Reebok sponsors

---

* Fireman, the third highest-paid executive in the country, bid to become majority owner of the New England Patriots in the spring of 1988.

a series of parties and celebrations in behalf of players to which it invites its dealers and distributors. Reebok management considers the marketing value to be greater when it places the company name exclusively before the select constituency of a less well-known event than when contributing to bigger events where the competition for visibility is more severe. As one Reebok executive stated, "We look for events that are unique, and which give us a special niche. The things we try to avoid are invisible promotions, 'black holes' where you sponsor something and you never know where your money goes. Event sponsorship is an inexact science, but we want to make certain that we get maximum value from our involvement."

One of Reebok's major investments in televised sports was its two-year agreement to become the official shoe and apparel sponsor of the U.S. Tennis Open, a major media and consumer event. Here, Reebok was more interested in the apparel identification than in shoes, primarily bcause logos on tennis clothes are more visible and easier to identify on camera. The U.S. Open, like many of today's major sports events, is heavily commercialized, and tournament sponsors sell anything that moves (or doesn't). In addition to its contract players who participated, Reebok also "bought" the ball boys and girls and lines judges, who all wore Reebok apparel during the two-week tournament.

Reebok banners placed strategically around the site (except for the center stadium, which was reserved for higher bidders in other consumer categories) were another part of the "official shoe and apparel" agreement. Reebok's center stadium exposure consisted of a listing on a sponsor board whose length made the credits of any normal TV program seem paltry by comparison.

Reebok considers the auspicious U.S. Open a way to reach thousands of on-site spectators and a vast television audience, as well as a means to merchandise and market its name and products at the tournament site. The company not only sold its apparel at three booth locations but also used the event to reach the important New York City retail community through player appearances at Manhattan stores and dealer seminars. Reebok also sponsored entertainment events at the tournament for retailers and Reebok distributors.

The Reebok sales success story, as its management clearly understands, is as much a matter of timing and good fortune as designing and manufacturing quality products. In recognizing the limitations of sports marketing, they remain realistic, pointing to the perhaps apocryphal story of the shoe company which spent heavily to be an "official shoe" at the 1984 Los Angeles Olympics. The company's post-event research, however, showed that most people confused the sponsor with a competitor.

In 1985, the John Hancock Company, once merely a staid life insurance company, began to dominate the field of marathon sponsorship as dramatically as the company's sparkling 59-story, all-glass office building dominates the Boston skyline. The country's fifth largest insurer, Hancock is now a major financial services organization with seventeen subsidiary agencies, managing more than $40 billion in assets. Under the astute leadership of its president and chief executive officer, E. James Morton, and David D'Alessandro, Senior Vice President for Corporate Comunications, the company sought to reshape its stodgy image by putting its name on events that project health. What could be better for a business that prospers most when its policy-holders live forever than an association with marathons?

When Hancock management announced its plan to become involved with the Boston Marathon, many saw the supreme irony of a profitable insurance company trying to breathe life into the oldest marathon in the country. The marathon had always been a matter of civic pride, a Boston institution in the same bigger-than-life fashion as Julia Child, Arthur Fiedler, and the Harvard Yard. Whether or not they ran, Bostonians always looked to the traditional April running of "the Boston" as a day that boosted the city's image and gave the sport of running what Child gave to French cooking, Fiedler to music, and the Yard to countless preppies—fun, festivity, and a touch of class.

By the mid-1980s, the Boston marathon seemed on the verge of extinction, much like a glamorous movie queen whose best days were behind her. Its future appeared particularly bleak under the administration of the Boston Athletic Association, whose leadership seemed more content to keep its collective running feet planted squarely in the nineteenth century than to adjust to the realities of the twenty-first. To B.A.A. officials, races were run as a matter of pride and endurance, not events to be tarnished by the crass commercialism of modern-day athletes. Race organizers went only so far in tolerating marathon sponsorship, allowing signs at the finish line and on pace cars. However, they scoffed at the idea of prize money which, by the 1970s, had become standard for virtually every other world class event.

While B.A.A. leadership clung to its ideals of pure amateurism, the once-prestigious race floundered, as international marathoners who earn their living by running no longer saw medals and olive wreaths as fitting rewards in lieu of prize money. Marathons are unlike other sports that place heavy physical demands on athletes over the course of a season. The 26-mile endurance test taxes runners so greatly that most can only compete in one or two events a year. Thus, appearance fees became as necessary an inducement as prize money to lure a field of "name" runners like Rob deCastella, Greg Meyer, Rosa Mota, Bill Rodgers, Joan Benoit Samuelson, Geoff Smith, Greta Waitz, and others. Top marathoners like these are no different from many foreign athletes who compete in the Olympics. They define the term "amateur" in a looser and more contemporary way.

Lack of prize money was not the only handicap facing "the Boston." Like promoters in most other sports who equate television exposure with excellence, marathon organizers feel that the lack of TV coverage often relegates their event to second-class status. The New York City Marathon, which regularly attracts nearly two million spectators who line the 26-mile course, was televised by ABC, capitalizing on the popularity of running as a fitness sport. Television gives this fall spectacle in New York a big-time look that brings its own rewards to the New York Road Runners, Inc., the event organizer, and to companies which sponsor the race. CBS has televised 90-minute edited versions of the Chicago Marathon that likewise give event sponsors and runners the glory and glamour that participants have come to expect. Network television coverage is conspicuous by its absence in Boston.

Like its stance on prize money, the Boston Athletic Association has taken a conservative view of television coverage, particularly if it meant moving the race from its traditional Monday date to the weekend, the only time the networks would consider. Traditionally, the Marathon has always been run on Patriot's Day, a Boston Monday holiday celebrating Paul Revere's midnight ride. To the B.A.A., moving the race to accommodate the networks would be sacrilegious.

Race organizers are not the only ones to shoulder the blame for lack of network TV coverage for "the Boston." The marathon course covers twenty-six miles which wind through eight cities and towns in eastern Massachusetts. Officials in each of these locales see TV rights fees as a way to recoup expenses that they encounter in providing security along the course and in cleaning up in the aftermath of the race. As far as the networks were concerned, no amount of rights fees are large enough to support the waiting hands of parochialism.

The John Hancock Company leaped into the midst of this fractious climate in 1985. On the surface, its move was one of great generosity bordering on charity; to cynics, it was an actuarial nightmare bordering on black humor—a major insurance company bestowing a ten-year life insurance policy on a frail and failing ninety-year-old client, nearly at the breaking point from stress and fatigue.

John Hancock's involvement is a classic example of corporate event sponsorship, even though Hancock was criticized by several competing marathon organizers who felt that Hancock was overly generous in spending considerably more on prize and appearance money than the runners' market warranted. In its deal, Hancock agreed to pay $1 million a year for ten years, nearly one-fourth of which went to prize and bonus money. Most of the rights fees went to the B.A.A., which administers the race now concluding at an elaborate finish line at Hancock's corporate headquarters in downtown Boston. In addition, Hancock agreed to compensate cities and towns along the marathon route to cover some of their race-related expenses.

The B.A.A.'s capitulation to offering prize money was a major victory for Hancock. However, the Association dug in the heels of its running shoes at the thought of paying appearance fees, which the insurer still felt necessary to attract top-flight runners who might finish out of the prize money. In a stroke of diplomatic and strategic genius, Hancock signed a number of world class marathoners to personal services contracts for the purpose of conducting running and fitness clinics at several locations across the country. The contract does not mandate that these runners compete in Boston, but it precludes them from appearing in other races within sixty days on either side of the April event.

While the Monday running rules out network coverage, Hancock has attracted start-to-finish race coverage on ESPN by buying nearly half of the air time. The race is also carried live by three Boston commercial TV stations.

The effectiveness of corporate sponsorship of a sports event is difficult to measure, but Hancock has developed a formula to quantify results. It gives an equivalent advertising dollar value to the tremendous amount of print and TV publicity Hancock received since its first announcement. It took the documented print clips and TV exposures, assigned a length or a time span to them, and assigned a dollar figure of what these same exposures would have cost in advertising rates. While company management felt that the results are "not precisely scientific," they computed a value of $8.2 million in the first year of its ten year, $10 million investment.

In 1987 Hancock signed a three-year agreement to sponsor the New York City Marathon which ABC televises. In explaining Hancock's interest in expanding its involvement in marathons, one top company executive said, "The network agreement was huge in that it opens up a market and increases our visibility in the Northeast where we do a large percentage of our business. We can enhance Boston's (marathon) reputation in New York without the pain of getting involved in the race."

Under the terms of the agreement, Hancock paid $500,000 per year in return for advertising exclusivity of its products on the telecast. In return, Hancock buys one-third of the total advertising spots in the telecast, and is designated by ABC as the official presenter on all network billboards and promotional announcements.

As a major postscript to its Boston and New York ventures, Hancock signed a five-year agreement in early 1988 to sponsor the Los Angeles Marathon. In order to attract top runners to each of these three events, Hancock planned to award between $100,000 and $250,000 in prizes to any runner who consecutively won the three races (a challenging feat given the short time—one month—between the Los Angeles race and the one in Boston.) By adding yet another major road race to its portfolio, the insurance/financial services company has laid claim to "owning" the only triple crown grand prix of marathons.

If the John Hancock Company saved a dying marathon, even more so did the company gain credit for rescuing a football classic that was all but dead.

The Sun Bowl in El Paso, Texas, founded in 1935, is the oldest independent college bowl in the country. It had become the culminating event in a festival that starts in October and ends in January, and includes golf tournaments, parades, and endless parties. When TV rights began to dry up in the mid-1980s, the Sun Bowl was one of the victims, as CBS cut back on paying for sports events that had only marginal value. CBS had televised the Sun Bowl for eighteen years but saw the TV ratings drop considerably between 1983 and 1985 because of competition from other, better-known bowl games, and from NFL playoff games. The Sun Bowl was not alone in facing the threat of extinction. In 1985, ABC dropped the Gator Bowl and the $800,000 rights fee that went with it.

For approximately 2000 volunteers in El Paso who worked on the three-month community event, the imminent death of the Sun Bowl was a matter of civic bereavement. For El Paso's municipal and business leaders who ran the Sun Bowl and its attendant festival, the sight of the big, good-hearted insurance company from the East coming to their rescue must have been reminiscent of a scene in the last reel of an old-fashioned western movie.

For Hancock, sponsorship was not a matter of charity. It was good business for a national financial services company riding a hot streak of good publicity following its Boston marathon involvement.

Beginning in 1986, Hancock paid $500,000 a year for three years' rights to the El Paso event, with a two-year option to renew. In return, the company received a variety of merchandising benefits in El Paso, including free game tickets, parties, and considerable on-site exposure for the Hancock logo. More important, Hancock gained exclusive entry into the small but influential southwestern TV market in which there are no major league franchises in any sport and where the Sun Bowl is the major sports activity. While CBS agreed to continue televising the game since Hancock was now paying most of the rights fee, the use of Hancock's logo on the field became a matter of serious contention.

The contract between Hancock and the network allowed the company to paint its famous script logo on the artificial surface of the Sun Bowl. The logo extends twenty yards at midfield between the two forty-yard lines, and is in a pivotal location that makes it visible for about half the game.

There were several other important matters to be negotiated before the three-way deal was consummated. One involved the change in the official name of the event to The John Hancock Sun Bowl. In return for the obvious name recognition, CBS required that Hancock purchase 25 percent of the commercial advertising time in return for being the exclusive advertiser in the financial service company category. CBS also guaranteed a 10 rating and at least a minimum amount of on-air promotion for the game.

The final serious negotiating hurdle to cross was the actual scheduling of the game. With major bowls dominating New Year's Day, most of the other secondary post-season college games were forced to pick alternate dates. One or two chose a weekend day before Christmas and New Year's, while others felt they would benefit by playing the game during the holiday break. Stung by poor late December ratings, Sun Bowl officials and CBS agreed to televise the El Paso game on Christmas Day. But when? For CBS traditionally an NBA game started at noon on Christmas Day, and so it suggested that the Sun Bowl now precede the basketball game. The suggestion received a cool reception from Sun Bowl and Hancock officials who loathed the idea of a noon-time start (Eastern time), which would reach West Coast viewers at 9:00 a.m. More than that, Hancock and bowl leadership courted the church-going audience and felt uncomfortable with the idea of their football game beginning at the same time as noon Mass. Football, television, and the Lord make strange bedfellows. After serious negotiations, CBS agreed to continue starting the professional basketball game at noon, followed by the Sun Bowl. This arrangement pleased Hancock management and its ad agency because more people watch television later in the day.

In evaluating its involvement in the 1986–87 Sun Bowl Festival, Hancock again applied the ad dollar equivalency formula. It found the return in terms of the gross impressions made through newspaper, magazine and TV publicity outlets to be approximately the same in dollar value as one year's rights fee. These impressions did not include the impact and value that Hancock derived from CBS promotions and actual game coverage. As a further index of its success, Hancock paid the lowest cost-per-thousand of all bowl games in the Christmas game of 1986–87. The game drew a rating of 11.5 (double the previous year's non-Christmas Day game), and Hancock paid $20,300 per commercial, the most efficient commercial buy of all televised bowl games that year.

While TV advertising has been a major part of John Hancock's marketing strategy, the company has thrived on the public relations values it has gained from carefully selecting sports events and paying for exclusivity. The staid insurance company needs no further testimony to the value of sports marketing than the comment made by one of its agents in the Southwest who said, "I cannot imagine anyone in El Paso not buying a John Hancock insurance policy or related financial service after what you've done for this city."

The two-story office building across from the railroad station in downtown Greenwich, Connecticut, does not look like a place where major sports deals are made. Such matters usually come out of Manhattan's cluster of skyscrapers that house network sports divisions, ad agencies, and the headquarters of most major leagues. Instead, this pleasant locale, where civility dictates that young police officers along Greenwich Avenue stand guard at street crossings to protect the passing parade of suburban maids and matrons from morning traffic, is the home of Sports Marketing & Television International (SMTI), marketing representative for the Breeders' Cup. In a relatively short time, this Super Bowl of thoroughbred horse racing has prompted the *Boston Globe* to rhapsodize that "the Breeders' Cup program is like having the Derby, the English Oaks, the Prix du Jockey Club, the Arc de Triomphe and the Jockey Club Gold Cup all staged at the same track on the same day." Not bad testimony for thoroughbred racing, a sport whose image was crafted more by Damon Runyon than by the public relations machinations of Peter Ueberroth and Pete Rozelle.

SMTI is headed by Mike Trager, a former NBC Sports vice president and advertising veteran who was in charge of all marketing and television activities for Anheuser-Busch while executive vice president of the D'Arcy MacManus Masius advertising agency in New York. While at the agency, Trager was responsible for developing the ABC-TV package of USFL games, and was exclusive representative for the sponsorship and marketing in the United States of the 1984 Sarajevo Olympic Games. To Trager and his SMTI associates, marketing the Breeders' Cup for a national TV audience posed a challenge even greater than that of the ill-fated USFL.

In the early 1980s, horse racing in the United States was on the decline. Track attendance and betting were down for both thoroughbred and harness racing, while television coverage was primarily devoted to the big three events—the Kentucky Derby, the Preakness, and the Belmont Stakes. As a big-time sport, thoroughbred racing traditionally lacked a focus. Unlike other major league sports, racing has no commissioner who can articulate a singular point of view about the sport, or who represents the collective interests of the various components that comprise the racing industry. Instead of being a single league under one umbrella, thoroughbred racing is more of an uneasy alliance of breeders, track owners, and racing associations and other self-governing bodies. Each has different goals and concerns. One of Trager's challenges was to help the thoroughbred racing industry avoid the pitfall that has faced virtually every other sport, namely, to keep self-interest from standing in the way of success.

Racing's decline in the television age has also been attributed to a lack of identity. In other sports, spectators pay to see performers who are generally the focus of media attention. From these ranks come living legends. In racing, however, the stars can't talk (which may be a blessing, given the level of most post-game locker room discourse). Instead, jockeys, trainers, and owners speak for the "athletes" and are identified with the sport, a forced identity at best.

At a pre-Kentucky Derby meeting in 1982, John Gaines, one of the industry's leading breeders of thoroughbreds, challenged his fellow breeders to agree to a plan which would at once raise the level of the sport and assure its future. Gaines suggested that they all work together to create an event, or series of events, to culminate in a championship like baseball's World Series or football's Super Bowl.

In deliberations that rivaled a U.N. General Assembly session, the majority of breeders agreed to raise approximately $20 million for prize and promotion money for a series of championship races in seven thoroughbred divisions. The breeders envisioned an event so important that TV could hardly ignore it. Enter Mike Trager and SMTI. The dynamic young TV and marketing professional had the requisite television and advertising experience. In addition, his ability to get USFL football off the ground in the wake of the NFL's network dominance could not help but cast him as a thoroughbred in the world of wealthy, success-driven race horse breeders.

Trager had to sell the Breeders' Cup to the networks, and once the steering committee settled on the concept of one seven-race day and a way to finance the enormous undertaking, timing was everything. From the point of view of the breeders, spring would have been an ideal time to hold the event, based on the racing season. However, this would inevitably conflict with the running of the Derby, the Preakness, and the Belmont.

From TV's standpoint, Trager knew that his best chance for selling the Breeders' Cup to the networks would be for a fall telecast, which even then stacked the odds against him.

First, there was the matter of weather. Thoroughbred racing on the East Coast in November always poses a risk. While more than a dozen tracks submitted proposals, for that reason alone the Breeders' Cup steering committee selected Hollywood Park for the first year. The selection proved wise in light of the second year, when the races were held at Aqueduct in New York. There, a steady drizzle and overcast day robbed the event of much of its glamour.

Trager approached each of the three networks with carefully structured business plans tailored to each of their needs. He knew that ABC and CBS had more experience than NBC in televising horse racing. He also knew that ABC and CBS were saddled with college football on Saturday afternoons and that his best chance rested with NBC, which carried a lower-rated smorgasbord of sports anthologies and professional bowling matches at that time. Although Trager would have preferred January and February from an audience standpoint when HUT (households using television) levels are higher, he also felt that his best bet for getting network clearance was in late fall.

From the beginning, Trager's strategy was to convince the networks that the Breeders' Cup had the potential to become a major world-class event. Approaching them with an all-or-nothing bravado, he insisted on a multi-year deal to establish credibility. He argued that the network which bought the rights could not pick and choose which of the day's races it would televise. Usually, the seventh race of a racing card is the most important, carries the biggest payoff, and attracts the biggest audience. Trager wanted the network to televise the full day—seven championship races run over four hours—even though each race only lasts about two minutes. The networks are often criticized for padding their 90-minute telecasts of Triple Crown events with inane and frequently boring material. The Breeders' Cup would run a race every thirty minutes. To him, filling time and sustaining audience were minor details. After all, Super Bowl Sundays virtually start the Saturday night before the game because advertisers know that enough sports junkies are willing to watch the endless parade of pre-game interviews and features. Even though the first race had yet to be run, Trager was convinced that the Breeders' Cup had "big time" potential that would one day put it in the Super Bowl class.

The approximate seven-figure rights fee was based on a projected 4 rating. (The Breeders' Cup actually averaged a 5 rating in its first year, although subsequent audiences were slightly smaller.) Other factors involved in establishing the rights fee were the fall air date, network production costs and profit expectations, the demographic appeal of the Breeders' Cup telecast, and the depressed state of the broadcast advertising market in the early 1980s.

NBC signed a three-year contract to televise the Breeders' Cup beginning in 1984. Rights fees would gradually accelerate each year. After two years, NBC was sufficiently satisfied with the results and extended its contract to run through 1989 with a two-year option to renew.

The success of the Breeders' Cup telecasts has been largely due to NBC's heavy on-air promotion and to production values which elevated the event to a level approximating Trager's vision. In 1986 the network used 18 cameras and a roster of notable thoroughbred racing analysts to provide commentary. The $10 million production budget to cover the live event approximated that of the Super Bowl.

Also, SMTI engineered an extraordinary marketing campaign which contributed to the event's success. By 1986 its efforts led to ESPN's carrying special pre-event programs: feature films and newsclips being fed to TV stations and other broadcast and cable networks; and race tracks across the country carrying live satellite feeds of each race on Race Day.

The unprecedented advertising, promotion, and publicity blitz created an aura designed to attract what NBC promotion called "an upscale, affluent group of active consumers." SMTI's search for event sponsors was buoyed by research which confirmed this audience profile to be more than network hype.

From the outset, Trager felt that the Breeders' Cup would be better off without a corporate sponsor to attach its name and title to the overall event. He was more interested in marketing each race separately, selling seven individual sponsorships to companies interested in reaching both the track and the TV audiences. Each race would carry its own sponsor's corporate name. He suggested to NBC that the four-hour telecast be produced like seven mini-programs, each tied to one of the day's races. Corporate sponsors would have to buy advertising time in the telecast. (As it turned out, SMTI's race sponsors accounted for nearly 50 percent of the commercial time sold in the first year's telecast.) In return the sponsors got product exclusivity in their category. For example, if Anheuser-Busch sponsored the fourth race, it was assured that NBC would not carry competing beer commercials for thirty minutes on either side of that race.

The mini-programs were introduced by an opening billboard identifying the race sponsor whose commercials bracketed the actual running of the race. Each mini-program concluded with an awards ceremony at which one of the sponsor's executives presented prize money to the winning owner and jockey.

The cost of sponsoring a race was based on the potential size of each event's TV audience and the resultant exposure. The first five races, which each offered a $1 million purse, were less attractive than the last two races, which offered bigger purses and ostensibly commanded a bigger audience. For example, the $2 million sixth race, the Breeders' Cup Turf, cost sponsors slightly more than the first five races, and the seventh race, the Breeders' Cup Classic, had a $3 million purse and was priced the highest.

In identifying potential race sponsors, Trager looked mostly, but not exclusively, to the traditional categories of sports advertisers—automotives, beers, financial planning services, and oil companies. He was encouraged by research, based on the TV audience which watched Triple Crown events, that showed a near 50–50 split between men and women, many in higher income levels. First year sponsors were Anheuser-Busch (Michelob), Chrysler Corporation, De Beers Consolidated Mines Ltd., First Jersey Securities, and Mobil Oil. After the first year, De Beers dropped out because of problems in South Africa. Chrysler left the Breeders' Cup to sponsor the Bob Hope Golf Classic. Seagram Distilleries (Mumm Champagne) became a Breeders' Cup sponsor in its second year.

In addition to exclusivity, numerous on-air identifications, and publicity exposure, Trager and his Breeders' Cup colleagues offered sponsors a number of other benefits. As part of the package, they got announcements on the trackside message board and over the track's public address system; signs, banners, and product displays at various track locations; a full-page, four-color advertisement in the official race program; and free reserved seats on race day. In addition they were provided accommodations for entertaining VIPs and clients at hospitality locations at the track and at local hotels during the festive race week. Hospitality and complimentary tickets are major inducements to attracting corporate sponsors at virtually every major sporting event.

One of Trager's biggest sponsor success stories involved the ubiquitous Anheuser-Busch after just two years' experience with the Breeders' Cup week. In addition to its Breeders' Cup race sponsorship, A-B signed a multi-year agreement in 1986 to sponsor a series of thirty-eight races to run at different U.S. and Canadian race tracks during the year. These races were part of "The $3 Million Breeders' Cup Budweiser Special Stakes Program," which not only promoted the brewery, but gave the Breeders' Cup valuable year-long exposure.

Just as the World Series or Super Bowl is preceded by season-long press coverage, Trager coveted the opportunity that the Budweiser Stakes provided to keep the Breeders' Cup races in front of the public. In addition to these events, he and the Breeders' Cup organizers created other activities that they hoped would give thoroughbred racing year-round attention. In 1986, they initiated a special Premium Awards Program in which $12 million was distributed to racing associations to enhance existing stakes at thoroughbred tracks across the country. The Breeders' Cup hierarchy saw this kind of activity as yet another way to support thoroughbred racing, and to give the sport the focus it lacked.

Someone once said that marketing is nothing more than the art of making something out of nothing. The Breeders' Cup is living testimony to this. What began as a gimmick to pump life into the slowly fading thoroughbred racing industry became an institution in only three years, through the marriage of television and sports marketing. One can only wonder what the odds were in 1982 when John Gaines and his fellow breeders bet that the Super Bowl of horse racing would finish so far ahead in the money.

10

WHO SHOT THE MESSENGER?
Journalism and the Bottom Line

THE WOEFUL STATE of television sports journalism should come as no surprise to the average fan. It has long been this way, and the fans themselves have been, both implicitly and explicitly, one of the most conservative influences restraining anything resembling unfettered journalism. For nearly forty years, television sports executives have shied away from the very tenets of free and enterprising reporting practiced by print journalists, and in doing so have cited their fear of upsetting either the viewing public on one hand, or the sports entrepreneurs and rights-holders they had to negotiate with, on the other. In short, the journalist, by nature a boat-rocker and disturber of the established order, is regarded with considerable suspicion, not only by his targets but by his employers as well.

No one likes to hear such bad news as the tragic, cocaine-induced death of University of Maryland basketball star Len Bias, payoff scandals at Southern Methodist University, academic "ghettoes" for athletes at the University of Georgia, or of the raft of athletes with drug, alcohol, and financial problems. Athletes and sports executives often react worst when the news is broken by a seemingly friendly source, a sports reporter. There is often a very real sense of betrayal, accompanied by a feeling that one's privacy has been violated by the very people who should have been guarding the secrets most assiduously, and who, in fact, have long benefited from association with the sports business. It is as though an unwritten gentlemen's agreement has been violated by a member of the inner circle within the club.

All journalists face formidable barriers in their attempts to understand and describe the sports business. Teams and organizations are generally closed-mouthed and protective of their employees, suspicious of the motives of many in the press, and wont to regard all mass media as partners, or adjuncts to beneficial public relations. Television sports remains a most difficult environment for an honest journalist because so many of the support systems available to "straight" news reporters—demanding readers, experienced editors, financial resources, space in the newspaper or magazine, and most critically, independence from conflicts of interest or commercial entanglements—are thoroughly compromised in television sports.

Compared with most television program formats, sports journalism is not expensive to produce. The expenses entailed are relatively high, however, when measured against the rate of return the company might expect, as a result of low ratings. Good journalism anywhere is reasonably expensive, requiring as it does highly trained support personnel, considerable time to develop stories, extensive and careful research, and editing. Worse, only a few good stories can be generated in a year, and they are difficult to put into the predictable, prescribed program formats of commercial television: when a good serious story (e.g., "Drugs in High School Sports") is ready for air the choice is either to drop it into the middle of a ball game, or other essentially escapist programming, or to pre-empt the network schedule to air a sports journalism special. The former never seems appropriate to the subject matter, and the latter is a sure ratings disaster. Through the years, various journalistically minded reporters and producers have fought for, and received, their own time slot for enterprise reporting. The almost inevitable results have been a gaggle of awards, some attention-getting publicity, and a hearty pat on the back from the network programmers when they cancel the program due to low ratings.

It would be easy to state that the historical root of the problem is money: the financial partnership between television and sports, which binds the success of one to the other, as well as spawning a host of in-house inhibitions and prohibitions concerning the role, function, and range of journalism. In fact, the growth of financial interdependence has made the problems infinitely more intractable: as Huntington Williams points out in the "Gannett Center Journal," with the flow of TV money "sports progressed from relative penury into a complex world of free-agency and super-marketing, of legitimate and illegitimate betting, of drugs and the right-to-privacy issue, and of racism, antitrust law and eminent domain." However, the most basic problems stem from the earliest days of broadcasting and sports, and from the widely held belief that broadcast sports were (and are) entertainment programs, staged and performed for the amusement and interest of fans, and that as privately controlled entities they were immune from the usual intrusions of journalists into topics other than what took place on the playing field.

Despite the basically entertaining nature of sports, the early CBS and NBC radio networks assigned the "description and accounts" of the games to News, since it traditionally covered "live" events. Williams notes the distinction between news and sports was muddied by the fact that several of the most prominent on-air commentators covered both types of events interchangeably: Graham McNamee sandwiched the 1924 Democratic National Convention and President Calvin Coolidge's inauguration between calls of the 1923 and 1925 World Series. At CBS, as always, tradition died hardest, lasting at least through 1960, when Walter Cronkite, looking slightly ill at ease, hosted the Squaw Valley Olympics. On the other hand, newborn ABC, having no tradition of covering much of anything in the fifties and early sixties, bought itself a Sports division by acquiring an independent production company; the result was a young and aggressive ABC Sports, independent of the stodgier News, which could cheerfully cover sports as entertainment. In an ironic turnabout, the later triumphs of ABC Sports would propel Roone Arledge to the presidency of News, where it must have seemed to many old hands that the tail was now wagging the dog.

The public traditionally has demanded very little, if anything, in the way of journalism from broadcasting. Radio and television sports have always been described as the ultimate escapist fare—the kind of programming one tuned into precisely to escape the cares and troubles in the rest of the world. In an era in which athletes were regarded as heroes and role models for youth, very few people wished to hear about Babe Ruth's drinking and wenching, the gambling habits of players, owners' treatment of their employees, the obvious racism of sports, labor-management problems, salary disputes, or a host of issues we now take for granted. Neither newspapers nor broadcasters saw fit to mention these indelicate subjects, and many actively participated in hushing up scandals of one sort or another, "for the good of the game," but also because they were afraid of their own audience's reactions to such disclosures.

It was a very cozy relationship, as the writers and broadcasters traveled with (and sometimes lived with) the teams, frequently on the team's payroll. Expenses were covered, meals and lodging provided, and a host of other courtesies extended to the journalists, who saw themselves in many instances as extensions of the team itself. Players and managers, owners and fans could afford to lower their defenses in front of these reporters, secure in the knowledge that, as "one of the boys," the reporters would protect their image, thoroughly sanitizing the scruffy, roustabout realities of sports.

Nearly everyone involved in professional sports, including players, managers, and owners, was less attuned to the challenges and opportunities presented by the press, and hardly understood the role of the mass media in shaping imagery or in generating revenues. Many athletes were semi-educated and came from small towns throughout the country. Some, in fact, couldn't read the very newspapers that were writing about them. Unsophisticated, naive, but fiercely proud of their prowess and privacy, they expected reporters and broadcasters to act as public relations men; often they were not disappointed. Reporters rarely strayed from a formulaic presentation of the athlete as grizzled veteran or winsome youth, making his way through American society by dint of dedication, hard work, God-given talent, respect for the system which so blessed him, and a sense of obligation to the fans, the owners, and the nation.

Whatever real reporting was being done appeared in newspapers, but subject matter and content were vastly different from those of today. Sports pages were filled with detailed play-by-play reporting of games; some well-known columnists appeared frequently to comment on the proceedings. There were, however almost no feature articles, adversarial reports, "background stories," or investigations of anything save the on-field activities. Radio and television did not then have the technical capacity now taken for granted, which enables them to dissect a play, or entire game, through a series of replay, slow-motion, and still-frame devices. Nor did there exist the enormous local broadcast newscasts, each containing its own sports segment, complete with scoreboards, replays, highlights, and other breaking news. The sheer tonnage of material available through broadcasting, combined with its immediacy and ability to beat most newspaper deadlines by hours, eventually forced a change on newspaper sports sections.

Faced with the realization that any avid sports fan would already have seen and heard described virtually every important happening in a game long before he read the next morning's newspaper, print editors and reporters began to shift to a more analytic approach. Their stories started to delve into the behind-the-scenes aspects of sports, and they began to reveal the complexity and turmoil that had long been just below the surface. The newspapers and magazines eventually made a virtue of their long deadlines, and devoted themselves to the kind of story which broadcasters, in their relentless rush to be first and fastest, could not cover with any grace or comprehensiveness.

In the mid-eighties the "national" newspaper *USA Today* appeared, featuring a flashy sports section emphasizing colorful graphics, personality features, short, breezy stories, and an extensive statistical rundown of the previous day's events in sports. Some press critics were moved to comment that *USA Today* had successfully mimicked the stylistic elements which had made television sports so popular. In fact, an important element of the paper's format was its prominent coverage of television sports.

In many respects, the growth of the modern newspaper sports page, and magazines such as *Sports Illustrated,* can be credited to the broadcasters' pushing breaking sports news into the farthest reaches of the nation, greatly popularizing the topic, and spreading interest wherever their signals reached. Newspapers and magazines now give millions of readers a chance to reflect on the events they have already seen, and to do so armed with a fuller, more varied, and thoughtful assemblage of fact and opinion. Broadcasting sells a lot of newspapers and magazines. In what may seem a gentlemen's agreement to divide the territory, broadcasters frequently use the existence of newspapers and magazines as justification for their own abdication of much journalistic responsibility. They concede the superiority of print reporting, bemoan their own lack of air time, and usually leave the field without a fight.

Sports news is often controversial, since it commonly entails some elements of criticism about highly trained popular athletes, their performance in a very public arena, and other factors which might have bearing on their performance, including salaries, personal habits, family life, and relations with the fans. Encounters with reporters are often at very close quarters, as interviewers and their subjects may spend most of the year in proximity with each other. On very few other beats is the range so close, so sustained, and so directly personal. It is not difficult to understand why, inevitably, great friendships and great feuds spring up constantly between sports reporters and their subjects. Locker room confrontations are frequent, punctuated by the occasional punch-out.

The demands of modern journalism, dedicated as it is to changing the old ground rules and rattling all skeletons, have made the relationship particularly touchy. Perhaps, only a few years ago, it would have been possible for athletes or sports executives to evade reporters' inquiries, or brush them off with a laugh (or snarl)—or even by placing a call to the Sports Editor. Today such reactions would almost inevitably cause the reporters to redouble their efforts.

It is interesting to note that, while most newspaper and magazine readers appear to accept this inherently prickly relationship, television viewers are much less comfortable with their reporters and announcers acting in an aggressive or confrontational manner. Perhaps it is because they can actually see their reporters at work, experience the process of news-gathering, and hear the emotion contained in both questions and answers; newspaper readers only see the sanitized, printed results of that work. To the dismay of those few within broadcast sports who want to be regarded as serious journalists, their viewing audiences often seem offended when they act that way in pursuit of legitimate stories.

Television executives occasionally have resorted to a halfway solution: hiring print reporters to do the heavy work of broadcast reporting. At one time or another, excellent reporters such as Dick Schaap, Larry Merchant, Robert Lipsyte, Pete Axthelm, Will McDonough, and Frank Deford have been enlisted as on-air reporters and commentators. Unfortunately, their efforts have rarely earned a sustained audience, either because their own television skills are below those of full-time television announcers, or because of the audience's aversion to the material.

Perhaps this aversion can be traced to the drumbeat of promotional material which almost exclusively emphasizes the broadcaster's non-journalistic virtues: his enthusiasm, voice, appearance, comfort with the athletes, and, in the case of color commentators, his own athletic experience. It therefore seems very much out of character for these "good guys" to suddenly switch gears and come on like Ted Koppel. Television viewers of all sorts are eager to categorize the people they watch regularly, and to expect the on-air characters to remain true to form (or the script), and faithful to that character. Once you get a reputation as a friendly announcer, or conversely, a tough interviewer, viewers and television executives are reluctant to let you change roles. Newspaper reporters, however, can often switch from "straight" reporting to writing opinion columns, from supporting a team to knocking it, without readers' becoming unduly upset.

Perhaps, too, the viewing audience instinctively understands that much of the reporting and analysis offered up by on-air talent is simply not very good. Most announcers and commentators in sports are virtually without journalistic training, either in the mechanics and techniques of researching, writing, editing, interviewing, and reporting, or in the principles, attitudes, and philosophies of journalism. They often cannot identify and define a story, develop it, place it in an understandable context, or anticipate the audience's state of knowledge and mind. They get remarkably little training or support within their own organizations, and they face unremitting caution and wariness from their would-be subjects. Any cub reporter would be hard-pressed to survive under such conditions, and few sports announcers have had even that much journalistic preparation.

For many years, the audience had relatively little opportunity to compare broadcast announcers. Each city had its favorite, usually a veteran announcer who had broadcast the same team's games for years and who had developed a cult following for his unique, personalized presentation of events. The advent first of network, and later, cable television as national distributors of sports programming brought the voice and descriptions of many announcers from out-of-town teams into each other's markets. For the first time, for example, viewers could watch the same event on more than one cable channel simultaneously, or watch an event on television while listening to it on radio. The results are startling to the uninitiated. During the 1987 NBA Finals between the Boston Celtics and the Los Angeles Lakers, anyone wishing to hear a modulated, middle-of-the-road description of professional prowess could watch the CBS network broadcast, with its careful, balanced approach to the two teams. Those wishing to hear a description of the Lakers' natural, almost symphonic grace and coordination could tune to laid-back Chick Hearn. Those wishing to hear a morality play conducted against the background of a Pier Six brawl, with the fate of civilization as we know it at stake, could listen to the Celtics' legendary Johnny Most.

To say that the three descriptions were at some variance would be an insult to the hyperbolic talents of all three. And in each city, in each home, many members of the audience reveled in the clash of perceptions and realities; knowing they were being manipulated, flattered, appeased, and even lied to diminished the enjoyment not a whit. Biased reporting, especially at the local level, is accepted by the audience as a harmless part of the sports entertainment package.

In fact, the NBA and ABC Radio recogized the virtues of the dissonant gulf between Hearn and Most, pairing them for the broadcast of the 1988 All-Star Game. Perhaps attentive to the less distinctive tastes of a broad national audience, each tried to downplay the vocal idiosyncracies which had made him a regional favorite. Hearn perked up, brightening and sharpening his customary Californian placidity; Most, whose voice in full cry crackles, sputters, and screeches like a police scanner, contented himself with a dull roar. Both announcers opted for the middle of the road, thereby leaving many first-time listeners wondering just what all the fuss was about.

Audiences also distinguish between network announcers and reporters, and those employed by local stations. For the most part, the network announcers do not travel with, or establish personal relationships, with their subjects. They may fly to the site of an event the day before it takes place, and leave immediately thereafter for another assignment. Their role is really that of event host and announcer, and very little reporting is expected of them. However, the local station personnel not only follow the same teams all year, and report on them nightly, but are often the public's main link to the athletes and their organization. Additionally, they are working under the most adverse circumstances, as crowded locker rooms, planes, and buses are not the most congenial locations for serious reporting. Public relations specialists interpose themselves between reporters and their intended subject, often attempting to stage-manage the interviews, control their content, and influence the outcome. Players, coaches, and managers are instructed to be extremely cautious in their dealings with news media, and often receive coaching in interview techniques from specialists hired by their agents or employers.

This formidable list of obstacles and encumbrances to good reporting would discourage many a serious reporter in the best of circumstances. Given the meager journalistic qualifications of many broadcast on-air personnel, it is not surprising that so few have managed to assert themselves with sufficient professionalism and determination to establish reputations as television sports journalists. It requires toughness, an ability to break the conventions of attitude and behavior so ingrained in the sports business, the willingness to fight for resources and support within the relatively timid corridors of power in corporate television, and the pre-eminent ability to attract a sufficiently large and loyal audience to the effort. It may not require Howard Cosell per se, but his methods and personality were in many respects finely honed instruments completely appropriate for breaking the strictures other had long since learned to accept without quarrel.

Cosell was special, of course, for reasons of style, impact and precedence. Throughout his career, he tussled with his subjects, his employers, his on-air image, and his own true self. To those readers who only remember the later years of his remarkable career, when his ego and vainglorious pronouncements brought him into direct conflict with his employers and professional colleagues, it is important to restate the immense, seminal contributions he made to the field. Not only did he pioneer many journalistic techniques in broadcast sports, he widened the public agenda with his selection of topics, causes, and issues. He was controversial, but perhaps part of this was only in contrast to the pallid docility of so many others in the business. In addition, Cosell willingly took on the role that his employers felt most comfortable with—that of the outcast, the iconoclast, the crazed savant of ABC Sports. He was the man you hated to love, and loved to hate, and he stood out like a beacon amidst the somber gray landscape in network sports. Perhaps it could have been no other way: that to break through to the audience, to act as a journalist, he had first to accept the audience's discomfort with broadcast sports journalism, and become a character they could count on whenever he came on stage.

He spoke his mind and elevated many a debate by the force of his intellect and convictions. ABC always appeared somewhat baffled with his success and equally uncomfortable with his predilection for being an advocate, often of issues or personalities which made the television sports establishment edgy. Further, he was sometimes inconsistent, and rarely predictable, so that anticipating what he might say on the air, or in one of his books or columns, was always difficult for ABC; smoothing over the inevitable ruffled feathers among sports executives, advertisers, and rights-holders was a constant preoccupation. His feuds with the print press were many, heartfelt, and bitter; the television industry places enormous stock in the opinions of newspaper critics, and tries all manner of persuasion to effect favorable coverage.

Cosell violated this with impunity, bearding the lion in its own den with his unwillingness to cede the journalistic beat to newspapers, and by returning their criticism word for word (actually, Cosell rarely restrained himself, and usually returned ten words for every one flung his way). He broke all the rules for corporate deportment, and eventually paid the price of decline and exile. Perhaps his finest series of programs, ABC SportsBeat, finally succumbed to low ratings after four years of good work.

One of the many complaints lodged against Cosell was that he was too negative about the sports scene and was always poking around, looking for problems, or even creating them. It was sometimes said he did not really enjoy sports at all but was just using them as a platform for his own views. This last intimation seems a patently false one, as Cosell enjoyed the beauties, intricacies, and human virtues of sports as much as any fan. In addition, he was possessed of that famous encyclopedic recall, which was trotted out in anecdotes during dull broadcasts, as he recalled some obscure statistic or fact from his immense memory. However, the impression that he was always poking around, making things difficult for people in the business, was essentially true. That it should surprise anyone reveals much more about the television sports business than it does about Cosell. Had he been covering any other business endeavor, such as banking or manufacturing, his behavior would be the absolute, expected, professional norm. Executives in those industries would not expect reporters covering them to be "fans," only dispassionate observers, dedicated to a truthful, balanced, and unbiased examination of the issues under discussion.

Too many sports executives and athletes expect a free ride from the press, especially broadcasting, and all too often they get it. In the majority of broadcast contracts, the selection of announcers is either shared with, or granted outright to, the rights-holder. They want to take no chances with an announcer who criticizes the team or its management, who raises embarrassing issues, or who lacks the requisite enthusiasm for what he is witnessing. As a result, the landscape is littered with "homers"— utterly biased observers in the employ of the event they are supposed to be covering. Many are current or former employees, or players themselves, retaining close personal ties to the players and management. All know exactly whom they have to please to retain their job in broadcasting, and most make certain they err on the side of caution, should any opportunity to rock the boat arise. By controlling the microphone (or, by extension, the camera shots) they effectively control the agenda for discussion, and can withhold praise and criticism with relative impunity. This often brings them scorn from newspaper writers, who are rightly offended by the one-sided presentation. However, among the broadcast audience itself, which is, after all, the final arbiter of taste in these matters, home-team announcers are a cherished ornament to the presentation of the game.

Advertisers, too, have preferences in the coverage of teams or sports with which they may be associated. Most advertising and sponsorship commitments are made well in advance (sometimes several years) of the actual sports season or event. Advertisers are rightfully nervous about the future performance of a team in which they have invested their clients' budgets. Bad news is not something they or their clients wish to be associated with, whether it is the poor on-field performance of a team hopelessly eliminated from contention; some public relations gaffe or major management error which turns the community against the team; an outright scandal involving something like drug abuse; unforeseen roster changes involving players central to the advertising effort; or serious personal problems. They want the brightest, most optimistic face placed on everything, because, after all, they are not journalists, for they are trying to help sell their clients' products. Without satisfied clients, they have no business to bring to the rights-holders, stadium managers, or broadcast stations, all of whom are dependent to some degree on this crucial source of income.

In many instances, advertisers have some control over the selection of announcers, some of whom have their own endorsement contracts with the advertisers, or are featured as spokesman in the advertising campaign. This is not to say that advertisers directly muzzle aggressive reporters very often, because the situation only rarely occurs that such a move would be necessary. Very few announcers or reporters are ever hired in major local markets who do not already understand the rules, written and unwritten, of proper behavior and style. All the various parties with a financial stake in the success of the broadcasts help filter out the potential troublemakers.

And why not? As a business proposition, why should a television company shell out astounding amounts of money as guaranteed payments in a speculative bid for future broadcast rights and then permit one of its own employees in any way to diminish the potential return on that investment? We would expect no different from any other industry group; General Motors isn't expected to hire Ralph Nader as spokesman after all. The business of television sports is selling advertising and gathering subscriber revenues, and that is best accomplished under controlled circumstances. A carefully orchestrated blend of entertainment, promotion, journalism, and controversy creates popularity, and the master blenders are loathe to rewrite this recipe, or bend to outsiders' demands that they do so. It is strongly felt along the corridors of power in television sports that the least they can get for their money is some control over the description and accounts of the events goinng out over their signals.

The networks have an understandable tendency to avoid criticism of their contractual partners—the league and team owners from whom they have bought the television rights. The 1987 strike by the National Football League Players Association illustrated the problem quite clearly. The three broadcast networks plus ESPN were, of course, offering coverage and commentary on an event and a league of which they were major financial partners. In fact, since the networks provided over 50 percent of total NFL team revenues, they were "the true owners and promoter of the game." Coverage of the strike was, at first, assigned to Sports, which proceeded to guilelessly carry the "scab" games (thus subsidizing them, and thereby the owners) while simultaneously offering commentary on the "news" angle of events. As negotiations to settle the strike dragged on, stadium attendance fell off sharply, but the NFLPA was declared the loser, because television ratings declined less sharply, and television, after all, was the most important factor. By the time the strike collapsed and the chastened players returned to work, the victorious league had indicated it would rebate approximately $60 million to its network partners for any damage done to ratings and advertising revenues.

The conflict of interest is apparent, freely admitted by sophisticated observes inside and outside the industry, and probably insoluble. So long as sports events are considered private performances, to be sold by their rights-holders at their discretion, the broadcasts of those events will in no way intentionally resemble unfettered journalism. The practice of placing rights on the table for competitive bidding means the rights-holder can use a range of criteria in deciding to whom the prize is awarded. Certainly money is a critical element, but so is the "cooperativeness factor," by which each contending bidder is judged: what will they do to help sell the product, to popularize the sport, to enhance its image? Who will have final say in the selection and assignment of announcers?

No newspaper of any stature would accede to these demands, nor would its editors even discuss with potential subjects the assignment of reporters or negotiate a rights fee to cover the very same story. It is one of the unique characteristics of our system of sports journalism that two reporters can be sitting side by side in the press box, one constrained only by his popularity with readers and editors, the other by an interlocking web of business interests and accommodations. Perhaps the sports public, which is made up of people who both watch television sports and read newspaper sports sections, has acclimated itself to the duality of the situation and makes mental adjustments in evaluating the two sources of information. The public may possess a more innate, flexible, and ultimately forgiving understanding of and comfort with the differences between the two industries than most observers believe.

If, then, the public seems in no way insistent that television sports take a more professional journalistic approach to its subjects, where then comes the pressure? Part of the demand for better, more independent reporting comes from the newspapers—both as competitive examples to the broadcasters, and as the source of many interesting stories—which have enlarged their sports sections to include copious reporting on all manner of off-field issues. The pressure on broadcasters to take note of stories involving even the most secret business affairs of the sports organizations, and the private lives of their players, is dramatic, particularly after they have appeared in print. Newspapers frequently set the agenda for broadcasting, and the broadcasters are hard pressed to respond when covering subsequent events. An aggressive, independent follow-up to the newspaper stories may leave them outside the good graces of the rights-holders with whom they have contracted, but failure to do so may damage their credibility as independent observers and lend further credence to the belief they have been bought off.

Another source of strain comes, surprisingly, from within their own television companies. More and more often, the News department of a local station—or the News division of a network—will attempt to assert its prerogatives to cover sports news, just as they would any other topic area. Institutional jealousies and turf-building are common in broadcasting, and no division of such a company would happily step aside for another under these circumstances, particularly given the implicit message of the News people: if you want a journalistic job done right, don't leave it to those amateurs in Sports. It is not unknown, therefore, to have more than one team of production personnel, representing News and Sports separately, cover an event or story of any magnitude. Sports, as we have noted earlier, has rapidly outgrown its formerly narrow confines in the public eye, and is frequently associated with international affairs, politics, social change, and other issues of complexity and importance. Wherever and whenever this seems to be the case, broadcast executives are faced with the choice of whether to cover it as Sports or News, and to whom to give the assignments.

Sometimes, events overtake any preplanning which may have taken place, and Sports production teams suddenly find themselves at a News event. Perhaps the most dramatic example of this was the 1972 Munich Olympiad, which rapidly became the focus of international attention not as a sports event but as the site of the kidnapping and massacre of Israeli athletes. ABC Sports was there in force, prepared to telecast the usual golden images of Olympic competition, international goodwill, and the ideals of amateur sport at its best. When the crisis erupted within the Olympic Village, it caught everyone totally off guard, scrambling for information. To its immense credit, ABC converted a Sports production into News in an almost seamless transformation, and relayed both descriptions and accounts of the unfolding tragedy to a stunned world. When, finally, several crews of ABC News personnel arrived on the scene, and struggled to gain access to the suddenly high-security Olympic Village, they found their compatriots from Sports had already established so proficient and dedicated a team of deeply involved professionals, that there was little News could do, except step back, admire the job being done, and offer assistance as needed.

Such a confluence of events and the presence of Sports cameras is becoming more and more common. The greatly increased ability of portable equipment to travel virtually anywhere in the world and send back live, high-quality pictures, has virtually turned every Sports production crew into a potential News crew—at least in technical ability. Additionally, the knowledge that the cameras are, in fact, on scene, has encouraged a whole host of individuals and groups to seek out the cameras for the sake of demonstrating or publicizing their cause. The question of what to do in such a situation troubles Sports executives. They are torn between their responsibilities to the rights-holders, their contractual partners, and the Sports audience (which presumably tuned in only to be entertained) and the obligation to cover events taking place on their watch. It is really a question of self-definition: are they observers of specified, contracted events, or of the whole world around them, and on what basis do they distinguish events they want to cover, from those they feel they ought to cover, and those they (and News) feel they are capable of covering?

When NBC was preparing its coverage plans for the ill-fated 1980 Moscow Olympics, considerable debate erupted between News and Sports regarding the composition and mandate of the crews they planned to send to Moscow. Here was a unique, international Sports event of major importance to NBC Sports; it marked a hard-won victory over ABC. In exchange for which, it had entered into extensive and restrictive contracts with the Soviet Government. These agreements covered everything from the number and location of cameras, the amount of equipment NBC had to leave in Moscow permanently, and the hours of broadcasting, to the control of the necessary communications satellites (which rested firmly in the hands of the Soviets). And while the contract was, in theory, mutually enforceable, no one doubted that, should the worst come to pass, the Soviet Government held the upper hand: it could pull the plug whenever it wanted, expel NBC employees, or interfere in any number of ways. This was acknowledged by Sports, and by the most senior executives of the parent company who negotiated the contacts, but the opportunity was judged worth the risk.

To NBC News, the chance to insert dozens of personnel and scores of cameras in the very heart of the closed Soviet world, at a time when international tensions were high, and the prospects for potential news stories great, was irresistible. News was preparing to cover anything from demonstrations to dissidents, and within the company made no secret of its desire to be there in force, ready for anything. When the Soviets invaded Afghanistan, President Carter initiated a boycott of the Games, and pulled out the U.S. teams. This was quickly followed by a withdrawal of most American advertisers from the telecasts and a drastic cutback of NBC's ambitious plans. Only limited late-night weekend and early-morning highlights ever made it on the air in this country. News never got its chance to piggyback on Sports' hard-won window of opportunity, and some ill feelings persisted between the two divisions. These tensions are now common in all the networks, as international sports become more and more intertwined with international news, and often in most unexpected ways. Preplanning for future Olympics, in particular, involves careful assessment of the relative interests of News and Sports, sometimes as collaborators, sometimes as competitors. The 1988 Summer Games in Seoul were the focus of agonizing reappraisals and emergency planning at the seemingly star-crossed NBC when persistent antigovernment riots broke out in early 1987.

Some sports events seem to take on a life of their own, far exceeding in public interest what they might "deserve" as news events, usually as a result of intense promotion. In these instances, television sometimes finds itself following public opinion, and covering events in detail because the public can't seem to get enough. The prime example of this phenomenon is the Super Bowl, which now dominates a two-week period of Sports and News attention even before the game itself is played. There are countless stories about even the most trivial aspects of team preparation, mob interviews with star players, individual interviews with everyone from the water-boy's parents to the man who paints the end zone. There are, naturally, plenty of stories about the explosion of coverage itself, and stories about the dearth of good stories. Reporters cover reporters covering other reporters, and newspaper critics cover them all. Much of the material is facile, shallow, and meant more to display each station or network's reporters hard at work on the scene than to provide any real reporting or insight. In short, the event has become a promotional showpiece for all involved, and it receives so much coverage because everyone in the television business benefits from that coverage.

The National Football League is, of course, the most skilled and experienced large-scale manipulator of television sports yet seen. Commissioner Pete Rozelle's legendary negotiating skills are augmented by a public relations apparatus that includes, in addition to the squads of helpful publicists, a marketing company, film outfit, archives, video production crews, technical advisers, writers, speech-makers, lobbyists, and lawyers. When he gets it all cranked up, as in the case of the Super Bowl, the cumulative effect is an irresistible tide of interest in the penultimate game of the year and all the hoopla surrounding it. Whether it is the tail wagging the dog, the television industry nevertheless turns out in full force to record the events, establishing by their presence the legitimacy of the whole process. In theory, anyway, ratings will rise if you cover Super Bowl Week (although how they can rise when everyone is covering the same thing is a mystery to statisticians), and the audience will be served. In fact, the prime beneficiary of all the publicity is the one network which will telecast the actual game itself, since all its competitors attentions will build audience anticipation for the game. It may not be an accident that Rozelle's promotional efforts deliver increased audiences to that network, partly as a reward for having paid all that extra money for the broadcast rights, and partly to drive the next contract's price even higher.

It sometimes seems that television sports is working at crosspurposes when it covers the mega-events, especially events it has helped publicize. On one hand, all sorts of planning, energy, and money will be spent on a drumbeat of promotions and publicity to enhance interest and ratings. The purpose of the campaign is, of course, to attract as much media attention, including that carried on competing outlets, as possible. What sometimes happens, though, is that, when the event finally begins, the broadcasters holding exclusive rights will attempt to forbid or restrict coverage by the very horde of competitors their own publicity campaign succeeded in recruiting. And the broadcast rights-holder can be very testy about any infringement on its rights. During the 1984 Winter Olympics from Sarajevo, ABC actually initiated legal action against NBC because NBC aired ten seconds of an Olympic flag-raising ceremony on a news program. The invitation to a public event, particularly when (in this case) ABC had done everything in its power to increase the media attention focused on it, and the denial of competing journalists' rights to show even a tiny, uninformative segment of that event, had never seemed so arbitrary.

International events such as the Olympics are increasingly available to viewers in the United States, thanks to the liberating effects of portable communications technology and satellite relay systems. As a consequence, events which would have been videotaped only a few years ago are now capable of being broadcast live in this country. This availability of programming from the other side of the globe is a mixed blessing for two related reasons, both stemming from the difference in time zones. Some events take place when it is three in the morning in the eastern United States, a time virtually devoid of audiences, and thereby worthless to most programmers. The most common alternative adopted by these programmers is to offer the event on tape-delay later that same day, when American audiences are awake. This time-shifting is a fine technical solution to the first problem, but it often creates a secondary, journalistic issue: how to embargo or restrict news of the event's outcome before the videotape airs.

Once again, the size and scale of the event have to be pretty grand or U.S. television would not have gone to the effort of covering it in the first place; its grandeur will be further promoted to build audiences and attract attention. To the chagrin of the broadcast rights-holder, the results will have been available to wire services, newspapers, and radio hours before the time-shifted air time. Even more disturbing to the broadcast rights-holder, those results (but not the actual footage) will be available to its broadcast competitors, which are likely to undercut the program's value by announcing the results well in advance of air time. There have even been instances when a network's Sports division has attempted to prevail on its own News division not to divulge any information which might lower ratings for the subsequent Sports program. Is it fair to control such information to maximize ratings? Is it really possible to succeed in the effort? It is just another version of an increasingly common situation: how can you differentiate between news, which is in the public domain, and proprietary information, bought and paid for by a corporation, to dispense or withhold at its pleasure?

The networks show a definite preference for big events, large audiences, and major metropolitan markets. It is no secret that they root for teams from major cities to make it through the regular season, and hopefully, into the various championship games. The continued interest of audiences in the ten largest markets constitutes an absolutely vital ingredient in the success of any sports program, and the networks would happily trade most of the rest of the nation for those top ten. There is pressure, some subtle, some not so, for leagues to maintain the competitive excellence and promotable high profile of teams in those markets. When, for example, the New York Knicks, Chicago White Sox, Philadelphia Phillies, Detroit Lions, or other major-market teams suffer long periods of drought, the networks are not pleased, and say so.

They want to schedule big-town, big-name teams, featuring attractive star players and interesting personalities. They also root for the longest possible series of championship games, as each means more income from advertisers, spread over a longer period of time, and therefore more opportunity to offset the enormous rights fees. If they can help promote these interests without obviously seeking to play favorites, they will do so, although any serious fan cannot help but notice that certain teams appear again and again, forming almost a league within a league, while others exist only in the small print of newspaper summaries and standings. This is, in the eyes of the television industry, a prudent economic strategy, which has created a secondary, journalistic issue.

It is, of course, in the enlightened self-interest of television to promote the events it will carry, and to maximize whatever audience potential might exist. In several unhappy instances, however, the urge to build and retain audiences has strained the ethical fabric of network sports and cast grave doubts on their integrity. It is one thing to publicize an upcoming event which is owned by someone else, and which you are just telecasting, and quite another to be the actual financial promoter of the event or participants. In the mid-1970s in particular the networks rushed to sign exclusive contracts with young boxers, often the members of the recently successful 1976 Olympic team. Their contracts were owned in part or outright by the individual networks, which had the exclusive rights to televise a certain number of their bouts. Audiences were never explicitly told that these boxers were, in effect, employees of the telecasting network, and the matches (made or approved by the network) were telecast without disclaimer. Needless to say, audiences may have benefited from such knowledge, both in evaluating the quality of the boxers and their opponents. One could be sure that the networks, like any other reasonable businessmen, were not anxious to jeopardize their considerable investment in their fighters by having them lose in the ring, while their television contracts still had several bouts remaining.

Boxing provided other difficulties for television during the 1970s, most importantly for ABC Sports. The sport itself had always had a checkered history on television, waxing and waning as famous fighters appeared on the scene, and as overexposure wreaked cyclical havoc on ratings. Further, the very dangerous and dark nature of the sport was occasionally displayed before a shocked audience, witness to a particularly bloody or even fatal fight. Audiences tended to diminish, and advertisers disappear altogether following one of these bouts, and reclaiming them took time. In addition, the permanent vexing problem of how to deal with boxing's own shady reputation and nefarious characters has bedeviled television for years and has tended to taint its carefully maintained posture of honesty and integrity. The problems may be endemic to the sport, and accepted by its participants as the price of doing business, but they are not subject to the same kind of federal oversight and regulation as the television industry and so can afford to offend more constituencies.

ABC Sports, in conjunction with a group of boxing promoters, decided to stage and televise a series of matches leading to the awarding of a championship. The boxers were selected by the promoters and various officials of boxing sanctioning organizations. As the matches progressed, rumors of discrepancies in the boxers' records, as well as the outcome of some matches, began to surface. ABC at first tried to ride out the growing storm of criticism, but as more and more evidence came to light that some of the boxers had not only changed names but had records that were utterly fanciful to boot, ABC had to act. One of the sharpest critics was a young ABC employee, Alex Wallou, who had through extensive research documented many of the problems. For some weeks, ABC ignored or downplayed Wallou's evidence—at least in public. Eventually, though, the network withdrew from the championship, apologized for its lack of oversight and thoroughness, and vindicated Wallou by placing him in charge of checking out any future bouts. Much public attention was directed at ABC, and charges of deliberate falsification flew, from newspapers to the halls of Congress.

At about the same time, CBS found itself in similarly uncomfortable circumstances. It had initiated a series of "winner take all" professional tennis matches, usually staged in Las Vegas, featuring prominent stars on the tour. It seemed to offer all the benefits of televised tennis, with none of the drawbacks: no long draws of qualifying matches which might bore the audience or eliminate the best players, plenty of time to promote the matches and the individual personalities of the contestants, a unique, one-time-only match between two promotable stars sure to appeal to advertisers, and a format scheduled precisely for television.

The only trouble was that the matches weren't really "winner take all." The truth of the matter, CBS later was forced to admit, was that both players received a very considerable guaranteed "appearance and travel" payment, sometimes as high as a quarter of a million dollars, just for showing up. The prize money was extra.

In golf, that most genteel of television sports, the problems of long, drawn-out tournaments could not so easily be avoided (not, at least, until a decade later, when TV latched onto The Skins Game for that purpose). Covering 72 holes, and lasting several days, the tournaments provided ample opportunities for any number of golfers to forge into the lead and even win. It is a sport characterized by an almost endless number of virtually interchangeable young men in polyester slacks, and dominated by a few identifiable, "bankable" stars. The networks had little interest in the former but a very considerable in the latter, as they believed very few people would tune in to wach the faceless army play, but many would be certain to watch a head-to-head duel by the masters. Accordingly, network promotional announcements were written to feature the appearance of the big-name golfers: "Watch Jack Nicklaus and Arnold Palmer on Sunday's coverage of The Masters!" the announcement might say. Unfortunately, the announcements were found to have been recorded not only several days before the event took place, but they often continued to run long after the golfers in question had faded from competition, missed the cut, or retired due to injury. More fuel was added to the critics' fire, as they became convinced that television had ignored accepted standards of integrity and full disclosure in favor of short-term promotional benefits.

As the glare of publicity and criticism fell on television sports, other common practices within the industry came in for scrutiny. It had been routine, for many years, for television to record on videotape time-consuming events such as auto racing and later edit the videotape for inclusion in a specified format. The method used was simple: the entire event was recorded live, with announcers doing their best play-by-play description of events as they transpired. Later, of course, when whole segments of the race were clipped from the tape to eliminate long, boring stretches, any commentary on those segments of tape was also lost. Consequently, to make a smooth edited tape that made sense to listen to as well as watch, the announcers would enter a recording booth, and renarrate the edited version on videotape. Naturally, since this took place hours or even days after the real race (and well before the air date), their ability to anticipate events in the race, or comment on something which might happen (and usually did), was greatly enhanced. It is certainly hard to look bad when you are calling a videotape not a race. Was this deceptive or simply a necessary adjustment to the time constraints placed on Sports? Was it a disservice to the audience, and a sneaky one at that, or one of the prices of doing business?

Other races presented related problems. Skiing, for example, which featured long lines of foreigners whooshing down slopes somewhere in Europe, had to be made suspenseful and climactic for the American television audience. Who would watch, after all, if the most famous racer, say Jean-Claude Killy, went first, shattered the record, and wasn't about to be overtaken by any of the dozens of remaining competitors? How much better it would be if he appeared late in the broadcast of the race, to stage a brilliant comeback, and overtake the previous leader. That, in fact, is what network television sometimes made happen. By editing the videotape, and thereby altering who raced when, they were able to extend the suspense, provide a boffo finish, and burnish the image of television sports for having captured so exciting a moment. The viewers, the greatest majority of whom had never heard of most of the racers much less comprehend the actual running of the tournament itself, were none the wiser, and probably enjoyed the artificial suspense. Was this practice, too, merely an intelligent utilization of televison technology to enhance its audiences' enjoyment, or was it a charade which undercut the pretense of journalism and objectivity? Ironically, it seems that those farthest from the affair, especially newspaper critics, elected officials, and academics, were most bothered by these questionable techniques, while the average fan just shrugged.

Another problem was created by the liberal employment of expert commentators who wore more than one hat. Typically, it would be someone like Dick Button, the ice-skating commentator, who doubled as a major executive in his own production company, a promoter of events, and friend and associate of many officials of the skating world. Another, Donald Dell, long a favorite tennis commentator, had at least as many entanglements and was a major organizer of the professional tour itself, as well as the bargaining agent for individual players, many of whom appeared on his telecasts. Both gentlemen, as it happens, were reasonably tasteful in their behavior and resisted the obvious temptations to boost their own private interests at the expense of others. When queried about the apparent conflicts of interest, they would respond that their work on television was clearly in the public domain, and the public would be able to judge for itself the appropriateness of their contributions to the programs. The real problem might have been their network's unwillingness to disclose these conflicts during the telecasts, so that viewers could, indeed, decide whether their existence was bothersome.

Eventually, the gathering criticism achieved sufficient momentum to generate Congressional hearings on the practices and policies of network sports. The Communications Subcommittee of the House Commerce Committee assembled a staff, commissioned research, and invited witnesses from within the networks and from among their sharpest critics. The hearings themselves were distinguished by the very entertaining presence of so many television heavyweights, including Sports presidents, commentators, and the inimitable Howard Cosell. As is usual in cases when the television industry seems threatened by Congressional oversight and its potential for more restrictive regulations, the witnesses were, for the most part, contrite, promising to review, clean up, and codify their procedures and policies. A few sacrificial lambs were offered up by the networks as several important executives lost their jobs or were shifted out of the glare of publicity. Interestingly, all of them have long since rebounded into prominent executive positions, especially in Sports; Robert Wussler lost his presidency at CBS, later to reappear as president of Superstation TBS. Perhaps the highlight of the hearings was the sight of erstwhile lawmakers sternly questioning the witnesses, only to surge forward as autograph hunters as soon as the day's testimony was complete. Cosell was besieged by requests for an autograph or picture, and to say he relished the atmospherics would be to understate the case greatly.

The networks, properly scalded by their brush with hot water, turned inward, and at the urging of their own lawyers and advisers, began formulating official standards for company policies in these delicate areas. This concept of adopting self-regulation, inhibition, and internal codes of conduct was nothing new to network television. Most reputable News divisions had long since adopted similar guidebooks, which specified not only the dos and don'ts of various situations but set out specific procedures to be followed and reported. In fact, each network had an entire in-house division called, variously, Standards and Practices or Network Practices, acting as overseer of anything controversial which might appear on air. Their mandate covered everything from problems of deception and unethical behavior to stereotyping of characters in entertainment scripts, commercial content, vulgarity, or any other potentially offensive element. The Standards and Practices people took a hard look at Sports, and in the wake of the Congressional hearings, corrected and codified many of the policies and operational procedures which had caused the fuss in the first place.

Shortly thereafter, viewers with keen eyesight and even more acute hearing would begin to notice tiny announcements accompanying various sports programs; the notices were, in effect, disclaimers and consumer warnings. We now take them for granted, and most viewers never give a second thought to the reasons why they are necessary, or seem terribly impressed by their import. Among the most common are the announcement (or graphic) which tells the audience that the announcers have been selected by or with the approval of the rights-holder; that certain athletes appearing in pre-taped promotional spots are "scheduled to compete"; that some of the events have been "recorded and edited for television"; and that all elements of the program, whether actual or simulated, "represent authenticated facts"; that certain athletes or commentators appear courtesy of another production company, and that certain programs themselves have been produced "in association with" an independent producer. A cynic might be tempted to remark that, translated into simple English, these mean: "the announcers can't speak freely"; "we can't tell who'll actually compete in the event we televise"; "we have monkeyed with the videotape to make better television"; "some things have been faked because it was easier than taping "the real thing"; "we had to hire certain commentators to get the rights to the event"; and "don't blame us—we didn't even produce the program."

Whether any viewers pay the slightest attention to these announcements is a moot point. They serve the purposes for which they were designed: to ease the job of corporate attorneys and diminish the chance of again running afoul of legislators. What they manifestly do not do is uphold a serious standard of journalist independence or inquiry. While it may be laudable to publicly admit (however furtively) that they are not meeting the same standards as News, the differences between the two divisions' attitude and approach are stark. Television sports, particularly at the big advertiser-supported networks, will never be News, even as events and issues compel a greater and greater dedication of air time, facilities, and talent to that end. In fact, not even the elevation of Roone Arledge to the dual position of president of ABC Sports and News had any real impact on the problem. Eventually, after Cap Cities took over ABC, he gave up the Sports position to concentrate on News. Sports suffered the dismissal, defection, or demotion of various senior executives and the loss of Cosell, its most irritating in-house scold and prod. The ratings were in decline, costs were up, and by 1988 journalism seemed more secondary than ever.

All may not be lost, however, as changes within the television industry indicate at least an opportunity to produce successful sports journalism in the 1990s. Proponents of the format are curiously buoyed by the fact that the increasingly fragmented television audience is leaving network television in droves, heading towards cable, independent producers, local television and videocassette. As a result, network shares of total audiences are dropping, even for popular, major league events. The scaled-down ratings expectations of network programmers make the relatively low ratings for sports journalism less worrisome. Additionally, as the costs of live, event-oriented programs rises to stratospheric levels, the comparatively puny budgets required by sports journalists seem positively attractive. Because these programs cost so much less to make, they need bring in proportionally less revenue. The growth of cable has opened up a vast available inventory in what had fomerly been the most precious commodity in the television business—air time. All across the cable dial, huge blocks of time are available to low-cost, low-budget programs, some produced in-house and some by independents and syndicators, many of which adopt a news-related formula including interviews, profiles, debate, and discussion.

ESPN naturally plays the most prominent role in providing sports air time to these programs. Its own Sports Center concept features a revolving cast of reporters, commentators, and guests discussing the days events, as well as some longer-range stories of interest. The network also airs, but does not produce, Mazda Sports Look, hosted by Roy Firestone, the winner of several awards for interviewing and reporting, and other programs dedicated to criticism and analysis of the world of sports. Even the seemingly staid Financial News Network carries a significant amount of sports programming, some of it insightful, as part of its program mix: money and sports go hand in hand more naturally at FNN (given its wealthy, specialized audience of investors) than almost anywhere else. Cable News Network, its sister CNN Headline News, and Superstation TBS (all operated by Turner Broadcasting) offer a range of programs and program elements that emphasize sports news, often cross-promoting events seen somewhere on the family of broadcast outlets, such as the Goodwill Games, a Turner invention. Sports journalism benefits from the multiplicity of channels available on cable, because many cable companies don't have the financial war-chest to compete for the rights to expensive events, but can afford the comparatively low cost of studio-based sports news and talk. Equally significant, the vast number of channels dilutes the ratings pool for all cable programmers, and they are often satisfied with ratings too low to be tolerated by ABC, CBS, or NBC.

Even ABC was emboldened to try yet again. In the early summer of 1987, it launched the quirkily named Monday Sportsnite, as a late-night follow-up to Ted Koppel's popular Nightline program. Al Trautwig, hardly a major star in the ABC Sports firmament, was installed as host and given the unenviable task of bucking years of history which showed that the format, the audience, and the hour were all wrong. ABC initially projected ratings so small (an average rating of 2) that they would normally cause network executives to swoon in despair, but that was based on the hard realities of the situation. Cosell's last major shot at producing such a program, the often excellent Sportsbeat, had been canceled after averaging a 2.7 rating over four years.

The significant difference, according to the "optimists" at ABC, was that the Sportsbeat ratings had been achieved in the daytime, when much greater potential audiences were available, while Trautwig would be fishing in a very shallow pond, in which no one could garner high ratings, regardless of format or content. There was much less downside risk, as the program began in the basement, with nowhere to go but up. The "pessimists" at ABC were already preparing replacement programming when Monday Sportsnite began its initial fourteen-week run.

Whatever the future may hold for serious sports journalism on television, its prospects will not be significantly improved under current circumstances. In an era of tightening network Sports budgets, the fragmentation of viewing audiences, and intense competition for ratings, the networks' tolerance of mediocre ratings will be lower than ever. Journalism will be supported only after it has proven itself in the advertiser-supported medium. That, in turn, will happen only if some forty years of audience ambivalence is replaced by a sustained commitment to the programming format, and to the individuals performing the difficult job of real reporting.

11

THE FUTURE

PREDICTING what the television sports landscape will look like in the year 2000 requires equal amounts of imagination and courage; perhaps long-range forecasting should be left to meteorologists. Ideas that appear to be "sure things" in 1988 may well have been eclipsed by the end of the century, as communications technology, corporate policies, and government regulation undergo profound changes. Nevertheless, we have invited several prominent executives in broadcast and cable sports, and sports marketing, to share their thoughts on the future.

We are thus grateful to these contributors for braving the vagaries of the crystal ball, and daring to predict how their business may be affected by a rapidly evolving sports marketplace.

Seth G. Abraham, Senior Vice President, Sports
Home Box Office, Inc.

Talking about television in the motion picture *Network*, Peter Finch's character, Howard Beale ranted that "television is in the boredom-killing business."

Well, nothing kills boredom like a tingling ball game on television.

It wasn't always that way.

During the so-called Golden Age of Television in the 1950s, there was but a limited lineup of sports programming on television. It was only three decades ago that St. Louis was the westernmost frontier of Major League Baseball and NBA Basketball. American television viewers watched sports on the three commercial networks and a small number of independent stations.

Viewed against the television sports landscape of 1987, 1957 was the dark ages. Today, we can watch live-as-it-happens Davis Cup Tennis from Sweden, The Goodwill Games from Moscow, Wimbledon from London, and the Olympics from just about anywhere. Much has happened in these years to connect by television a worldwide community of sports fans.

Cable television has been a major factor in the explosion of sports on television. There are scores of networks—basic cable, pay cable, regional services, pay-per-view networks, and Ted Turner's TBS—that feature sports as programming fare. The expansion of sports since the 1950s and three channels may be one of the most significant developments in broadcast milestones since someone got the idea in the first place to put cameras on a ball game.

Sitcoms and soaps come and go on television, but sports is constant. It engenders loyalties of all kinds: fan loyalties to players; loyalties to teams are mainstays of sports. This very basic appeal of sports has enabled dozens of networks to prosper with viewers tuning in with startling regularity.

The beneficiary of this loaded lineup of televised sports is, of course, the fan. The fan now has a remarkable choice of sports selections from which to watch.

When Henry Ford rolled the first Model Ts off his assembly line in Dearborn, Michigan, the industrialist singlehandedly freed Americans from their sitting rooms and parlor rooms. America could travel.

Similarly, cable television allowed American television viewers to "travel" around their television dial to watch an ever-expanding array of sports. Consider the TV sports junkie, who can watch a marathon of twenty-four hours a day of sports on ESPN, World Championship Boxing on HBO, Major League Baseball on TBS, or United States Tennis Open Championships on the USA Network. The contemporary definition of "seventh inning stretch" is getting up from your easy chair to visit the refrigerator or bathroom.

Truly, the fan at home has become his or her own television programmer. It is not at all unusual to see a fan with cable television watching two or three events on two or three sets at the same time .

One of the modern-day wonders of the world is the sports gaming room at the Las Vegas Hilton with 75 screens telecasting 75 different sports events.

Is this the "arena" of the future? What exactly is the future of sports on television? What will we be watching at the turn of the century, the twenty-first century?

Certainly, we will be watching *more*. It simply may be that the sports fans' appetite for ball games on television is insatiable. Seasons of sports come and go—Baseball begets Football which begets Basketball and the College Football Bowl Games, NCCA Basketball Championships, and the cycle begins anew with Spring Training.

At HBO, sports programming is among our most popular events. I have never received a letter from a subscriber claiming that "more sports on HBO is too much." Generally, the opposite is true.

My favorite letter in 10 years at HBO came from a man in Harrisburg, Pennsylvania, who wanted more prizefights on HBO because "I have lots of time on my hands." He signed it with his inmate number from the Harrisburg Correctional Institute. Prisoners are sports fans, too—#9986501 reminded me.

In the year 2000, ABC, CBS, and GE will continue to televise sports in much the same pattern they do today—mostly weekend afternoons. The World Series and The Super Bowl (XXXIV) will continue to be seen on free TV. Politics and Congressional watchdogs will make sure of that.

But many other sports will find homes on cable television. Collegiate Football and Basketball, Major League Baseball, NFL, Olympics, Golf, Tennis, World Championship Boxing are and will be staples of cable television in shared contracts with commercial networks. HBO, USA, ESPN, and TBS will capture the "thrill of victory, the agony of defeat" just as ABC so professionally does. Regional sports networks will expand with programming lineups fashioned around the home teams. Those loyalties never die (see "Brooklyn, New York," where some baseball fans still hold out to root for the *Brooklyn* Dodgers).

ESPN will be around too, successfully. New fathers or mothers will find that ESPN is a very handy thing to have around the house when your infant child has you up at the wee hours. Two years ago, when my daughter was born, ESPN brought me to Sweden to watch USA-Sweden Davis Cup action at 4:00 a.m. My daughter drank a bottle; I drank in the wonderful play of John McEnroe.

Perhaps the biggest change, however, will be the fact that fans' living rooms will become extensions of the "ticket gate" with the spread of broadcast technology known as pay-per-view. Simply put, pay-per-view means that a viewer pays a charge to view a single event via cable television. In 1988, there are approximately 10 million TV sets with the ability to receive this pay-per-view technology. Most often the events seen with a pay-per-view charge are recent theatrical movies, World Championship Boxing, and special musical concerts. In recent years, multi-million dollar "gates" have been generated by pay-per-view (and closed circuit) coverage of bouts, such as Marvin Hagler vs. Ray Leonard, Larry Holmes vs. Gerry Cooney, Hagler vs. Thomas Hearns. Viewers were generally charged about $30 per fight to view them.

In the year 2000, countless more viewers will be able to order up events on their television sets. We are not talking about Flash Gordon sci-fi tricks. This technology exists and will be more available as the costs to transmit, receive, and bill viewers goes down.

So the living room will become the twenty-first century arena as viewers push buttons on their television set, buy their "ticket" and watch a ball game. Instead of concessionaires hawking peanuts, popcorn, and crackerjacks, all you have to do is visit your own refrigerator.

The economics of sport foretell more sports on pay television and pay-per-view television. Franchise owners (teams) and rights-holders (events) simply will not be able to take more money out of the fans by raising ticket prices. You will not see a price of $75.00 on a box seat for a baseball game. Additional revenues to meet higher operating costs will come from television revenues. So, fans will pay more, but in the form of a television ticket, not a ball game ticket.

This hardly means that all sports will migrate off "free" television. These cable technologies will give birth to new events, new leagues, new forms of competition. What might we be watching in 2000?

Why not a Collegiate Football Championship Game?

In Major League Baseball, viewers may see inter-league games as part of regular season play.

What about "Professional Olympics" in which pros play pros in basketball, baseball, soccer?

Whatever the sport, the fan is the winner because there will be more choices, more diversity when the fan walks into his living room and says, "Let's go to the ballgame!"

Robert Apter, Vice President, Administration and Finance, ABC Sports

At ABC we reached the absolute pinnacle in the summer of 1984 during the Los Angeles Games. Every four years, when we do an Olympics, everybody just rises to the occasion. It's a feeling that you can never duplicate: it's more exciting than any other event in television. But we came out of Los Angeles just as high as could be, and that is when suddenly the economy took a turn for the worse in sports television. The end of 1984 and 1985 were extremely difficult years. We really didn't have an inkling of the Cap Cities takeover until it actually happened. Of course, we had heard rumors about it, and we looked at CBS, but we never expected it to happen at ABC. It suddenly happened, and for at least a few months we thought maybe we were going to be out of businss—maybe Cap Cities is mean and lean—maybe they're not going to want a Sports Department.

From having made so much money in 1984, we were losing almost the same amount in 1985 and the beginning of 1986, and we thought this was perhaps the end of network television sports, at least at ABC. What happened? Cap Cities brought in Dennis Swanson, and it was like we were reborn. If anything, we're on the upturn right now, and we do see the light at the end of the tunnel. Yes, this place is upbeat; we are not going out of business. We have gone from having some forty events losing money in 1986, to only two losing money in 1987, the big one being baseball; if we could just break even on that, we'd be making a pretty good profit.

As regards revenues: they are cyclical, and there is nothing we can do about that. Advertisers spent all their money in 1984 on the Olympics, and then they had nothing to spend at the end of the year. They got very cautious in 1985, and I think they also knew that it was the time to exert their pressure on the networks. They literally said, "What we've been paying for the last twenty years is too much, and this is what we are willing to pay in 1985." We all took it very much on the chin in 1985; though right now things seem to be coming back somewhat.

I would expect that the Olympics are not going to be split up between networks—it may be split within corporations, but not networks. We will get the rights to 1992, and we'll make money on it, or we'll come darn close to making money. I think the Olympic committees recognize that $309 million was on their wish list, and they got it. There's no way that a Winter Games not taking place in the United States is worth that much, although we think Calgary will be great. It's a perfect time zone situation . . . perfect. It will be the best Olympic coverage on television.

The current NFL contract is the first to include cable, and I believe the next will be similar, even though the cable industry has not grown as fast as people expected it to. The three networks still find the NFL a jewel they like to have, perhaps at a somewhat lower level. It may be that there will be no pre-season on the networks, but I still think you are going to have regular season and post-season on free television.

The Future

It seems that every time we have made a new contract with a group like the NFL, or an NBA deal, it was always going to be the last one for free television. Nevertheless, the best of the NFL, the best of the NBA, the best of baseball is still on free television, and I just have a feeling that ten years from now that is still going to be the case. More and more regular season games will be on cable, but the playoffs and championships of each major sport, including the Super Bowl and World Series, will stay on broadcast television.

If it's up to NBC, they'll do baseball until the year 3000, and I guess CBS won't touch it until that year. I am not sure that there will be too many new leagues on television, but boxing still has a home, and I expect all three networks to remain involved. Other kinds of shows—the Wide Worlds, CBS Sports Saturdays—those can just keep on going so long as they are profitable, and (at least at ABC) they are on the comeback trail.

Wide World of Sports, which was our backbone for years and years, is really on the comeback trail in its 28th year. This is a result of our changing the way we program it: it used to be just taped programs, and when Wide World was the only game in town, there was no competition, so we could get away with events which had been taped the day before, a year before air date. The viewer was none the wiser. Now, however, our emphasis is on live events whenever possible—interspersing into that some taped events as well as a live host—so that it not only has the anthology nature that it used to have, but it is also a sports news show with the latest information and scores. I think Wide World can just keep on going well into the year 2000. In addition, I believe you are going to see the return of shows like The American Sportsman, which were very popular in the sixties. We have already indicated that by bringing back the Mutual of Omaha adventure series, which has done pretty well in the ratings, and I think you might even find the title "American Sportsman" back on television someday.

So far as other sources of revenues are concerned, the big thing now is fully and/or partially sponsored client events. We resisted it for years, but we saw it happening; we have to get on the bandwagon, or we aren't going to survive. It might be the beer companies, the insurance companies, or sporting goods companies, which are now getting into it: we think that corporate sponsorship is really the future of many sporting events. I'm not sure that we are going to have a Budweiser Super Bowl in the immediate future, but we will certainly see a lot of Budweiser boxing and many other sponsored events.

We widened our horizons in the last year. We realized that we can do more than just television programs. We are involving ourselves in the video cassette business. We have a new clothing line, which we hope will catch on and rival Coca Cola Clothing. We're interested in publishing ventures with third parties, and will be involved in interactive video and computer games. We are trying to get into any business which we feel enhances our image, and where we have the potential of making money. However, we won't get into anything that tarnishes our image, even if it can make us some money. In other words, we are definitely widening our horizons, but we are still a television production company, and that is our main focus.

We believe the audience will basically be the same. What we are finding is an increase in the female audience on certain shows like the Monday Sportsnite show—not hard sports, because we recognize that there is a very large percentage of women watching late night television—which is why there are more soft sports pieces, and pieces involving Shirley Muldowney, Billie Jean King, or Paul Newman racing cars. We did one kids' show, recognizing that if we can get these 9- to 11-year-old kids watching ABC Sports at noon on Saturday, maybe we get them to watch sports at 4:30 in the afternoon, or on a Sunday afternoon as well. We are going to have to work to develop and keep a new audience, and it's not going to come the way it did years ago, when there were no other diversions. Today, people can record their shows and watch them later, or never watch them; they can watch rental videotapes. There are so many other activities that people are now involved in that we have to work hard to find and maintain new audiences.

We are open to more different ideas, or we wouldn't have attempted the kids' show, or brought back an adventure series with Mutual of Omaha. I think we are more adventurous than in the past; we are better prepared, because we certainly are not going to put a show on unless we have good revenue and cost information. But if a proposed show looks like it could make some money, or is worthwhile to do it just to break even, I think the door is wider than it ever was before.

I believe one of our problems was that we got very, very comfortable with the status quo: many of our shows made money, so why change? Well, we found out we had to change, because things were changing, and we were no longer making money. We had to change the look of our shows. We had to make Wide World more contemporary, and couldn't run demolition derby, figure skating, and wrist wrestling every week any more. We had to do things differently, and that meant spending more money. In the end, we felt it would have a positive effect on the programs, and we have been right in many cases. We still make mistakes, too, but the door is open wide to new and different ideas.

We don't want to look like everybody else. We want to look like ABC

Sports. That is what gave us our reputation in the sixties and seventies, and that is what we want to be our reputation in the late eighties and nineties.

J. William Grimes, President and C.E.O.,
ESPN, Inc.

In the year 2000 there will be even more sports on television, and more will be distributed on some form of pay television, whether it's basic cable as we understand today (which is what ESPN is, a video service that receives its revenues from both the advertiser and the home subscriber), or on some form of pay cable, where there is an incremental charge for the particular service or network. Therefore I would estimate that in the future there will be more total hours of sports available on television, and more of that being paid for by the viewer—with augmentation or incremental fees paid by the advertiser.

In the short term—the next five years or so—the broadcast networks will retain virtually any major sporting event that they care to retain. I think the cost of retaining those events is going to increase rather dramatically, although the rate of increase in the years 1986–91 will be lower than in 1980–86. With the new cost-conscious ownerships of ABC, CBS, and NBC there will be pressure on the people who run the Sports divisions of the three networks not to "overpay." By "overpay" I mean spending more money on the acquisitions of rights and the production of the sport than they can generate through their sole source of revenue: advertising. If they can convince their affiliates that instead of the networks' paying the affiliates for carrying programming, the networks provide them, the affiliates should pay the networks, that will affect their income, and to a degree their revenue; it is still, however, a business based only on advertising revenue. Beyond that, the events will increasingly go to cable, because not only will the economics be there, but so will the penetration or number of homes that can gain access to satellite delivered programming like ESPN. Whether it comes through the cable or comes direct to the home through satellites, the penetration will be high enough because it will be affordable and available to 95 percent of American homes in five years. I really believe the networks will be pretty much out of the business of major sports by 1995 or 2000.

There is room for new cable sports entities to succeed. Already there are probably six or seven regional sports networks distributed via cable that only showcase local or regional teams; there are a number of opportunities for those entities to strengthen themselves. One is for them to bind together more successfully so that they can buy the rights necessary to augment their local and regional coverage: that would provide competitive pressure on ESPN. Also, I think that, even on a more local basis, it is important to remember that the cable companies are merging and the industry consolidating, so, where three years ago the top twenty cable companies owned perhaps 30 percent of all subscribers, in 1987 they own 60 percent. I think we will see an increase in sports events on television as a result of that (the merger of geographically adjacent cable systems), because the attendant economics are such that more sports programming is feasible that way.

Any company that builds market share and enjoys success in a growth industry, which is what cable television has been—and ESPN has been a part of that in the sports area—must recognize that the day will come when that industry matures. When a growth industry's base business (which to us has been an advertiser-supported, subscriber-supported basic service, as I defined it earlier) matures, then the management of that entity must look and say, "with that growth maturing, we become more vulnerable to other kinds of distribution and marketing and competition, so what could we do?" Well, we could do a number of things.

One would be to invest in existing regional services, using our expertise and knowledge to make a viable contribution to the product that way. We could become more involved in pay-per-view sports; we have some experience in that already. We were an early pioneer, and like many early pioneers we lost our money. In fact, we've lost it twice: once with Don King on strictly a pay-per-view boxing event, a triple-header in 1983; we also did something different, which has a greater future potential, and that is what we call Season Ticket, in which we took Atlantic Coast Conference basketball and attempted to charge the cable operator an incremental fee for the subsciber who only wanted to see ACC basketball games. That mode of delivery is very attractive because the economics, combining the incremental fees to the homeowner, and the advertising in a sport like regional basketball, are sufficient to create a business on its own. Unlike a regional sports network, that mode of delivery is tailored to the basketball fan only, so you don't have somebody who likes baseball but doesn't like basketball dropping the regional sports network.

Those are two ways ESPN could expand. Of course the third area we are now making a lot of quiet progress in is international—we are doing almost five million dollars per year in the international sales of our programming. Those revenues are not only helpful in supporting our domestic growth, but they also provide relationships with foreign sports rights-holders who can deliver to ESPN for domestic distribution additional sports we don't have: this leads to yet a fourth possibility, which would be an ESPN II. Perhaps it would be a service of much more narrow-appeal sports, where the cost of acquisition is much, much lower; while we could not generate the same amount of advertising revenues or subscriber fees, it would be a service that we could do better than someone else, providing more customer value and also making it more difficult for a competitor to enter our market.

One of the reasons for our success is that we have been the low-cost sports television producer. However, with success comes increasing pressure to spend more money. It usually comes from the employee base—production personnel—and there is also the pressure of refurbishing the capital assets that enable you to produce events: mobile units are the major asset there. The question remains: how difficult will it be for us to remain the low cost producer? We believe we can manage it on the employee base because the networks remain hindered by expensive union agreements, under which it is not so much the employee cost that deters network efficiency, more importantly it is their inability to utilize their personnel to do more than one task. We believe if we manage our employees correctly, if we provide them with more salary and greater benefits—and perhaps more importantly, the opportunity to do many different things—we will maintain that edge in cost-efficiency.

While we acknowledge that we have to have high-marquee, broad-appeal (high-rated) sports programs on ESPN, we have always put the business of creating product value and becoming economically viable above the desire to acquire all major sports events, as others in this business have done.

Our business and our activities at ESPN are not really oriented to figuring out what the next "hot" sport should be. However, because of our origins, which were based in poverty and red ink, and because we are 24 hours or thereabouts in sports programming per day, we were—and remain—a haven for anyone with an idea. What we did over the years here—and what is a very big challenge for us to continue to do—is to say to anyone with an idea, "our doors are open, please come and sit with us." A perfect example, I think, is that in 1984 a guy by the name of Jim Foster came to see me and he said, "I have an idea: it's called Arena Football, it's football played indoors, it's eight men, and it's utilizing indoor hockey and basketball arenas in the summer." In 1987, we had four of these events on ESPN that averaged over a 2 rating with virtually no promotion. If it makes it, ESPN will have a five-year exclusive deal for Arena Football. And it would be a fabulous success story for us, like The America's Cup, only with continuity. I do not know who the next Jim Foster will be, but not a week goes by that we don't get mail from two, three, or four people with a new idea. We have to make certain that we give these sports ideas an opportunity to be exhibited on television, if they are attractive.

We have done several cooperative productions with the networks in recent years. With ABC, ESPN televised early rounds of U.S. Open, PGA, and British Open Golf. With NBC we have done the Nabisco and Dinah Shore golf tournaments. In 1986 we did the first two days of a golf tournament with CBS—the first time we had ever done anything with CBS—so that may bode well for the future. But it must be understood that for the over-the-air network, it's kind of a mixed bag: if ESPN pays them money for the rights to telecast Thursday and Friday, the networks are caught in an unappealing situation of competing with us for the very same advertisers. I don't think we will see a lot more of it.

At present, ESPN sports programming is really in three areas: sports events, sports news, and sports instructional/lifestyle. We have thought long and hard about creating a one-night-per-week sports movie during the summer, when we don't air baseball—perhaps from the end of NHL playoffs to the beginning of football. However, there are problems, one is cost, which have hindered these efforts.

The Olympics is a type of event which has very, very broad appeal that may well relate to some pay-per-sport augmented by tiers of events stripped off by the networks: that's one reason we do not have as high hopes for it on the basic ESPN as we might. The other reason is that we believe if we have to pay a lot of money for something on ESPN, we ought to have some continuity, more than two weeks. The problem with the Olympics (for us) is that it is great fun, but after two weeks it's gone. Remember, half our money is coming in through monthly subscribers, so we have got to offer some compelling programming all twelve months. Would we love to have some Olympics? Yes. Might we? I think there is a way we might participate, but we would do so on a very prudent basis, because it's not so important for us as it might be for someone else.

Finally, I would like to point out a major technological change that may benefit cable: the development of a higher-resolution television picture. In Japan now they are experimenting with television having 1300 lines, rather than our 550, and the viewer gets a much clearer picture. I have seen a demonstration of the high definition system, and it really is dramatically better than what you see on television now. There well may be a race between the cable and broadcast businesses to develop it. If cable wins that, it will be a tremendous competitive advantage, and would enable cable to increase its penetration of homes even faster than the present rate. That would drive audiences to cable, and might even drive rights-holders to get more distribution on a medium that gives the viewer such a tremendous picture.

Chester R. Simmons, Former President, NBC Sports,
President and CEO, ESPN, Inc. and Commissioner, USFL;
Sports/Media Consultant and Television Producer.

Sitting in front of our television sets in the year 2000 will be quite unlike anything we are used to in the eighties or what we will see in the nineties, especially in sports television. Unfortunately, most entertainment programming will remain the "cultural wasteland" former FCC Chairman Newton Minow called it years ago. I call it an abyss, a black hole into which tens of millions of dollars have been thrown without any visible cultural, entertainment, or creative benefits, and with few if any redeeming features. But not sport. The medium was made for sport (and news, for that matter); live, exciting programming at any time, from anywhere in the world.

Unfortunately, the networks relegate most sports to weekend daytime, usually compressed and packaged from 1:00 to 2:00 p.m. until 6:00 p.m. The occasional special event or short series gets into prime time, but for the most part sport has been the stepchild of the networks. Too many losing struggles with too many network presidents, chief financial officers, affiliate relations people, and the affiliates themselves proved the point, and exacerbated the frustration of network Sports executives. But by the year 2000 there will be many reasons for networks to take a new look at sports. The whole world will be the stage for the successors to Arthur Watson (NBC), Neal Pilson (CBS), and Dennis Swanson (ABC) The heir to Bill Grimes's chair at ESPN will have the best time of all.

If the networks have been unable to extract from the affiliates an additional half-hour for network news, how can a network Sports president expect to get hours of time? Once the gates are open to cable, however, the commercial networks will never recapture the programming they lose. The only factor inhibiting the shift of major events such as the World Series and Super Bowl is the level of cable penetration; that too will change.

Sports' platform will be the world: The NFL in London, Munich, and Sydney; the NBA in Rome, Madrid, and Tel Aviv; the NHL in Oslo, Stockholm, and Geneva; Major League Baseball in Tokyo, Mexico City, and Havana, and it might not end there. A great new era in television sports history will have begun. The international programming, including more true "world series," will attract more viewers, generating higher ratings and more advertising/sponsorship revenues. The viewer demand for more sports in a greater variety of time slots will cause network executives to look more favorably on this stepchild.

Not only will the broadening international aspect of sports affect the United States; just imagine what it will do for the countries that will become involved with the NFL, NBA, NHL, MLB, MISL, and perhaps even the son or daughter of the USFL (that very well could happen, and if given a chance prove very successful). Nor should we overlook the opportunity for intercollegiate competition on a worldwide basis. Privately owned commercial stations and networks are being developed all over Europe, the Far East, and Australia, and their appetite for programming is insatiable. Full-season availability of U.S. sports will bring top dollar, and interest will explode, particularly if local teams are involved as well.

All of this will benefit ABC, NBC, and CBS only if they keep a very careful eye on ESPN, and a watchful one on HBO. Strangely, the networks "allowed" Pete Rozelle to include ESPN in the 1987 NFL contract. ABC's clout and position probably won the day for ESPN over other serious bidders. It was strange because it brought an additional advertiser-supported network into competition for a pool of revenues depleted by disastrous ratings and sales in 1985–87. Rozelle could have given the cable deal to HBO, which would not have diluted the pool of advertising revenues. However, this setback will not inhibit HBO's interest in all forms of major sports rights. Another loser in the NFL bidding, the new Fox Network, will also be heard from again. ESPN, with its endless capacity for sports programming, can and will be a continuing source of serious concern to the broadcast networks as the international aspect of sports develops. Its programming schedules offer not only a tremendous amount of air time, but also great flexibility.

Two occurrences in 1987 pointed up dramatically the serious problem the three networks have in programming major long-form events: CBS's callous treatment of the Pan American Games from Indianapolis and NBC's coverage of the World Track and Field Championships from Rome. Both events were relegated to weekend coverage shoehorned in and around regular coverage of golf and baseball. To add insult to injury, weekday coverage and scheduled in late-night fringe-time periods. Edwin Moses's dramatic victory in the 400-meter hurdles was seen on tape at approximately 1:15 a.m. EDT. Even more reason for the networks to be concerned about cable and non-traditional network formats.

ESPN and/or TBS, HBO and Fox will have a piece of Major League Baseball, or a larger slice of the NBA, and significantly, they probably

246

will have a piece of the 1992 Olympics from Barcelona and Albertville. Cable's more flexible programming schedule will overcome the time-zone problems so evident in the Sarajevo and Seoul Games. Every moment available for telecast from an Olympic Games should be, can be, and eventually will be televised, no matter what time of day. Cable can play the role that the broadcast networks can't or aren't willing to play.

Increasing ratings will generate greater advertising revenue, which combined with subscriber fees, will give ESPN enough financial clout to begin competing in all venues, and winning many. Individually, or through a consortium, cable will be able to buy whatever they want, and will reach enough households to satisfy the promoters, sponsors, and the public. The impact of cable will cause rights fees to continue rising, but not as steeply as during the mad Olympic bidding wars of 1968–88.

So long as advertisers can reach their demographic targets they will continue to support sports on television in ever increasing numbers. But— and it's a big but—there must be an increasing extension of their media buys to maintain their level of expenditure. Everything will more than likely have a corporate name attached to it, with the possible exception of the Rose Bowl; I believe even the Olympics will be seduced by sports marketing. The advertisers' and sponsors' clout will become more and more apparent as live events become more desirable worldwide. The Europeans' early involvement and relative sophistication in sports marketing will stand their promoters in good stead for their involvement with American sports.

The extension of the media buy will be vital, and without the name-in-title, the banners, the tents, the trips and meals, advertisers and sponsors will be difficult to deal with. And there is really nothing wrong with corporate sponsorship, so long as good taste is observed. After all, the viewer benefits if an event gets on the air, if partly due to some banners and signs. The networks, despite some unease, will have to continue these practices started in the Eighties, because of their positive impact on the bottom line.

The sports anthology program has probably declined as a major ratings winner for the networks, although the three main existing programs will be continued—to bridge live programming. The networks will continue to attempt serious sports journalism, but with little success due to low ratings. Cable will undertake the burden of sports reporting with some success, and may win accolades from critics and the public. Should cable fail, it will have missed a wonderful opportunity.

New program formats will be increasingly hard to come by—although someone probably said the same thing ten years ago. In those ten years we have seen the development of Seniors Golf, The Skins Game, The

Breeders' Cup and Breeders' Crown series, America's Cup coverage (due to advances in technology and cable's time and money) and extended coverage of the NFL and NBA college player drafts (again, cable's great inventory of available air time). It is significant that all of these are live, exciting programs: that will be the keynote of the 2000s.

Michael Weisman, Executive Producer,
NBC Sports

Sports television in the year 2000—now *that* should be interesting. For starters, it may seem like the end of the century is only around the corner but actually it's further off in the distance than that. Consider that the very first televised sporting event took place in the 1930s; the first World Series on television was the 1947 classic; color television didn't become widespread until the 1960s. And the equipment that the networks utilize in 1988 is vastly different from that used ten years ago. In other words, technologically speaking, we're still in the formative stages of sports television. Who knows where we'll be in the year 2000?

Harry Coyle, the venerable NBC director who has handled thirty-two of the forty World Series that have been on television, has had a unique view of developments over the years. Harry tells a story about how he used to have three cameras to cover a baseball game. By a few innings into the game, however, only one or two cameras would still be functioning. So Harry would have to devise different game plans depending on which of the three cameras was working. Things have come a long way since then, but the lesson is clear. Even though the technology has changed dramatically—even though you can put a remote control camera on the goal post as NBC did at the 1984 Orange Bowl to offer that unique viewpoint of the action—you still have to make sure that the equipment works. An even more important fact is the phenomenal rate at which technology is advancing. Responsible sports producers have to ask whether or not the increased technology really enhances sports broadcasts or, at some point, does it simply become a matter of video overkill?

If you ask ten different sports television executives about the future of our industry, you're bound to elicit ten different responses. From my perspective, the technology is only as good as the people who harness it, and its value is measured not by the extent—or cost—of the technology but on how well it enhances the viewers' enjoyment of the game. One must remember that the purpose of network broadcasts is to cover games and entertain an audience.

The extent to which we as broadcasters can make viewers feel like they're in the ball park is, of course, limited. It is still an entirely different feeling to sit at Wrigley Field with its charm and ambience than it is to watch a broadcast of a baseball game from there. Even more dramatic is the difference between viewing an Indy car race from trackside as opposed to doing it in your living room. Television simply does not capture the 200-plus mile-per-hour speeds of a race car. But in 1988, TV sports is certainly a lot better than it was twelve years ago. And twelve years from now, it only promises to be even better yet.

Computers have had as huge an impact on the television industry as they have on most aspects of American society. In sports, computers allow us to put cameras in places where cameramen can't go, and to control the equipment from a different location. By the year 2000 this aspect of sports production figures to be even more refined. Micro-components might allow us to place cameras in locations never previously thought possible, cameras barely visible that hover above a stadium and are no bigger than a bottle cap.

Enhancements in audio also figure to be a significant part of sports television in the year 2000. Imagine the following scenario that combines several technological advences: A baseball manager walks out to the mound to talk with his pitcher. In 1988, you would see shots of the two men talking. The announcers in the booth would be conjecturing about the nature of the discussion. In the year 2000, however, the director might be able to get incredible closeups of the two, while a special device that not only reads lips but in turn triggers a graphics generator might be able to put the exact words being spoken onto the television screen.

Technology is only one aspect of the sports broadcasting business that will change come the year 2000. There are other significant developments to consider. The question, for instance, of where the cable television industry will be twelve years from now is perhaps most important. At one time, many people predicted that cable would dominate the sports television industry. That clearly is not yet the case. For starters, cable TV only reaches about half of America's homes. Just how far cable will go in saturating the country is still a matter of speculation at this point. There is an increasing sentiment that the really big events will be shown on some form of pay-per-view in the not too distant future. The networks have battled ferociously to keep the big events on free, over-the-air TV, and with the exception of major boxing matches, very few of the premier events in sports can be watched on cable. The Super Bowl, World Series, NBA Finals, and the Olympics are all still viewed on the commercial networks. It is simply an economic reality that, if 90 million TV homes can watch an event, this is worth more than if only 45 million can. Of course, this might change by the year 2000. The question involves the amount of rights fees that the networks can afford to pay for their premium programming. As the fees commanded by the National Football League and Major League Baseball escalated in the 1970s and 1980s, network officials became increasingly wary of paying the higher prices. This was particularly evident as advertising rates failed to keep pace with accelerating rights fees, and profits eroded. The equation of balancing rights payments with advertising revenues is still the major dilemma facing network sports, and an issue bound to perplex network sports divisions for the remainder of this century.

Will the networks manage to keep their slice of the pie? Contrary to some of the popular notions, it is the thought here that the networks *will* remain a force into the twenty-first century. The symbiotic relationship that the networks enjoy with the major sports leagues is sometimes underestimated. Major League baseball has grown *with* the networks. Pro and college basketball and football have also flourished just as have major golf and tennis events. While the profits aren't what they used to be, all of the participants in sports television are making adjustments to stay in tune with changing realities.

Perhaps the most important thing to remember about sports broadcasting as we head toward the year 2000 is that technology alone is not the answer to successful telecasts. Nor is it money or physical resources. The success and popularity of sports on television lies in the people who make it happen and the ingenuity they bring to their craft. Some of the best things produced in recent years at NBC Sports have been the least expensive. Innovations such as the ten-minute ticker which updates out-of-town scores throughout our telecasts have won us wide praise from viewers and critics alike. The "ticker" costs hardly anything to produce and has proven to be a valuable addition to our coverage. The "silent minute" in our coverage of the Super Bowl in 1986 was another attempt at inexpensive innovation. While it may have seemed more like a promotional stunt than a practical device, we felt our viewers needed a break from the constant barrage that goes with televising pro football's prime spectacle. So too with the audio-less game NBC tried several years ago. While the result may have been less than successful to many critics, these new approaches to presenting sports on television are simply examples of how ideas are often more memorable than an onslaught of costly electronic pyrotechnics. The experience and resourcefulness that we have seen demonstrated by many people in sports broadcasting allows us to approach the future with optimism.

BIBLIOGRAPHY
AND SELECTED READINGS

Robert Berry, William Gould, and Paul Staudohar. *Labor Relations in Professional Sports*. Dedham, Mass.: Auburn House, 1986.

Robert Berry and Glenn Wong. *Law and Business of the Sports Industries (Vol. II)*. Dover, Mass.: Auburn House, 1986.

Heywood Hale Broun. *Tumultuous Merriment*. New York: Richard Marek, 1979.

Jim Byrne. *The $1 League: The Rise and Fall of the USFL*. New York: Prentice-Hall Press, 1986.

David Chester. *The Olympics Games Handbook*. New York: Charles Scribner's Sons, 1975.

Howard Cosell. *Cosell*. New York: Pocket Books, 1974.

Howard Cosell (with Peter Bonventre). *I Never Played the Game*. New York: William Morrow, 1985.

Everette E. Dennis (Exec. Ed.), and Huntington Williams, III (Ed.). "Sports and Mass Media." *Gannett Center Journal*, Vol. 1, No. 2, Fall 1987.

Joseph Durso. *The All-American Dollar: The Big Business of Sports*. Boston: Houghton Mifflin, 1971.

Peter Gammons. *Beyond the Sixth Game*. Boston: Houghton Mifflin, 1985.

Robert Garrett and Philip Hochberg. "Sports Broadcasting and the Law." *Indiana Law Review*, Vol. 59, No. 2, 1984.

David Halberstam. *The Breaks of the Game*. New York: Knopf, 1981.

David Harris. *The League: The Rise and Decline of the NFL*. New York: Bantam Books, 1986.

William O. Johnson, Jr. *Super Spectator and the Electric Lilliputians*. Boston: Little, Brown, 1971.

Gene Klein and David Fisher. *First Down and a Billion*. New York: William Morrow, 1987.

Leonard Koppett. *Sports Illusion, Sports Reality*. Boston: Houghton Mifflin, 1981.

Don Kowett. *The Rich Who Own Sports*. New York: Random House, 1977.

Bowie Kuhn. *Hardball*. New York: Times Books, 1987.

Guy Lewis and Herb Appenzeller (eds.). *Successful Sports Management*. Charlottesville, Va.: Michie Law Publishers, 1985.

Robert Lipsyte. *SportsWorld*. New York: Quadrangle–New York Times Books, 1975.

Norman Marcus. *Broadcast and Cable Management*. Englewood Cliffs, N.J.: Prentice-Hall, 1986.

Martin Mayer. *About Television*. New York: Harper & Row, 1972.

James A. Michener. *Sports in America*. New York: Random House, 1976.

Roger Noll (Ed.). *Government and the Sports Business*. Washington, D.C.: Brookings Institution, 1974.

Ron Powers. *Super Tube*. New York: Coward-McCann, 1984.

Benjamin G. Rader. *In Its Own Image*. New York: Macmillan, 1984.

Bert Randolph Sugar. *"The Thrill of Victory."* New York: Hawthorn, 1978.

Tony Verna. *Live TV: An Inside Look at Directing and Producing*. Stoneham, Mass.: The Focal Press, 1987.

We acknowledge a debt of gratitude to the following television sports columnists whose regular and timely articles offered frequent updates and insights of great interest:

Jack Craig in *Boston Globe*
Stan Isaacs in *Newsday*
Rudy Martzke in *USA Today*
William Taaffe in *Sports Illustrated*

The following periodicals were also of some utility, particularly regarding short-term trends in contract neogtiations and programming policies:

Pay Tv Sports.
Carmel, California: Paul Kagan Associates.
CableSports.
Hartsdale, N.Y.: QV Publishing.
The Sports Executive.
Greensboro, N.C.: The Sports Executive, Inc.
Broadcasting
CableVision
Variety
The Sporting News
TV Guide
Television Age
Inside Sports
Television/Broadcast Communications

Several surveys and research studies were provided to us, either by the research firms themselves, or by their clients; others were cited by sources on a confidential basis. Among the companies whose research product was made available to us were: N. W. Ayer, Simmons, Katz Agency, A. C. Nielsen, Arbitron, McKinsey & Co., and Frank Magid Associates.